Reshaping Social Work Se

Series Editors: Robert Adams, Lena Dom

The **Reshaping Social Work** series aims
base for critical, reflective practitioners. ~~Each book~~ is designed to
support students on qualifying social work programmes and update
practitioners on crucial issues in today's social work, strengthening
research knowledge, critical analysis and skilled practice to shape
social work to meet future challenges.

Published titles

A Guide to Adult Social Care Law in England by John Williams, Gwyneth Roberts
and Aled Griffiths

Anti-Racist Practice in Social Work by Kish Bhatti-Sinclair

Critical Issues in Social Work with Older People by Mo Ray, Miriam Bernard and
Judith Phillips

Doing Radical Social Work by Colin Turbett

Social Care Practice in Context by Malcolm Payne

Social Work and Community Development by Catherine Forde and Deborah Lynch

Social Work and Power by Roger Smith

Social Work Research for Social Justice by Beth Humphries

Social Work and Social Policy under Austerity by Bill Jordan and Mark Drakeford

Spirituality and Social Work by Margaret Holloway and Bernard Moss

Invitation to authors

The Series Editors welcome proposals for new books within the *Reshaping Social
Work* series. Please contact one of the series editors for an initial discussion:

- Lena Dominelli at lena.dominelli@durham.ac.uk
- Malcolm Payne at macolmpayne5@gmail.com

Reshaping Social Work
Series Editors: **Robert Adams, Lena Dominelli and Malcolm Payne**
Series Standing Order ISBN 978–1–4039–4878–6
(outside North America only)

You can receive future titles in this series as they are published by placing a standing
order. Please contact your bookseller or, in the case of difficulty, write to us at the address
below with your name and address, the title of the series and the ISBN quoted above.

Customer Services Department, Macmillan Distribution Ltd, Houndmills, Basingstoke,
Hampshire, RG21 6XS, UK

Social Work and Community Development

A Critical Practice Perspective

Catherine Forde and Deborah Lynch

First published 2015 by
PALGRAVE

Palgrave in the UK is an imprint of Macmillan Publishers Limited, registered in England, company number 785998, of 4 Crinan Street, London, N1 9XW.

Palgrave Macmillan in the US is a division of St Martin's Press LLC, 175 Fifth Avenue, New York, NY 10010.

Palgrave is a global imprint of the above companies and is represented throughout the world.

Palgrave® and Macmillan® are registered trademarks in the United States, the United Kingdom, Europe and other countries.

ISBN 978-1-137-30838-2   ISBN 978-1-137-30839-9 (eBook)
DOI 10.1007/978-1-137-30839-9

This book is printed on paper suitable for recycling and made from fully managed and sustained forest sources. Logging, pulping and manufacturing processes are expected to conform to the environmental regulations of the country of origin.

A catalogue record for this book is available from the British Library.

A catalog record for this book is available from the Library of Congress.

Contents

List of Illustrative Material

Research Boxes

Figures

Acknowledgements

We hope that this book will illuminate the practices of social workers who use community development approaches to facilitate social change. These practices, often deeply woven into the fabric of their day-to-day work, demonstrate active engagement in dialogue with communities to resist inequalities and injustices and seek broader change at community and societal level. This is our dedicated space to acknowledge and thank you, particularly those practitioners who participated so enthusiastically in our research and whose voices emerge from these pages with such clarity, strength and purpose. Thank you too, to the social work and community development practitioners, theorists and writers (and book draft reviewers!) whose ideas and sustained engagement continue to inspire and re-ignite work in our fields of practice.

The co-authorship of this book as social work educators has been important to us, as it brings our disciplinary traditions together: social work and community development. We acknowledge our students on the social work programmes at our universities; students' questions, reflections and insights were an intrinsic part of the development of this book project. Thank you to our colleagues and to both our universities, University College Cork, and the University of Queensland, for supporting the book project in so many ways. In particular we thank the College of Arts, Celtic Studies and Social Sciences at University College Cork for their timely contribution from the Research Publication Fund.

We acknowledge the gently encouraging style, support and practical guidance of Peter Hooper at Palgrave – we have learned much from your approach and experience. Thank you to India Annette-Woodgate and Alex Antidius for handling our questions and managing matters of production.

We now turn to those closest to us, and to those who 'lived' the project. Sean, Maria, Sandie, Finbarr and Kiran – thank you for your enduring support. Your generosity (in time and space), understanding, care and patience were what it took to complete the book.

The authors and publishers would like to thank Pearson and Jim Ife for Figure 3.1, 'Ife's Framework of Human Service Delivery', from J. Ife, *Rethinking Social Work* (1997); Policy Press for Figure 5.1, 'Spiral of Learning and Action', from M. Ledwith and J. Springett, *Participatory Practice: Community Based Action for Transformative Change* (2010); Oxford University Press for Figure 6.1, 'Policy Practice Engagement (PPE) Conceptual Framework', from J. Gal and I. Weiss-Gal, 'The "Why" and the "How" of Policy Practice: An Eight-Country Comparison', in *The British Journal of Social Work* (2013).

Social work and community development: An introduction

The connections between social work and community work are long-standing and multifarious. Some of these connections are well known and documented, such as shared historical origins, a common value base and grounding in diverse bodies of theoretical and practice knowledge. Other links, while less evident, are equally significant. Both disciplines have professionalised within the last fifty years and now have a distinct occupational status in many countries. Furthermore, both have constantly been shaped and reshaped by societal events. This is particularly evident in the early years of the twenty-first century as social work and community work grapple with a complex and challenging policy environment that demands new and innovative responses to a range of multifaceted social, economic and environmental problems.

The authors are well positioned to explore the relationship between social work and community work. One is a social worker with experience of working in child protection practice in Australia, as a development worker in Indonesia and Nepal, and as a social work educator in Ireland and Australia. The other has worked as a community worker, researcher and community work educator in Ireland. These experiences, coupled with eleven years of co-teaching community work on a Master of Social Work qualifying degree, have given us insights into the possibilities and challenges of using community work approaches in social work practice. We recognise that social work students set out with the desire to effect positive change through their work and are eager for ideas and approaches that will enable them to achieve this. Some have prior experience of community work approaches, through voluntary or paid work in a range of organisations and groups. Their social work training equips them with many of the skills and ideas necessary to harness community work approaches in practice, but they require insights into how they may be used in social work settings, and the encouragement to do so. The findings of a recent research project which we conducted indicate that social workers can and do find ways to use these approaches in their practice in a range of different settings and despite pressures and challenges. This book seeks to encourage social work students to identify both means and opportunities by which they can practice in similar ways.

The aim of this text is to offer readers an understanding and analysis of the relevance and importance of community work ideas and approaches in social work practice. It argues that community work approaches offer a form of critical practice that connects well with social work traditions, values and ideas. The book provides a robust comparative perspective on social work and community work experience in a number of countries, including in particular the United Kingdom, the United States, Australia, Sweden and Ireland. This comparative dimension offers opportunities for learning about the theory, policy and practice of social work and community work in each of these contexts.

The book is written for students on qualifying and post-qualifying social work courses. It will be of interest to social work students who are undertaking community work and community practice modules on their courses, students and practitioners who already have community work experience and those who are keen to explore the relevance of community work approaches for social work practice. It is also aimed at social work students, practitioners and educators who may have little or no experience of community work but who are interested to discover its potential for an engaged and critical practice.

Change and continuity in social work

Throughout its history, social work has undergone continuous change and development. This evolution has occurred in response to events and in accordance with changing policy imperatives. Parton (1994) and Harris (2008) describe the progression of social work from its origins in nineteenth-century philanthropy to its formalisation and absorption into the machinery of the state in the late nineteenth and early twentieth centuries, and the development of the social work profession in conjunction with the emergence of the welfare state in the second half of the last century. In its positioning between the state and its client groups social work has always been 'contingent, complex and contested' (Dickens, 2011, p. 36; Parton, 1994).

Different places, different practice

Social work is an international occupation with different manifestations in different places, depending on local conditions, policies and welfare systems. For instance, in the UK and Ireland social work has become a 'distinct occupational entity' (Harlow, Berg, Barry and Chandler, 2012, p. 11) with a specialised focus, while in the Nordic countries social work practice is more generalist in nature and has yet to secure a specific professional identity (Hallstedt and Hogstrom, 2009; Kullberg, 2013). While the demands of professionalisation, managerialism and high-profile child protection cases have led to the detachment of community work from social work training and practice in England and Wales (Dominelli, 2004a; Stepney and Popple, 2012), this has not occurred to the same extent in countries such as Australia, South Africa and the US, where community work still features in social work training and social workers use community work approaches in their practice (see for example Mendes, 2007, 2008b).

Regional differences are also significant. The nature and focus of social work practice and education in England is qualitatively different from practice in other parts of the UK such as Scotland. In England the reorganisation of social service provision under New Labour led to a narrowing of the social work role to a concentration on risk and protection rather than prevention (Parton, 2009, 2014b), while community work has all but disappeared on social work courses (Dominelli, 2004a). Recent reforms to English social work education, specifically the Professional Capabilities Framework (PCF) which was introduced by the Social Work Reform Board in 2011, offer a broader conception of the social work role (for example the PCF underlines the importance of social justice, equality and inclusion to social work practice) but have been criticised for not adequately taking into account the realities of practice, particularly in child services (Higgins and Goodyer, 2014; Higgins, Popple and Crichton, 2014). In post-devolution Scotland, preventative approaches like community work have been emphasised in social work policy, although social work writers express concern that the wider UK policy environment may undermine these aspirations (McGhee and Waterhouse, 2011; Ritchie and Woodward, 2009). These international and regional differences afford opportunities for comparison and learning between contexts.

The changing landscape of social work practice

Over the last forty years the increasing pace of social change has given rise to ever greater challenges for social work and the social professions. The rise of the neo-liberal ideology since the 1970s has led to an emphasis in many countries on the primacy of the market and the corporation; the liberalisation of trade and welfare systems; an emphasis on individual rights, freedoms and interests; curtailment of welfare states and the relocation of social concerns such as the provision of care to the private sphere of the individual, family and community (Clarke, 2004; Ife, 2013; Lorenz, 2001). Growing uncertainty and awareness of a range of risks (Denney, 2008; Webb, 2006) have given rise to rationalism in the form of managerialist processes that demand that all organisations, regardless of type, operate in a 'business-like' (Buckley, 2008; Clarke, 2004, p. 36) manner.

Social workers have been cast 'as managers of family life for certain sections of the population' (Dominelli, 2004b; Parton, 1994, p. 26).

Globalisation has enabled freer movement across territorial borders, growing diversity in many countries, and technological advances such as the internet. There has been an 'internationalization of social problems' (Dominelli, 2004b, p. 164; Dominelli, 2010a; Fell and Fell, 2014; Midgley, 2004) as refugees and asylum seekers enter Western countries, women and children are trafficked across borders and child abuse becomes an international phenomenon facilitated by the internet. Reports (Barnardos, 2012; Stacey, 2009) into the increase of child trafficking in England and Wales and the use of online networks to facilitate movement of trafficked children highlight the scale and complexity of the problems that social workers and related professions face. Along with these challenges the international social work profession is confronted with 'voluminous child protection notifications' (Lonne, Harries and Lantz, 2012, p. 2), criticism of the profession for a perceived failure to respond appropriately and adequately to these problems (O'Brien, 2012; Parton, 2009), and an increasingly pressured workforce (Dickens, 2011).

Continuity within change

While social work has experienced constant change, it has also demonstrated a high degree of continuity. In the first place, it continues to be concerned with the 'social' or the condition and welfare of human beings and their relationship to their environment (Jones, 2014; Vickers and Dominelli, 2014). The International Federation of Social Workers (IFSW) (2013) suggests that social workers 'should be concerned with the whole person, within the family, community, societal and natural environments'. While changing circumstances have pulled social work towards individual and family work and away from an engagement with communities and society, there is much in current social work theory, policy and practice to facilitate the restoration of a broader outlook. Mendes (2008a, p. 249) points out that the introduction of structural and systems perspectives into social work education has facilitated a focus on 'the relationship between individuals and broader social and community structures and networks'. From a policy perspective, the profession's commitment to social justice and equality is embedded in the *Global Agenda for Social Work and Social Development: A Commitment for Action* (IFSW, IASSW and ICSW, 2012). The Agenda, which is a joint initiative of the IFSW, the International Association of Schools of Social Work (IASSW) and the International Council on Social Welfare (ICSW) reiterates social work's commitment to the achievement of 'a people-focused global economy that is regulated to protect and promote social justice, human rights and sustainable development' (IFSW, IASSW and ICSW, 2012, p. 2). Commitments of the Agenda for the period 2012–2016 include the promotion of social and economic equality, ensuring the dignity and worth of the person, ensuring an appropriate environment for practice, and promoting wellbeing through sustainable human relationships. All of these commitments underline the importance of working with communities and other professions to address injustice and inequality in a range of areas. In practice terms, the contingent and complex (Dickens, 2011) nature of social work provides social workers with opportunities to identify and use a range of approaches.

Social work and community

Readers may be aware that there is a voluminous literature on 'community', a concept that has existed since ancient times but which is characterised by considerable elasticity (Somerville, 2011). Yerbury (2012) points out that early sociologists differed in how they conceptualised community, and in their turn these interpretations diverge from those of contemporary thinkers. Some of these contemporary understandings are based on the complexity of contemporary society and encompass, for example, the idea of 'virtual' communities, generated via the internet.

Community is popularly thought of as place, in geographical terms. It may also be understood in terms of bonds or ties between people, or what Putnam (2000) refers to as social capital. While there are limitations to this dual interpretation of community as place and bonding, it has acquired a fresh legitimacy in the context of globalisation and the challenges associated with it. Community theorists have argued that both conceptions of community are important at this time of 'global crisis' (Chaskin, 2008; DeFilippis, Fisher and Shragge, 2006; Kuecker, Mulligan and Nadarajah, 2011, p. 248; Tovey, 2009), and that a renewed focus on locality and local agency is necessary to both address and counter the challenges posed by the economic crisis that has affected much of the world. In the international literature there are many examples of local community action in the face of social change and external threats. Dominelli (2012a) writes about the struggle of Indigenous peoples around the globe to maintain their ways of life, cultures and traditional rights against a range of risks including land grabbing, ecological degradation and attempted assimilation. Pyles (2009; Pyles and Harding, 2012) has documented the use of community organising strategies in post-Hurricane Katrina New Orleans, and Caniglia and Trotman (2011) have explored the role of community work in efforts to recover from the January 2011 floods in Queensland, Australia. Leonard (2007) and Slevin (2010) discuss the efforts of the transnational Shell to Sea movement to resist the construction of an underground gas pipeline in an unspoiled part of the West of Ireland. While these studies illustrate the enduring and redemptive validity of 'community' as place and as a set of social relationships, they avoid romanticising communities and the challenges they face in countering economic, social and environmental risks. They also point to a third useful perspective on community: community as a *political* unit or 'a basis for representation, collective deliberation, mobilisation and action' (Chaskin, 2013, p. 112). This perspective encompasses communities as sites of community mobilisation and social action.

Another interpretation of community is important in this discussion. Late-modern or post-modern ideas which emphasise the critical questioning of accepted or taken-for-granted assumptions about the world (Fawcett, 2009) enable us to envisage identity and 'community' as constructs that emanate from individuals rather than having a separate or objective existence. In an Australian study on young people's attitudes towards 'community', Yerbury (2012) discovered that they valued the idea of community but had quite different and individualised ideas about what constitutes 'community'. For them, community represents different things, both intrinsic and extrinsic. These include a sense of self, relationships with other people and belonging, and social action. Community therefore 'begins with the individual' (Yerbury, 2012, p. 196).

The idea that the impetus to engage with others and to act comes from within the individual, not from without, may help to explain why the imposition of external constructs of 'community' is often problematic. For example, neo-liberalism and economic problems have led governments to advance particular ideas about community for a range of policy purposes. The concepts of 'community empowerment' and 'Big Society' that have been harnessed by the New Labour and Coalition governments in the UK offer unitary, simplistic or totalising ideas of 'community' that fail to acknowledge individuals' differing reasons for participation or non-participation or to explain why some individuals and communities are failing to 'thrive' (Somerville, 2011). These prevailing ideas tend to reify community rather than acknowledging its complexities and contradictions (Arvanitakis, 2008; Cleaver, 2001; Somerville, 2011), and this reification has implications for the practice of social workers and other professionals who work with individuals, families and communities.

A typology of community as place, bonding and agency is useful in considering the relationship between social work and community. Social workers operate within communities of place, whether in localities or in other places such as hospitals or care settings. They are also change agents who routinely seek to build relationships with individuals, families and communities, including other professionals. They have first-hand knowledge of the situations, challenges and problems that face people and their communities. They regularly practice in deeply divided 'communities' and particularly with 'minority communities' (Mantle and Backwith,

2010, p. 2382). For example, in the context of urban regeneration projects such as those in Dublin's inner city; in Ireland social workers and community workers engage with communities experiencing significant inequalities and ongoing social and economic exclusion (Share, 2010). Social workers are also 'network thinkers' and understand the significance of social and relational dimensions of community that are not necessarily spatially bounded. Ennis and West (2013) describe how a social worker applied a network approach to bring people and organisations together to build positive social connections across different cultural groups within suburban Northern Australia. Hawkins and Maurer (2010) show how ideas of social capital were applied by social workers in rebuilding lives and communities in New Orleans following Hurricane Katrina.

All of these characteristics provide social workers with opportunities to engage as 'agents of progressive social change' (Stepney and Popple, 2008, p. 11). Despite facing particular challenges in realising this role, including the current 'obsession with individual needs' (Teater and Baldwin, 2012, p. 9) in much of social work practice, the impetus for change can emerge from individual practitioners and groups of practitioners, working together and with other change agents (Martin, Hanson and Fontaine, 2007; Mendes, 2007). For example, Mendes's research (2007) shows us that social workers engage in social action at informal levels in everyday practice within their organisations and communities, as well as within more formal structures such as professional organisations. It is the purpose of this book to argue that social workers in all settings can and do find opportunities to act as progressive change agents in communities.

Questions 1.1

Meanings of community

1. What does 'community' mean for you?
2. What are some of the positive or negative aspects of community, in your experience?
3. What specific understandings of 'community' as outlined in this chapter resonate with you? Why do they resonate?

Community work and community development

Like 'community', community work is a contested concept that does not have a universally accepted meaning. There are benefits and disadvantages to such elasticity. The benefits include the richness of community work practice, which can draw on a wide range of approaches and methods to achieve its aims. Conversely, the contested nature of community work has facilitated its exploitation over time by different interest groups for very different purposes.

Defining 'community work' is a more challenging task than it may initially appear. In the first place, a distinction is often made between 'community work' and 'community development', although the terms are sometimes used interchangeably. Sometimes community work is envisaged as an umbrella term for a range of approaches that centre on communities. Keith Popple's (1995; see also Dominelli, 2004a) analysis of community work models is a well known example of such a typology. These typologies facilitate an understanding of the breadth and depth of community work activity, but do not necessarily reflect the reality or 'messiness' of practice in which these models are usually employed 'in multiple variant forms' (Green, 2008, p. 53).

In many accounts the concept of 'community development' is used instead of 'community work'. Community development is a mutable concept that has been interpreted and used variously depending on time and context. It is often classified into different types, in a similar manner to community work. For example, the American writer John J. Green (2008) refers to three broad models of community development: self-help, technical assistance and conflict. Self-help may refer to action by residents of a locality or members of a community in the pursuit of specific goals in the interest of the community, such as the acquisition of a building for communal use, the establishment of a not-for-profit enter-prise, or the development of a playground for children. Technical assistance is concerned with accessing information, resources and techni-cal knowledge in order to undertake development goals. In this case professional community workers are likely to be employed for their skills and knowledge; for instance, a community worker may provide a commu-nity group with the technical assistance or knowledge it needs to identify and access funds for a development project. The self-help and technical assistance models may be located in the functionalist or consensus ideol-ogy, which seeks change without necessarily challenging or changing the way society is organised (Shragge, 2013). The third model, conflict community development or community action, is centrally concerned with bringing about fundamental social change through exposing and confronting 'the root causes of poverty and injustice' (Gilchrist and Taylor, 2011, p. 16; Ledwith, 2001), based on collective action which may build from the local to the global. The examples of community mobilisa-tion in the previous section exemplify this approach. Again, the seeming neatness of the typologies disguises the reality of practice, and it is not uncommon for community groups to engage in all of the activities that Green describes and to use a combination of consensus and conflict approaches to achieve their goals (Ohmer and Brooks, 2013).

In the UK, Gilchrist and Taylor (2011) identify three main approaches to community development: making the existing structures work more smoothly, rebalancing the system to be fairer and more democratic, and fundamentally changing the way society operates. Like Green's typology, these approaches range across the ideological spectrum from consensus/ functionalist to conflict.

As the typologies suggest, community development has a long history as both a grassroots movement and as an intervention. As a grassroots movement, it may be defined as a bottom-up participatory process that is initiated by communities and seeks to effect change at the local, national or global levels. Currently and in many parts of the world, conflict community development is being hampered by the shift to neo-liberalism and the incorporation of community development approaches to achieve social and economic objectives, while community development groups and agencies face a difficult choice between accepting and challenging the system (Burkett, 2011a). Despite these challenges, conflict community development or community action endures and may be found at local, national and global levels (Shragge, 2013). For instance, in 2001 large numbers of protestors campaigned to prevent Glasgow City Council from closing the Govanhill swimming pool. Mooney (2006) points out that the campaign to save the pool was one part of a wider protest against the degradation and shutting down of public services in working-class areas of Glasgow.

Governments, state bodies and voluntary organisations have been amongst the agencies that have exploited community development as an intervention in a range of social and economic problems, and there has always been interplay between these actors and community groups. In the last forty years, this interchange has increased as governments have increasingly sought community-based solutions to the problems that have accompanied globalisation, neoliberal economic policies and social change. Governments in the UK, the US, Australia and the Republic of Ireland have harnessed community development ideas to encourage community involvement in self-help and service provision in the context of growing social problems, the rolling back of the state and fiscal retrenchment (Forde, 2009; Fremeaux, 2005; Gilchrist and Taylor, 2011; Hodgson, 2004; Mendes, 2009; Shaw, 2003; Shragge, 2013). These initiatives are 'top-down' rather than bottom-up or stemming from the grassroots; 'top-down' refers to a development that is 'instigated or prescribed by state agencies as a managerial procedure and with formally established processes for involvement' (Paterson, 2010, p. 78). The effect of growing state engagement in community development has been multi-faceted. Since the 1990s, unprecedented levels of state, private and philanthropic funding for community development activity (Gilchrist and Taylor, 2011) have enabled governments and other funders to dictate large parts of the community development agenda (Shragge, 2013). As community groups and projects respond to macro imperatives and funding opportunities, service provision and enterprise have consequently become prominent features of the community development landscape. This has led to an emphasis on consensus-based practice and compromised community autonomy and control. In the US, for example, Sites, Chaskin and Parks (2007, p. 529) describe how over time community development corporations (CDCs) have shifted from traditional ideas of community development based on 'community participation and accountability' to a focus on 'entrepreneurial inventiveness' in response to a challenging fiscal climate. This represents a movement away from community development as a developmental process and towards community development as a set of tangible and evidence-based outcomes, and from accountability to the local community to inter-agency cooperation.

The breadth of contemporary community development activity may give rise to a perception that community development is practically *everything* that happens in a community (Gilchrist, 2003). This is a risky assumption that needs to be challenged. Recently, community development organisations have sought to reclaim the concept of community development by identifying its specificity and key characteristics; this is discussed in the next section.

The starting point for our understanding of community development is that the 'ultimate power of community, or of any community practice, lies not in its status as a distinct sector of activity but in the extent to which it contributes to social justice' (Sites, Chaskin and Parks, 2007, p. 533). Community development is therefore not everything that goes on in a community, but is rather activity that strives for social justice goals. Social justice is the pre-eminent value because 'injustice invariably devalues all the others' (Solas, 2008b, p. 133). The associated characteristics of community development are presented in Box 1.1.

Text Box 1.1

Community development

Community development is a *critical form of practice* that identifies and attempts to address unequal relations of power. It is inalienably *value-based* and seeks *social change* 'founded on social justice, equality and inclusion' (Federation for Community Development Learning, UK National Occupational Standards for Community Development, 2009).

Community development is *transformative* in nature because it seeks change rather than stasis. The change process builds from the smaller- to the larger-scale, involving greater numbers of people as it proceeds. This transformative potential distinguishes community development as an approach (Ledwith and Springett, 2010). Transformational practice is value based, democratic and collaborative, and links the local with the global.

Since social change is most effectively achieved through the actions of groups and collectives, *collective action* is the fourth distinguishing characteristic of community development. It may be argued that action 'that is framed solely in individualistic terms is not legitimate territory for community development' (Shaw, 2011, p. 141), but in reality much community development practice begins with individual initiative and draws in more participants as it progresses.

Community development is a *preventive* approach that anticipates issues and situations and seeks to address them before they turn into problems. In fact, a good deal of community development practice is simply about working creatively with people to enjoy and celebrate community life, but in so doing communities also seek to avoid or address some of the problems that affect them. Practice in the community is therefore about 'improving the well-being of all community members' (Gamble and Hoff, 2013, p. 217).

The final characteristic of community development is that it is an *educational process*. It is typically an informal type of education, based on learning by doing, but formal education sometimes plays a part (Freire, 1997). Teater and Baldwin (2012) make the point that 'Social or community workers engaged in community development have this role of community education, enabling communities to develop critical autonomy and voice in their struggle with those in power' (p. 30).

Community development and social work: Connections in practice, values, and knowledge

There has been a relationship between social work and community development since the earliest examples of social work practice. Community development is a separate and distinct discipline from social work but is also an important dimension of 'holistic and effective' (Mendes and Binns, 2012, p. 606) social work practice. This relationship will be explored in detail throughout the book, while for now we will explore the key connections between social work and community development, in the areas of practice, theory, values, knowledge and skills.

Practice

Internationally and historically, social work has had enduring links with community work, although the influence of community work has varied

from country to country. In the nineteenth century, Charity Organisation Societies (COS) and the Settlement Movement sought to engage
middle-class volunteers with the problems of poor urban areas in the UK
and later in the US (Bradley, 2012; Brueggemann, 2013). While the focus
of the COS was charitable and individualised, leading to the development
of casework approaches, the Settlements based their work on a structural
analysis of poverty, research and policy advocacy and the encouragement
of solidarity amongst poor and disadvantaged groups. These early differences in orientation have persisted in social work and have undergone
shifts in popularity, marking 'continuities and discontinuities' (Dominelli,
2004a, p. 10) in social work practice over time.

From the late 1960s a growing awareness of the importance of community led to the development of community social work, an approach
which was used in parts of the UK but did not become substantially
embedded in practice (Dominelli, 2010a; Stepney and Popple, 2012),
despite receiving recurring attention in the social work literature. The
emergence of radical social work in the UK in the 1970s led to the introduction of community work approaches on social work curricula and in
practice, and while the progress of radical social work was undermined by
the ascendance of the neo-liberal political ideology, several of its ideas
have continued to exert influence in social work practice (Ferguson and
Woodward, 2009; Healy, 2012).

Looking beyond the US and the UK, we can see that social work has had
a strong connection with community work in Scandinavia and in southern
hemisphere states including Australia, New Zealand and South Africa. This
connection endures despite the pressures that social work is experiencing
in each of these countries (Aimers and Walker, 2011; Allen-Kelly, 2010;
Gray and Lombard, 2007; van Heugten and Daniels, 2001; McDonald and
Chenoweth, 2009; Mendes and Binns, 2012).

Values and principles

Social work and community development are underpinned by a similar
set of *values and principles*. In the first place, both are based on humanistic
values that prioritise the welfare of human beings (Mendes, 2008a).
According to the International Federation of Social Workers (2014), social
work is based on the principles of human rights, social justice, social
inclusion and solidarity with the disadvantaged, while community development 'is a moral activity' that contributes to 'the creation of a better
and fairer world' (Shaw, 2011, p. 141). These principles provide the foundation for a practice that challenges inequality and injustice at both
agency and societal levels. Other values tend to be associated primarily
with either social work or community development. For instance, collective action is essential to community development practice, but does not

feature in most lists of social work values, despite the reality that many social workers have experience of working on a group or collective basis.

Anchoring values

Anchoring practice in the values of social work and community development achieves a number of purposes. It provides practitioners with a set of ethical benchmarks that guide their actions and enable 'good practice'. It reminds them that the fundamental purpose of social work and community development is about human well-being. On a practical basis, it helps to identify the aims and focus of the work from the start; it enables the setting and attainment of particular development goals; and it facilitates the establishment of ways of working. Most significantly, it helps to reconnect practitioners with the values that distinguish social work and community development from other areas of work. This is particularly apposite at a time when both disciplines are under severe pressure from the competing demands of the state, ideology and increasingly complex social problems. In community development, these demands are due to

> the great variety of contexts in which we work; the numerous practice approaches that abound; the various and fragmented theoretical underpinnings and the social policy contexts that inform the work; and also the diverse language that is used to discuss practice. (Lathouras, 2010, p. 16)

Social workers experience similar pressures, often to a greater extent because of the legal dimension of their work and the necessity of familiarity with the theory and practice of the law, sometimes in strained circumstances such as child protection work.

Gamble and Weil (2010) distinguish between the codes of ethics that professional and representative bodies develop to identify the key ethics and values that underpin professional practice and the values and principles that inform everyday practice in social work and community development. Social work practice is informed by the ethics and values identified by the IFSW (http://ifsw.org/policies/statement-of-ethical-principles/) and by those espoused by national social work codes of ethics, such as those of the National Association of Social Workers USA and the Australian Association of Social Workers (AASW) (see Australian Association of Social Workers, 2010). In the mission statement of the International Association for Community Development (IACD) social justice is identified as the core value of community development and the associated practice principles include local leadership, respect for local values, a collaborative approach and diversity, equality and social inclusion. National umbrella associations for community development also produce their own sets of values and principles. The Federation for Community Development Learning in the UK lists the values of community development as equality and anti-discrimination, social justice, collective action, community empowerment and working and learning together (www.fcdl.org.uk).

While international and national codes of ethics are important, there are likely to be some variations between practice principles based on the local context to community development practice. In each context particular principles will be pre-eminent while local values have to be taken into account, as the IACD practice principles acknowledge. Lathouras (2010) describes the values and principles that underpin the work of the Nambour Community Centre on Australia's Sunshine Coast. The values include human dignity and worth, belonging, reconciliation, cultural diversity and social justice. The principles include cooperation, sharing resources, education, responsiveness and sustainability. Several of the values and principles relate specifically to the local context. In particular, the values of reconciliation and cultural diversity recognise that Nambour is a mixed community of Indigenous Australians, Torres Strait Islanders and white Australians of different national and cultural backgrounds. The values and practice principles were specifically developed to match the development needs of the Nambour community. The starting point for community development practice is to reflect on the goals, values and principles that will guide and inform the work in accordance with community needs.

Unpacking values

The values that attend social work and community development are complex and contested in their own right and require some unpacking. Here we explore the principal values that underpin practice in both disciplines and consider the impact of values on practice.

All values, including those of social work and community development, are pliable entities that can be interpreted and harnessed to meet a range of different and sometimes opposing objectives. For instance, 'social justice' is a complex concept that is understood quite differently in different times, places and cultures. Reisch, Ife and Weil (2013) point out that social justice does not have a single, universal meaning but has been understood and operationalised very differently at different times and in different places. To illustrate, Kenny, Fanany and Rahayu (2012) explore differing understandings of social justice amongst grassroots community development projects in Indonesia. While the projects share a commitment to social justice they emphasise different elements of social justice depending on the activities in which they engage. Faith-based Muslim projects are concerned with the pursuit of human rights and specifically with issues of 'gender, freedom of speech, local production and the environment' (Kenny, Fanany and Rahayu, 2013, p. 287). Village co-operatives, on the other hand, understand social justice in terms of economic security and self-determination.

Brian Barry refers to the need for a 'right theory of social justice' (2005, p. 4) that is based on a clear set of principles, and that avoids pernicious effects. Solas' (2008b) vision of social justice, written for the AASW, provides a model and a set of principles that are applicable to both social work and community development practice. As we have seen, Solas considers social justice to be a 'cardinal' value (2008b, p. 133) of social work and based on the principles of equality or a recognition that injustice 'resides in the social order, not people' (ibid., p. 134). Other characteristics include the capability to lead a 'dignified life' (ibid., p. 134), upholding of difference and diversity, and the inviolability of collective rights in the cultural, economic, political and social areas.

Empowerment is another concept that is central to both social work and community development practice. Ife (2013, p. 63) refers to the centrality of empowerment in community work and the manner in which 'many community workers would choose to define their role in terms of an empowerment process'; many social workers may describe their work in similar terms. In reality, however, empowerment is a contested concept that is used in very different ways and to fulfil diverse agendas. Those who have power invoke 'empowerment' in restrictive ways that are aimed at maintaining their own hegemony. In this way, people may be empowered to be

> citizens of the institutions of the modern state; as consumers in the increasingly global market; as responsible patients in the health system; as rational farmers increasing GNP; as participants in the labour market, and so on.
> (Henkel and Stirrat, 2001, p. 182; see also Gray, Stepney and Webb, 2012)

Henkel and Stirrat's argument is that people can be empowered to conform to orthodox, dominant or hegemonic ideas about society and how it should be organised. Thus empowerment is sometimes used to maintain the status quo rather than in a critical manner to change it.

We understand empowerment as a 'bottom-up' process that individuals and groups undergo in order to seek social justice. The first stage in the process is consciousness-raising or the development of a critical awareness of the individual or group's situation. Empowerment is achieved in a number of ways but principally through consciousness-raising, an educative process aimed at bringing about change. Consciousness-raising is the means by which people begin to become aware of their situation and make connections between their own experience and that of others who are experiencing similar challenges, either in the same community or elsewhere in the world. They may then use the power at their disposal to seek immediate changes to their situation or strive towards change in the longer term. The critical approach to case work that we describe in Chapter 3 is an example of how individual consciousness-raising may occur; consciousness-raising is also explored in more detail in Chapter 5. Ledwith and Springett (2010, p. 19) suggest that 'True empowerment... is not an individual state, but a collective state'. While we are inclined to agree with this view we acknowledge that empowerment begins with the individual and may then broaden to collective action. Communities can use creative ways of seeking and celebrating empowerment, including music, art and drama (Gamble and Weil, 2010; Landvogt, 2012).

The final value that we explore is *participation*, which is also common to social work and community development. Like 'empowerment', participation is a much used and contested concept within community work and in the wider society. Meagher (2006, p. 31) considers some of the reasons for this:

> Enthusiasm for participation is present across the political spectrum and there is a measure of agreement about its value. For the Left it presents a solution to the problems of alienation and marginalisation, for those in the Centre it is a means to improve decision-making and service delivery and for the Right it means freedom and individual choice.

As Meagher suggests, 'participation' is a malleable idea that can be mobilised to justify a range of agendas and, as a result, is at risk of being rendered meaningless.

For us, participation is concerned with *who* becomes involved in efforts to achieve social justice, *how* participation is achieved and *what* it achieves. While it is impossible, and probably unnecessary, to involve everyone in the community development process, it is important that people have the opportunity to become involved if they want to. It is particularly important that those on whom the work is focused become involved and have their own voice, rather than having someone else such as a professional speak or act for them. Participation is therefore about building involvement from the bottom up or grassroots:

> It can be viewed as a continuum of activity that can start from information sharing through capacity building and empowerment to active engagement and meaningful participation in democratic processes. It recognises that people have the right to participate in decisions and structures that affect their lives. (Community Workers Co-operative, 2008, p. 26)

A number of different characteristics of participation may be discerned from this definition. In the first place, participation is manifest in and may be built up from small-scale activities such as information sharing and participation and decision-making in a group to much larger-scale activities, including the achievement by groups of 'a central role in the definition of public policy' (Meade, 2009, p. 68). Secondly, participation is an educative process and individuals' and groups' capacity to participate can be encouraged and enhanced through experience and through education, a role that can be undertaken by the social or community development worker, depending on their position in a group and the stage of the group's development. Kenny and Clarke (2010, p. 256) write about the potential of critical capacity building to achieve 'collective self-determination and the realisation of human rights'. Gamble and Weil (2010) identify and describe education and training roles in their wide-ranging discussion of the roles of social and community practice workers. Westoby and Shevellar (2012) explore community-based education and training approaches in a range of international contexts such as Papua New Guinea, Cambodia and South Africa.

Finally, participation is about outcomes as well as process. As our discussion of empowerment indicated, people may be encouraged to participate in initiatives that seek maintenance of the status quo. The goal of participation needs to be 'positive effects on economic, identity/cultural and political opportunities' (Davies, Gray and Webb, 2014, p. 126) for those who participate and the communities they represent. It takes time and considerable effort to work towards this goal, which cannot be reached by 'waving a magic participation wand' (Cornwall, 2008, p. 278).

Theoretical perspective

It is helpful to locate social work and community development practice within a specific theoretical framework. The perspective put forward here is a critical one, for several reasons. First, a critical perspective is compatible with the origins of social work and community work practice. While social work theory has experienced 'continuities and discontinuities' (Dominelli, 2004a, p. 10) over time, critical ideas have been drawn on since the earliest manifestations of the work in the nineteenth century (ibid.). The use of these theories has been more marked in recent years as anti-racist, anti-oppressive and post-colonialist perspectives have developed as a response to inadequacies in existing theories (Weil and Ohmer, 2013) and issues posed by growing diversity and inequality. Second, while critical theories themselves represent a hybrid of different traditions and ideas, they are based on the unifying principle of change or transformation, and the 'most useful theories for community practice focus on change' (ibid., p. 127).

Critical practice, which derives from critical theory, is a term that is common to social work and community development. While a familiar term in social work, critical practice is also a hotly contested concept and requires some unpacking to enable clarity. Stepney and Popple (2008) identify two principal strands of critical practice: critical postmodernist practice and critical realist practice. While the terminology is intimidating, these two conceptions represent forms of practice that are familiar to social workers, at least in theory. Critical post-modernist practice emphasises social change through a bottom-up approach in which the worker uses critical reflection to identify the presence of unequal relations of power and knowledge in their practice with service users and changes their practice accordingly. Conversely, the starting point for critical realist practice is that while individuals experience inequality and injustice in a very real way, the causes of inequality and injustice are structural rather than located in the individual. Structures are 'relatively durable interlocking... social/material relations' (Sayer, 2012, p. 186) of power between the powerful and those who are in relatively powerless positions. Sayer uses land ownership as an example of a structure; landlords or property owners can levy rents on tenants who do not own land or dwellings, and their power to do so may be further upheld by property rights enforced by the state, which is itself another structure. Structures generate real 'gender, class and racial stratifications' (Houston, 2014, p. 10), while discourse and knowledge are also mediated by structures.

Given that structures are generated by humans, it is through human endeavour that they can be resisted, challenged and countered. Resistance cannot be taken for granted, however, as people often accept the forces to which they are subject (Sayer, 2012). Critical realist practice, therefore, depends upon critical analysis based on challenging 'taken for granted knowledge and popular assumptions' (Stepney, 2012, p. 25) that may obscure the reality of situations or deflect the necessity for action. It acknowledges the effects of structures on the lives of individuals but recognises that people can 'take action to achieve change and address structures and discourses of inequality and oppression' (Ife, 2010, p. 143; Houston, 2001). Significantly for social work, critical realism recognises that inequality and injustice need to be 'addressed through strategies of prevention as well as protection' (Stepney and Popple, 2008, p. 163). This focus on prevention and protection is a realistic one and recognises the complexities and 'high-risk' (Stepney and Popple, 2008) nature of much of social work practice.

A critical realist perspective most closely fits the project of this book, although we do not use the term 'critical realist' and favour simply 'critical practice'. Stepney and Popple's (2008) argument that critical realism facilitates a hybrid form of practice encompassing a range of different approaches fits with our contention that community development has a place in social work practice. Notwithstanding the consensus-based nature of much of contemporary community development, it still offers approaches that are considerably more critical than the 'individualising and pathologising nature of care management and risk assessment' (Baldwin, 2011, p. 193), and acknowledge the importance of both structure and agency in recognising and addressing social problems. The recognition of the structure-agency dialectic opens possibilities for social workers and community workers, who are de facto *social actors* and *change agents* in the lives of individuals, groups and communities. Change can be small-scale in nature, but small changes 'can still have a real impact on the lives of those involved' (Ferguson and Woodward, 2009, p. 138). Sometimes small-scale or local change may lead to change on a wider scale. Furthermore, as discussed earlier, change can start with the individual and build into collective activity. This resonates with social work, where the starting point is often the individual, usually the individual social worker and service user, but there is potential to move beyond working on an individual basis to working with groups and communities.

Skills and knowledge

Social work and community development also have a similar skills and knowledge base, or what Aimers and Walker (2011) refer to as 'knowledge intersections'. While there is a statutory dimension to social work knowledge that community development does not share, the two disciplines draw on remarkably similar bodies of skills and information. This knowledge base is primarily humanistic in nature and drawn from 'sociological, political, anthropological, psychological, economic and critical theory frameworks' (Weil and Ohmer, 2013, p. 136). Both disciplines also draw on macro or explanatory theory and micro or practice theory, which is concerned with action and change. Both also use tacit theory (ibid., p. 136), or the common and everyday knowledge that all practitioners build up through their lives, experiences and relationships. Writing in a South African context, Ferguson and Smith (2012) make some interesting points about social work students' use of theory and skills on non-traditional social work practice placements in campaigning organisations and social movements. They point out that the students used a range of social work and community work skills, and that both sets of skills were helpful in approaching the work effectively. They also drew on systems and strengths perspectives, but to a much lesser extent on critical or structural explanatory theories. These findings are thought provoking in two ways. Firstly, they illustrate that social work and community development have a common and almost wholly interchangeable skills base. Social workers therefore have the capacity to use community development approaches in their practice without moving outside their established knowledge and skills frameworks. Secondly, they signify the pre-eminence of 'a conservative neo-liberal ideological context' (ibid., p. 991) that discourages critical and structural perspectives in both social work and community development practice and inhibits social workers from considering the potential of critical approaches in their work. The ideological and policy context to social work and community development practice is explored in Chapter 2.

Questions 1.2

Social work and community development: Shared values, knowledge and skills

1. What do you see as the main 'connections' between social work and community development?
2. Debate the role of community development in social work practice. Use examples to justify your arguments.

Chapter outline

Initial chapters explore the influence of macro developments on social work theory, policy and practice and consider the corresponding impact of these developments on social work and community development. Chapter 1 has looked at the contested nature of 'community' and 'community development', which are variously understood in contemporary theory, policy and practice, explored the historical connections between social work and community development, and identified some of the values, skills and knowledge that social work and community development share. Chapter 2 considers the impact of a rapidly changing policy environment on social work and community development practice, and examines the implications and challenges for social work engagement with communities. The focus of Chapter 3 is the potential of discourses to forge links between social work and community development. The chapter locates critical community development within a community discourse, and discusses how new and developing areas of social work practice offer opportunities for critical practice.

Chapters 4, 5 and 6 concentrate on the connections between social work and community development approaches and investigate the possibilities of critical practice. Aspects of contemporary social work practice theory are the subject of Chapter 4, which considers both the potential and challenges that these practice theories offer for social workers' engagement with critical community development approaches in local and global contexts. Theoretical approaches addressed in the chapter are: radical and structural social work, systems theories, post-modern approaches and critical realism.

Chapter 5 critically analyses the origins of community development as a grassroots approach and an intervention. The chapter unpicks the community development process, its broad scope and critical or transformational potential. Chapter 6 evaluates some of the ways in which social workers can effect change through critical or 'creative activism' – innovative ways in which social workers can engage in critical community development practice. The chapter argues that opportunities to undertake critical practice exist in all social work practice settings and that social workers should be prepared to identify and seize these opportunities through their own agency or through engagement with others.

Identification and explication of some of the ways in which social workers can prepare for and scaffold their critical practice is the focal point of Chapter 7. The chapter explores the value of personal practice frameworks, evaluation, 'reflection in action' and practitioner, transformational and participatory research for social work practitioners.

The Conclusion draws together the key elements of the book and addresses the challenges and opportunities for social work practitioners, educators and academics, students and researchers in engaging with community development ideas and approaches.

- Social workers and community development workers are *social actors* and *change agents* in the lives of individuals, groups and communities.

- Social work and community development share similar values, knowledge and skills sets, including a commitment to social justice in theory and practice.

- Community development approaches offer possibilities for a critical and engaged social work practice.

- Identify a community issue that you feel very strongly about. What are the parameters of the issue and what challenges does it pose?
- Consider how a community development approach might assist you as a practitioner to address this issue.
- Identify and explore the values and principles that may underpin your approach to the issue. How will these values and principles guide your practice? What skills will be beneficial?
- What do you see as some of the challenges or barriers to using a community development approach in social work practice? In your discussion, consider a range of social work practice contexts such as statutory child protection, a probation service, a small non-governmental agency working with refugees and migrants.

- Chaskin, R.J. (2013) 'Theories of Community' in M. Weil (ed) *The Handbook of Community Practice*, 2nd edn, Thousand Oaks, CA: Sage.
- Dominelli, L. (2004a) *Social Work: Theory and Practice for a Changing Profession*, Cambridge: Polity Press.
- Ife, J. (2010) *Human Rights from Below: Achieving Rights through Community Development*, Cambridge: Cambridge University Press.
- Lathouras, A. (2010) 'Chapter 2: Community Development Work – A Method' in A. Ingamells, A Lathouras, R, Wiseman, P. Westoby and F. Caniglia (eds) *Community Development Practice: Stories, Method and Meaning*, Australia: Common Ground Publishing Pty Ltd.
- Parton, N. (1994) '"Problematics of Government", (Post) Modernity and Social Work', *British Journal of Social Work*, 24, pp. 9–32.
- Stepney, P. and Popple, K. (2008) *Social Work and the Community: A Critical Context for Practice*, Basingstoke: Palgrave Macmillan.
- Weil, M. and Ohmer, M.L. (2013) 'Applying Practice Theories in Community Work' in M. Weil (ed) *The Handbook of Community Practice*, 2nd edn, Thousand Oaks, CA: Sage.
- Yerbury, H. (2012) 'Vocabularies of Community', *Community Development Journal*, 47(2), pp. 184–198.

Online Resources

- UK Federation for Community Development Learning (2009). *National Occupational Standards for Community Development*, available online at www.fcdl.org.uk [Accessed 4 March 2015].
- International Federation of Social Workers, IASSW and ICSW (2012). *The Global Agenda for Social Work and Social Development Commitment to Action*, available online at www.cdnifsw.org/assets/ globalagenda2012.pdf [Accessed 4 March 2015].
- International Federation of Social Workers (2014). 'Definition of Social Work', available online at http://ifsw.org/policies/definition- of-social-work/ [Accessed 4 March 2015].

2 Ideology, policy and community

Introduction

In this chapter we explore the main macro influences on social work and the social professions in the twentieth and early twenty-first centuries and consider some of the challenges that these influences pose. The chapter begins with an overview of the impact of the neo-liberal ideology on economic policy internationally and considers how economic crisis, welfare reform, modernisation and managerialism have affected the provision of social and public services, particularly social work. The chapter proceeds to examine how many governments have coupled neo-liberalism with a communitarian agenda, producing policies such as the Third Way and Big Society, and looks at the effect of this on communities and community development activity in a number of countries. It then considers some of the challenges and possibilities of prevailing policy frameworks for social work and community development practice.

The international policy context 1950–2013

After the cataclysm of the Second World War (1939–1945), governments in a number of countries, particularly those directly affected by the war, instigated a range of social and economic reforms with twin aims: to address the post-war legacy of poverty and deprivation and to move away from the predominance of low interventionist or laissez-faire capitalism (Beech, 2012) towards greater state intervention in economy and society. Interventionist government became known as 'welfare capitalism' (ibid., p. 90) or the 'welfare state'. From the late 1940s welfare states were being developed in several countries although the nature and extent of the welfare state differed from place to place. The central idea behind the welfare state is of 'welfare rights ... as social rights enjoyed by virtue of entitlement' (O'Sullivan, 2012, p. 22); welfare as entitlement differed from previous forms of welfare which were reserved only for the destitute. Hayward (2012) identifies four principal types of welfare state: Scandinavian, Anglo-American or neo-liberal residual, continental European and ex-Communist. While these are ideal types the most comprehensive welfare states have been the Scandinavian ones, while the least extensive are the neo-liberal residual welfare states of the 'Anglophone' countries (Hayward, 2012), including the US, the UK and, in more recent times, Australia.

From the early 1970s welfare states began to come under pressure as governments faced a series of fiscal difficulties. The oil crises of 1973 and 1978 led to rising inflation which, coupled with rising wage costs and increasing unemployment (O'Sullivan, 2012), led governments in Europe, the US and Australasia to relinquish or roll back on policies based on principles of state intervention and expenditure. These policies were replaced with the 'singular goal' (Lingam, 2013, p. 207) of 'economic growth coupled with liberalization, deregulation, and privatization' (ibid.). These represent key characteristics of neo-liberalism, an ideology that predated the 1970s but failed to gain significant purchase in the aftermath of the Second World War. Other key characteristics of neo-liberalism include 'a limited and non-interventionist role for the state' (Hay, 2004, p. 508), the curtailment of welfare benefits in favour of participation in the labour market (ibid.), and an emphasis on individual freedoms and concomitant responsibilities (Harvey, 2005). Since the 1970s, neo-liberalism has been the over-riding ideology in the Global North and initially the cultivation of global markets, the relatively free movement of trade and investment internationally and the deregulation of financial systems led to unprecedented economic growth and prosperity and to greater movement of human beings across geographical boundaries than ever before. While the economic crash of 2008–2009 has forced nation states and supra-national institutions like the European Union into austerity and reregulation (Lee and Woodward, 2012), neo-liberalism remains the over-riding force in the economic sphere and exerts an ongoing influence in the social one, as we will now explore.

Changing welfare states: The marginalisation of welfare

Internationally, welfare states have undergone change and retrenchment due to successive fiscal crises and mounting state debt. Under the rubric of neo-liberalism each type of welfare state, from the comprehensive Scandinavian model to the residual Anglo-American, has been subjected to increasing reform. While the nature and extent of the reform has varied from country to country, the trend has been to move away from universalistic policies in favour of contingency planning for risks such as unemployment, poverty, illness and disability (Webb, 2006). Labour activation policies have sought to curtail unemployment, press 'responsibilisation' or the principle of work as duty as well as right, and ensure a 'reserve army' (van Berkel and Hornemann Moller, 2002, p. 59) of labour to be mobilised during times of economic growth. Paradoxically, as welfare states became more residual, governments began to intervene to address perceived risks in areas that previously occupied the private sphere. These include the provision of early years care and education for children, the introduction of health policies such as the ban on smoking in public places, and increasing surveillance measures in the prevention of crime. In the UK, for instance, the announcement in 2013 of compulsory supervision orders for minor offenders after release from prison is evidence of unprecedented state intervention in the criminal justice process and in the lives of those who have served their time in prison (Travis and Watt, 2013). Meanwhile, the public services that work on the frontline of these areas, including social work, are subject to greater prescription, regulation and control (Lorenz, 2001).

Welfare policies championed by successive UK Conservative governments from the 1970s to the 1990s were adopted by New Labour and continue to be pursued by the Coalition government. Gray, Stepney and Webb (2012, p. 264) describe a form of 'welfare governance', whereby the state behaves in a paternalistic manner towards those in receipt of welfare, treating them as customers or clients and forcing them into labour activation schemes in order to 'make them *productive* members of society or *economic participants*' (ibid., their italics). The personalisation or individualisation of social care, which is characterised by the introduction of personal budgets and direct payments for recipients of care, has been criticised for embodying the neo-liberal ideology of personal choice, individualism and consumerism, undermining the collectivist principle of the welfare state (Lymbery, 2012a, 2012b), as well as for failing to be as efficient or effective as envisaged (Spicker, 2012). The individualisation and personalisation of welfare policy facilitate a movement away from structural and critical explanations for poverty and open the way for an alternative narrative that places the blame for a failure to prosper on the poor and disadvantaged. Slater (2012) suggests that David Cameron's slogan 'broken Britain' represents a moral panic that simultaneously undermines ideas of big government and the welfare state, pathologises the poor and vulnerable and justifies the radical cutting of welfare budgets while promoting narrow forms of citizenship that encourage people 'to volunteer and donate ... in order to help vulnerable people change their ways' (p. 17).

In the US the welfare state has always been residual, but welfare provision has become increasingly marginal over the last thirty years. Uluorta (2008) attributes this to the collapse of the Soviet Union, the financial 'boom' of the late twentieth century and the September 11 attacks, all of which combined to underscore a sense of American supremacy and the rightness of policy based on neo-liberal principles. The election of Ronald Reagan in 1980 introduced a thirty-year period of reduced government intervention, deregulation of the financial sector and championing of business, and the restriction of the rights of ordinary workers (Schaffner Goldberg, 2012). 'Increasingly, the state and its institutional apparatuses are reluctant to reclaim social spaces' (Schaffner Goldberg, 2012, p. 251). Workfare policies have forced welfare recipients into poorly paid, often 'dead-end' jobs that afford little prospect of social mobility. In addition, privatisation, devolution and increasingly bureaucratic and systematised work practices have changed the complexion of public services (Reisch and Jani, 2012).

Retrenchment has led to significant welfare reform in the Nordic countries, which have traditionally operated the most extensive and progressive welfare states. The comprehensive Nordic welfare state has been characterised as a 'social shock absorber' (Hayward, 2012, p. 10) that helps to maintain social and economic stability. Since the 1990s all of the Nordic countries, apart from Iceland, have experienced growing unemployment and reduced tax income (Johansson and Hvinden, 2007) and have responded by adjusting their welfare systems, primarily through the introduction of capacity-building or activation programmes to encourage re-entry to the workforce of the long-term unemployed, young people and members of minority groups such as people with disabilities and immigrants. Harlow, Berg, Barry and Chandler (2012, p. 7) point out that Sweden has 'embraced neoliberal thinking'; this has occurred through the extension of its existing labour activation policy, benefit reductions (Johansson and Hvinden, 2007), an escalation in the privatisation and outsourcing of some social services, financial restraints and the introduction of New Public Management (NPM) procedures (Harlow, Berg, Barry and Chandler, 2012).

Like other capitalist countries in the northern hemisphere, over the last thirty years Australia has undergone a process of sweeping welfare reform. The combination of a globalised economy and neo-liberal politics has broken the traditional reliance on centralised wage bargaining and placed an emphasis on liberalising the labour market, labour market activation programmes (McDonald and Chenoweth, 2009), the privatisation and marketisation of some public services, and large-scale public sector reform (Germov, 2005). Cumulatively, these developments have precipitated the establishment of 'a new regime characterized by paternalism and coercion' (McDonald and Chenoweth, 2009, p. 147), the transformation from an extensive to a neo-liberal residual welfare state, and 'fractured the dependent population back into the categories of deserving and undeserving poor' (ibid., p. 146). The introduction of severe anti-immigration policies and the growth of opposition to non-white immigration to Australia are symptomatic of a growing conservatism and perhaps a concern that immigration threatens the country's economic and cultural interests (Louis, Duck, Terry and Lalonde, 2010).

Consequences of the neo-liberal 'turn': New public management

In many countries, the neo-liberal 'turn' has been accompanied by the influence of managerialism or NPM in the public sector. While there are some differences in the manifestation of managerialism in each place, the rationale for its introduction is typically associated with a drive to economise, modernise and render public services more efficient and responsive. Parallel with these developments, social services including social work are increasingly run in accordance with NPM codes of practice. These codes are wide-ranging in nature, and include privatisation or semi-privatisation of aspects of services, the planning and evaluation of services using performance indicators and research, and the use of consumer/customer charters. In an 'insidious twist' (Lorenz, 2008, p. 16), language is used strategically to advance the process of change and encourage the complicity of service user and service provider alike. Accordingly, service users are now often referred to as 'consumers' who have rights but concomitant responsibilities, such as the responsibility to look for work if unemployed and the responsibility to oversee the health care system in the case of patients and patients' groups (Tonkens, 2011).

Whatever the benefits of NPM codes of practice, and undoubtedly greater transparency for service users may be considered advantageous, it is apparent that there are several significant drawbacks. In the first place, the promotion of increased productivity and cost-saving may jeopardise both quality and equality of service delivery and of care (Germov, 2005). Secondly, a concentration on the technical aspects of practice via performance indicators and audits may detract attention from the wider context in which practice takes place and be detrimental to a broader consideration of the causes of the problems and issues that service users experience. Thirdly, concern with *how* a task is performed may lead to 'a loss of the critical judgement' (Jordan and Drakeford, 2012, p. 73) that is crucial to occupations such as social work. Finally, and equally importantly, managerialism or the 'contractual model' (ibid., p. 72) may downplay the importance of empathy, compassion and caring in human service work. The consequences of such a loss can be calamitous, as the breakdown of care in the Mid Staffordshire Hospital (see Francis, 2010) and the recent scandals concerning the mistreatment of older people in the UK and Ireland (Commission for Social Care Inspection, 2008; Donnelly, 2008; Age Action Ireland, 2011) have illustrated (see Case Study 2.1).

Elder mistreatment and abuse in the UK

In 2007 the UK National Centre for Social Research published an audit of mistreatment and abuse of older people at home. The report catalogued a range of physical and psychological abuses inflicted on older people by spouses, family members and carers at home. The report concluded that approximately one in forty people (or roughly 266,000 people) aged sixty-six and older had experienced mistreatment or abuse in their homes. Spouses were the principal abusers (51%), followed by other family members (49%), care workers (13%) and friends (5%).

In 2008 a study by the group Action on Elder Abuse into adult protection referrals to local authorities in England discovered considerable alleged physical abuse of older people by care workers, followed by family members (Manthorpe, Stevens, Hussein, Neath and Lievesley, 2011). These reports demonstrate a growing awareness of the problem of elder abuse in the home and in care settings including hospitals and care homes. Manthorpe, Stevens, Hussein, Neath and Lievesley also refer to the Francis Report into Mid Staffs Hospital. The report

> emphasised that patients, mostly older people, were the people who had borne the brunt of the failings of this hospital where staff were not supported to be open and learn from mistakes, where many staff at all levels did not focus on quality care, where organisational and individual ambitions were a priority, and where systems failed to share information on risk and to work collaboratively. (ibid., p. 62)

The impact of managerialism on social work

There have been serious repercussions for social work from the shift towards neo-liberalism, managerialism and responsibilisation. Some of these repercussions are quite predictable, others less so. There is a preoccupation with 'performance targets, national service standards and a league table culture' (Stepney and Popple, 2008, p. 102), or what Webb (2006) refers to as the regulation *of* social work (his italics).

Changing social work practice in the UK

In the UK, a number of key developments have had a significant impact on social work policy and practice, although certain differences between the four countries within the UK must be borne in mind. A complex set of events initiated by successive Conservative governments in the 1980s and progressed by the subsequent New Labour government has transformed the social work landscape, introducing a 'managerial revolution' (Harris, 2008, p. 855) and resulting in a mixed bag of both opportunities and costs. The individualisation of welfare initiated by New Labour in 1997 and pursued by the Coalition government appeared to offer new opportunities to social workers to exercise key aspects of their role (Lorenz, 2001), including the upholding of human rights and social justice, but the reality of the shift to individualisation has been more problematic. Social work commentators including Lymbery (2010, 2012a, 2012b), Ferguson (2007) and Houston (2010a) have criticised the implementation of personalisation and argued that it represents a shift towards consumerism rather than a recognition and realisation of the core elements of citizenship, including collective rights, redistribution and equality. Lymbery (2012a) illustrates by pointing to the difficulties that personalisation poses for many service users who have physical and mental disabilities that may restrict their capacity to exercise the choice that the policy holds out for them. In turn, this creates problems for social work, 'an occupation that ought primarily to be concerned with those people who have the lowest levels of capacity to act as self-actualising consumers' (ibid., p. 788). Recent research provides evidence of some innovative local personalisation practices that enable service users to determine their own needs, but suggests that a tension exists between these practices and 'top-down, prescriptive directives for personalisation' (Brookes, Callaghan, Netten and Fox, 2015, p. 101).

Personal and social relationships have always been integral to social work practice but the shifting policy environment of the last fifteen years has changed the nature of this relationship considerably and rendered it much more complex (Lymbery, 2014; Rogowski, 2011, 2012). Social work departments have become responsible for the implementation of a range of policies and for the regulation of individuals and communities, or social work *as* regulating (Gray, Stepney and Webb, 2012; Webb, 2006). It remains to be seen whether the findings of the Munro Review of Child Protection (2011) will help to reverse this trend, but recent evidence suggests that this has not yet happened (Cooper, 2013).

Webb (2006) argues that risk assessment has become dominant in social work practice, as social workers attempt to identify, analyse and counter the risks to a range of populations, including children, people with mental health issues and older people. In children's services, prevention and early intervention have become pre-eminent, and there has been a fragmentation or hiving off to other professions of more expansive and 'non-authoritarian' (Harlow, 2003; Harlow, Berg, Barry and Chandler, 2012; Munro, 2011; Welbourne, 2011, p. 409) roles previously undertaken by social workers, such as parental support, which is now principally delivered by family support workers. Similarly, managerialism has removed many social workers from front-line activities and repositioned them in more co-ordinating and managerial areas of work (Carey, 2009; Dominelli, 2004b); this contributes to deskilling and the neglect of hands-on practice. In the process, the 'pursuit of social justice and empowering social work' has been severely hampered (Welbourne, 2011, p. 409) while service users may be reduced to statistics and 'waste-products of the game' (Webb, 2006, p. 77) rather than thinking agents and members of communities capable of understanding and acting upon their situations, both on their own and on a collective basis with others. Social workers are encouraged to, or compelled to, view service users as categories of risk, such as 'homeless' or 'offender' or 'asylum seeker', rather than members of the community. These 'othering' (Dominelli, 2004a, p. 76; Lorenz, 2001) perspectives on communities have had distancing effects on social work practice.

In the UK, the job dissatisfaction that results from these combined developments has led to a movement of social workers out of the public sector and the growth of employment in private agencies that are contracted by government (Harlow, Berg, Barry and Chandler, 2012; see also Price and Simpson, 2007). Parton (2014a) argues that the recent proposal to privatise children's services in England represents a return to the charitable provision of services in the nineteenth century and is part of a wider movement towards the commercialisation of the state. These developments, together with cutbacks to public services in the context of austerity, have reduced numbers of social workers in the UK and curtailed the capacity of social work to offer a 'proactive and positive supporting role' (Lymbery, 2012a, p. 789) at a time when this is most needed. Comparable developments have occurred in the Nordic countries where, as in the UK, most social workers are employed in the public sector and work in municipal authorities at local level and where NPM has been implemented and embraced by all actors including social workers (Johansson, 2012; Stepney, 2006). Social work managers are increasingly required to 'focus on administration, finance, budget cuts and market adaptation instead of leadership and efforts to meet the staff's social needs' (Kullberg, 2013, pp. 4–5), while social workers have very limited influence on operational decision making and policy making (Johansson, 2012).

Changing social work practice around the world

Social work has been strongly affected by the unrolling of managerialist policy and practice, sometimes in unexpected places. In China, social work has been discussed as a means of social control in the context of radical social change over the last ten years (Leung, Yip, Huang and Wu, 2012). As capitalism has been introduced to the one-party Communist state, national and local government have sought ways to address the social issues and problems that accompany massive economic growth, and social workers have been recruited in large numbers to contribute to shoring up social cohesion and service provision. Leung, Yip, Huang and Wu (2012, p. 1050) suggest that in China 'social work presents a sophisticated, handy and seemingly manageable technology for governing at a distance'. While the Chinese context is a specific one, there is evidence of parallels with social work in Western democracies, where social work's 'traditional mandate of care and control' (ibid., p. 1054) has nudged inexorably towards control over the last thirty years.

The exercise of control may also be applied to social work in the US, but predictably takes a very different form from that in China. American social work reflects the national values of individualism and privatisation, but perversely control is manifested in specific ways. Pozzuto and Arnd-Caddigan (2008) point out that evidence-based practice (EBP) based on randomised controlled trials is heavily used in US social work. They cite the example of a state mental health agency in North Carolina which has used EBP based on randomised controlled trials to explore the effectiveness of specific treatments. These are the only treatments that are funded by the state, so that those who find these treatments ineffectual must fund alternatives themselves. Economic rationalism is the main criterion for choice of treatment and there is 'a paternalistic tacit assumption' (Pozzuto and Arnd-Caddigan, 2008, p. 67) about what service users need, rather than a concern to establish the most suitable intervention for each individual. Pozzuto and Arnd-Caddigan argue that economic imperatives also drive social workers, many of whom establish for-profit services after qualification, and concentrate on work that will yield the most funding, rather than that which responds to the needs of clients. These forms of 'domination' (ibid., p. 69) are the antithesis of the social work values explored in Chapter 1.

In Australia, extensive reform of state welfare services and the adoption of NPM codes of practice appear to have had an impact on how social work is delivered, although Wallace and Pease (2011) point out that research evidence of its impact remains slim. Research Box 2.1 describes McDonald and Chenoweth's (2009) study of the impact of NPM practices on the Centrelink agency in Australia.

Private social work in New Zealand and Australia grew during the 1980s, although it has not reached the extent of privatisation of American social work. The move towards privatisation was due in part to a move to liberalisation of both economies and the marketisation of a range of activities, including social work and other traditionally public sector services (van Heugten and Daniels, 2001). In New Zealand the growth of private social work practice was partly due to social workers' frustration with the uncertainty caused by the constant reorganisation of public services and partly to the growing acceptability of enterprise and profit in a country that had a traditionally 'ambivalent attitude towards private enterprise and business' (ibid., p. 746). Since the 1980s similar developments have taken place in Australia, where cuts in public spending and contracting out of services have provided opportunities for private social work practice.

Social work in Centrelink: Professional dilemmas

McDonald and Chenoweth (2009) describe the transformation of Centrelink, an agency that delivers a range of services to welfare recipients, from 'a traditional bureaucracy to a contemporary corporation' (p. 149) in the context of Australia's transition from a traditionally welfare state to a workfare economy. The NPM reforms introduced by Centrelink include the adoption of consumerist language and procedures, including the designation of service users as 'customers' and the employment of a range of mechanisms to measure customer satisfaction.

Centrelink is the largest employer of social workers in Australia, and McDonald and Chenoweth map the effect of the changes to Centrelink on the social workers' roles and engagement with service users. In the context of the reorganisation of Centrelink, the social workers were required to specify what they could contribute to the new agency. Their chosen roles were crisis intervention via operation of Centrelink call centres and disaster recovery work. McDonald and Chenoweth's study reveals that the Centrelink social workers have encountered a series of 'clashes in institutional rationalities' (ibid., p. 157), or conflicts and ethical predicaments caused by differences between social work values and the values espoused by the new Centrelink. These include a decrease in their professional autonomy, the erosion of client confidentiality, and a constriction of the functions they undertook before the reorganisation, notably a reduction in their scope to engage in community development and social justice work. Some of the social workers appear to have accepted and readily conformed to several of the practices of NPM, including the use of the term 'customer' in place of 'service user' or 'client'. Some have actively attempted to reconcile their new ways of working with the principles and values of social work, rather than identifying any disconnect between their previous and current ways of working. Others have engaged in both active and passive resistance.

While McDonald and Chenoweth acknowledge that Centrelink is a unique organisation and that not all social workers operate in similar settings, they point out that social workers in other practice contexts are not immune from similar dilemmas and suggest that workfare and NPM together represent one of the most significant challenges for social work and that 'ongoing critical observation, evaluation and engagement are, at a minimum, desirable' (ibid., p. 158).

Questions

1. What challenges does NPM pose for social workers and community development workers? Draw on your own experience in addressing this question.
2. In your view what are the implications for social work practice of a reduction in capacity to undertake community development and social justice work?
3. What is your opinion of the strategies that the social workers in Centrelink use to respond to NPM?

Lorenz (2008) argues that NPM codes enable the maintenance and further development of '"traditional" social work methods' (Lorenz, 2008, p. 16) such as case management while in its turn case management claims to satisfy NPM's 'Zeitgeist of rationality, efficiency, and individualism' (ibid., p. 16). NPM represents a concern with guaranteeing 'a reliable and compliant workforce who will simply work at the will of employers through managers' (Rogowski, 2011, p. 9). The Centrelink example suggests that there is a more nuanced picture in practice; social workers respond to managerialism in various ways, by rationalising it and accepting it into their frames of reference, by resisting it or by challenging it. None of these responses is passive or compliant; each involves a conscious choice about a course of action.

The 'turn' to community in international policy

We have seen how the relationship of social workers to families, groups and communities has changed under neo-liberalism and with the development of managerialism. This is part of a broader movement towards community-based solutions as governments, semi-state agencies, voluntary bodies and commercial interests look to respond to the challenges and risks that accompany neo-liberalism and globalisation. As the discussion in Chapter 1 emphasised, there are different conceptions of 'community' and each has legitimacy, from spatial understandings to those that emphasise relationships and people's capacity to exert agency over their environment. A conception that has received considerable attention in the twentieth century and into the new one is community as an entity or locale for addressing issues and effecting change. This section will explore the reasons for the 'turn' to community and consider some of the ways in which community has increasingly been used as a site for community development and social work activity.

Community as intervention: Communitarianism

Chaskin (2013) refers to three ways in which community is used as a basis for action. In the first place, community is what Chaskin refers to as a 'unit of identity and action' (p. 115), in which different actors seek to build the capacity of the community to facilitate and encourage change, or attempt to mobilise the community to seek change from the state or the market. Highlighted in Chapter 1, this is the space in which community development activity occurs and in which there is a 'continued evolution of practice on the part of existing community organizations, activists and community initiatives responding to shifting circumstance' (Chaskin, 2013, p. 116). Grassroots community development activity constantly reacts to events in the community and to outside influences such as changing government policy and its impact on community members.

Secondly, community is viewed as a context in which planning and decision-making occurs. Communities are perceived as microcosms of society and as such act as sources of information and experience on which decisions can be based. Thirdly, and of most relevance to this discussion, communities have increasingly become the focus for 'top-down' intervention through targeted programmes instigated by the state, voluntary agencies or other actors to address public policy and service issues such as employment, housing, anti-social behaviour and the environment. Since the 1990s the focus on 'community' and the associated trend towards co-operation and partnership between the state and the voluntary sector in the delivery of human services have also been evident in countries including New Zealand (Aimers and Walker, 2011) and Australia, and in several European countries including the UK and Ireland. The interest of governments in community has been attributed to the influence of the communitarian discourse, which emphasises a strong and associational community life, a vibrant civil society that acts as a buffer between state and market, and the co-existence of rights and concomitant responsibilities that all individuals as members of a community hold. Strongly associated with the work of the American sociologist Amitai Etzioni, communitarianism emphasises positive and attractive values including 'strengthening relationships, enhancing processes of participation, developing the capacity for communal self-help, promoting feelings of empowerment and connectedness' (Sites, 1998, p. 58). Given these attributes it is unsurprising that communitarian ideas were taken up by a number of governments in the 1990s and continue to exert influence into the twenty-first century.

In several countries communitarian ideas were transmuted into the so-called 'Third Way' approach, or the 'political offspring' (Gwyther, 2000, p. 1) of communitarianism. Third Way policies were instigated in the US in the 1990s during Bill Clinton's presidency and variants were popularised in Europe by Tony Blair in the UK and in several other countries including Germany, Ireland, the Netherlands and the Nordic countries, and in New Zealand and Australia. Also described as the mixed economy of welfare or welfare pluralism, the Third Way is characterised by three principal policy approaches. These are the free movement of capital throughout the globe, the rolling back of the state via decreased expenditure on welfare and social services, and the reform and modernisation of welfare systems (Stepney, 2006; Stepney and Popple, 2008). The reform and modernisation of welfare systems involves greater reliance on voluntary and community provision of services, decentralisation of services, increased formalisation of relationships in and between welfare-providing organisations, and greater monitoring and inspection (Parton, 1994).

In the UK, New Labour notably appropriated the concept of 'community' and used it in an extensive range of policies. Initiatives such as the Urban Programme, New Deal for Communities (NDC) and Local Strategic Partnerships (LSPs) used a targeted and co-ordinated approach to the provision of a range of services in disadvantaged areas. In Ireland, an extensive network of area-based partnerships was introduced in the early 1990s to combat long-term unemployment in selected areas through co-ordination of service provision by the main state and semi-state organisations at municipal level (Forde, 2009). In both Ireland and the UK, engagement with communities was seen as a core feature of these initiatives.

Growing links between community, state and market have been noted by a number of American writers including Sites, Chaskin and Parks (2007) and Chaskin (2013). Brueggemann (2013) refers to 'new federal partnerships' (p. 42) between the state and community-based organisations, and suggests that co-operation 'between government and the voluntary social sector is now a central financial fact of life and has become the backbone of this country's human services delivery system' (ibid., p. 43). Recent examples include a number of anti-poverty programmes such as Promise Neighborhoods and Choice Neighborhoods which were introduced by the Obama administration in a large number of US cities to address poverty in an integrated manner through pooled funding and inter-agency initiative. According to Murphy (2011) advantages of such area-based initiatives include the potential to influence broader policy, while drawbacks include inadequate funding due to 'a political environment where concern for the poor is absent' (p. 1), and the small-scale nature of the initiatives relative to less progressive federal programmes such as the provision of food stamps.

Craig (2007) describes a number of initiatives in Australia and New Zealand including the development of partnerships in Western Australia to build relationships between Indigenous people and local governments, and efforts by the New Zealand government to establish relationships with the Maori people to address the problem of alcohol-related crime. Aimers and Walker (2008, p. 18) suggest that New Zealand government funding has been confined to 'those services that meet government priorities', to the detriment of schemes initiated by communities themselves.

Communitarianism: Issues and opportunities

Governments' espousal of communitarianism and the third way has been heavily criticised in the sociological and social policy literature on both economic and social grounds. From an economic perspective, Somerville (2011, p. 94) argues that in Britain, New Labour viewed communities in a utilitarian way as just one set of market actors within neo-liberalism, 'helping to shape that market in their own interest, through the choices they make as individual and collective consumers' (see also Reisch and Jani, 2012, writing about the US context). The welfare reforms described earlier in this chapter are indicative of these approaches. For instance, workfare policies regard welfare recipients as actors who will act rationally in order to obtain employment, and personalisation policy treats people with disabilities as consumers who can exercise choice about their own care arrangements. As these examples illustrate, 'community' has become a convenient facade for policies that are essentially individualist in nature and intent (Fremeaux, 2005), and a useful middle way between the harshness of neoliberalism and the interventionism of the left (Sage, 2012).

Mowbray (2005) and Craig (2005) note that the Australian government became very interested in the concept of 'community' in the last decade of the twentieth century, and initiated an array of programmes including 'community/capacity building, government-community partnerships, community and neighbourhood renewal' (Mowbray, 2005, p. 255). Mowbray argues that governments' engagement with communities represents an attempt to 'legitimate the state's continuing commitment to economic fundamentalism' (p. 255) rather than a genuine effort to co-operate with and learn from the experiences of community and voluntary actors. Governments have discovered that relatively small fiscal investments in programmes involving communities can yield considerable benefits in good publicity and improved public opinion.

A second set of critiques focuses on the social and communal effects of policy based on communitarian ideas. During times of reduced expenditure on welfare and social services, the involvement of communities as partners in service delivery with the state and private sectors ensures the targeting of much-needed funds to community and voluntary actors, but also serves to legitimise the state's actions. Ideas such as 'community', 'civil society', 'participation' and 'active citizenship' have become vehicles through which government policy is channelled. Civil society and the community groups that constitute it have become a tool or solution (Forde, 2009; Fremeaux, 2005; Hodgson, 2004) of the state for the provision of welfare. State discourse promotes 'induced self-help' (Shaw, 2003, p. 362) and, like individuals, communities and community and voluntary organisations are persuaded to take responsibility for issues and problems that were previously the remit of the state (see Practice Example 2.1).

Community development as welfare provision

Recently, in an interview with one of the authors, a community development worker in a state-funded community development project in Ireland described how she is required by the state to request and record the Personal Social Insurance numbers of everyone who uses the project. The purpose of this requirement is to quantify and justify the project's work, in terms of how many people use the project's programmes, services and drop-in facilities. There are obvious problems with this requirement. These include the limitations of employing quantitative measures to assess the performance of community development processes that are inherently qualitative.

In your view what are the other problems with this requirement?

The self-help or responsibilisation (Webb, 2006; see also Newman and Tonkens, 2011) discourse has served the state well but has had unforeseen and negative impacts on the communities involved, including increased formalisation or bureaucratisation of the relationship between the state and community groups and agencies, associated diminished autonomy for many of these groups and agencies, and the consequent '"imprisonment" rather than the liberation of local initiatives' (Hodgson, 2004, p. 157). Unprecedented levels of state funding have turned the focus of much community development activity from grassroots initiatives into interventions to address a range of issues identified and prioritised by the state. These issues include the provision of care and welfare, tackling crime and anti-social behaviour, and addressing the health, educational and social needs of community members. 'Community' is the prefix and the centre-point for many of these interventions – 'community safety, community policing, community health, community education, and so on' (Craig, 2007, p. 336). This terminology of community is also apparent in the employment by government of labels such as 'community cohesion' (Ratcliffe, 2012) and 'community capacity-building'. Craig (2005) suggests that employment of these terms enables governments to 'repackage' their interventions in different ways, while effectively retaining their control over communities and ceding little power. Terms such as 'community capacity-building' euphemistically describe

> what are effectively 'top-down' interventions where local communities are required to engage in programmes with predetermined goals... as a condition for receiving funding, approaches far removed from 'bottom-up' community development interventions. (Craig, 2007, p. 349)

In the UK, this burden has arguably increased since the introduction of the Big Society agenda, which has placed a greater onus on communities by relying 'much more on voluntarism and the replacement of publicly funded posts by local volunteers and the third sector' (Ratcliffe, 2012, p. 276) while simultaneously cutting their budgets (Barnard, 2010; see also Ishkanian and Szreter, 2012).

Westoby and Botes (2013) describe the dilemmas faced by state-employed community development workers in South Africa. These workers face constant tensions between political and professional agendas, between process versus output and between service delivery and developmental approaches. Westoby and Botes give the example of how citizens' sense of entitlement to goods and services from the state conflicts with the community workers' desire to mobilise citizens 'to make fair entitlement claims to the appropriate duty bearers' (ibid., p. 1304). They argue that these tensions derive from the equivocal position in which state-employed community development workers are placed and are based on

> knowing that one is working from the 'inside' of the state moving 'out' to communities, while recognising that many community groups are working in the other direction, with little concern for inside priorities. (ibid., p. 1308)

Like the social workers in Centrelink, community development workers have to find ways to navigate these dilemmas in order to meet the demands and expectations of both state and community.

In conclusion: Challenges and opportunities for social work and community development

This overview of policy developments in a range of countries has shed light on some common difficulties and challenges facing social work and community development internationally. In the first place it has shown how neo-liberalism and the advent of managerialism have wrought significant and comparable changes in the social work and community development landscapes in different countries. It has also explored the response of social workers to the new and emerging institutional landscape. This response has been complex. While the drive for the imposition of managerialist policies and practices is a structural one, it may be reasonably argued that social work has at least partially negotiated and accommodated these policies and practices, thereby enabling their operation and maintenance. Carey (2009) argues that possible reasons for this include the 'personal and professional aspirations' that propel social workers and other social professionals to embrace 'externally driven policies or... other forms of "disciplinary power" to acquire professional recognition' (p. 523). Further, in countries where most social workers and many community development workers are employed by the state, there is interdependence between the state and these areas of work (Carey, 2009); they cannot extricate themselves from this relationship and are forced to constantly negotiate it. As the examples of the Australian Centrelink agency and South African community development illustrate, this negotiation can present personal and professional dilemmas for many social workers and community development workers. How they may address these dilemmas and practise in a critical way is the subject of the remaining chapters.

- Since the 1970s neo-liberalism has been the over-riding ideology in capitalist countries. Characteristics of neo-liberalism include an emphasis on the primacy of the market, deregulation and the residualisation of welfare.

- Neo-liberal politics and the imposition of managerialism or New Public Management practices have bureaucratised social work practice and changed and challenged its relationship with individuals, groups and communities.

- The effects of neo-liberalism and NPM pose ongoing challenges for communities and for critical community development practice.

- Social workers and community development workers seek to respond to these challenges in meaningful and informed ways, not as passive recipients of policy.

stop and think

- Discuss some of the possible effects of neo-liberalism on individuals and communities.
- What has been the impact of (i) managerialist and (ii) communitarian policies on social work practice?
- In your view, how have social workers responded to these policies?
- How can social workers counter ideas and practices that label individuals, families and communities as dysfunctional, deviant or at risk?

- Berg, E., Harlow, E., Barry, J. and Chandler, J. (2012) 'Neoliberalism, Managerialism and the Reconfiguring of Social Work in Sweden and the United Kingdom', *Organization*, available online at http://org.sagepub.com/content/early/2012/06/21/1350508412448222.
- Chaskin, R. (2008) 'Resilience, Community and Resilient Communities: Conditioning Contexts and Collective Action', *Child Care in Practice,* 14(1), pp. 65–74.
- Craig, G. (2007) 'Community Capacity Building: Something Old, Something New...?', *Critical Social Policy*, 27(3), pp. 335–359.
- Dominelli, L. (2004b) 'Practising Social Work in a Globalizing World' in N. Tan and A. Rowlands (eds) *Social Work Around the World III*, Berne, Switzerland: International Federation of Social Workers.
- McDonald, C. and Chenoweth, L. (2009) '(Re)Shaping Social Work: An Australian Case Study', *British Journal of Social Work,* 39, pp. 144–160.
- Pozzuto, R. and Arnd-Caddigan, M. (2008) 'Social Work in the US: Sociohistorical Context and Contemporary Issues', *Australian Social Work,* 61(1), pp. 57–71.
- Westoby, P. and Botes, L. (2013) '"I work with the Community, Not the Parties!" The Political and Practical Dilemmas of South Africa's State-Employed Community Development Workers', *British Journal of Social Work,* 43, pp. 1294–1311.

3

chapter

Beyond dominant discourses: Challenges and opportunities

Introduction

So far we have explored some of the connections between social work and community development. Not only do they share a value and knowledge base, they have been considerably shaped by a changing societal and policy environment which has presented challenges and opportunities for both social work and community development. This chapter explores the major discourses that influence practice in contemporary settings and considers the implications for both social workers and community workers. We draw on examples where practitioners challenge dominant discourses and explore how critical approaches enable us to move 'beyond dominant discourses' and create opportunities for engaged, critical and creative practice within current practice settings as well as in new arenas of practice.

The chapter begins with a discussion of what we mean by the concept of 'discourse' and identifies the major discourses that have been influential in shaping social work ideas and practice in different practice contexts such as health, education and welfare. We then explore the influence of discourses of community on social work ideas and practice and argue that a critical community development practice is compatible with social work history, knowledge and values. We locate critical community development within the community discourse which we explore in depth, and we extend our discussion to developing areas of social work practice that offer new opportunities for both social work and community development practice.

What is discourse?

Discourses constitute the language and social practices (Thompson, 2010) which we use to understand and engage with the social world; they include the 'social subjects, social relations and systems of knowledge' (Humphries, 1997, p. 642) that make up our world and enable us to make sense of and function in it. These practices contribute to both the construction of reality as well as to its understanding by helping us to find ways to react to what happens in the world. Dominelli (2004a, p. 106) refers to this as 'the expression of agency', or people's capacity to respond to phenomena that they encounter in their lives. Discourses are therefore about both understanding and action.

Post-modern ideas about discourse emphasise the multi-layered and contested nature of reality, which is seen as a subjective entity that is constructed by individuals and understood using systems or discourses of meaning. Inevitably individuals and groups shape reality in ways that are beneficial to them, therefore power plays a significant role in discourse (Fook, 2012), and powerful groups use discourses to uphold their interests. Humphries (1997) points out that the 'most powerful discourses in our society have firm institutional or structural bases, in "normalizing" practices of the law for example, in social welfare, education, the organisation of the family and work' (p. 642). For instance, the law underpins dominant ideas about most aspects of life, from the right to life to the extent of people's rights to education, health and welfare provision. These ideas are reproduced and reinforced through other institutions such as schools and services. These prevailing ideas serve the interests of particular groups. Professions are formed and sustained on the basis of discourses that uphold and legitimise their claims to practice. Healy (2005) and Thompson (2010) both give the example of the biomedical discourse, in which doctors have traditionally been accorded considerable power, and patients respond in accordance with 'doctor's orders' (Thompson, 2010, p. 164). Similarly, as a profession, social work is sustained by a body of knowledge, professional education and sets of ideas that distinguish it from other professions (Fook, 2012) and enable social workers to claim expertise in a range of areas.

We can use the biomedical example to illuminate another characteristic of discourse. Given that reality is constantly shaped by individuals, and assuming that power is a diffuse entity (Foucault, 1980), it is inevitable that competing or 'countervailing' (Thompson, 2010, p. 166) discourses emerge to challenge dominant ones. These countervailing discourses often emanate from the groups who are subject to the dominant discourses. For instance, in recent times the patients' rights and social medical discourses have begun to challenge the supremacy of the biomedical model. The patients' rights discourse accords greater power to the voice of patients and facilitates the questioning of 'doctor's orders' and the assertion of patients' own knowledge and experience.

Discourse and social work

Unpicking the various discourses that underpin social work is a complex task, but Healy (2005) clearly identifies three sets of discourses that impinge significantly on social work practice. Her model provides insight into the multifaceted nature of social work, in policy, theoretical and practical terms. Social work practice is influenced by many sources of knowledge and experience and by several factors, including legal considerations and policy constraints, professional knowledge and authority, and knowledge and experience gained through practice. The three sets of discourses are:

- Institutional or dominant discourses, including public and organisational policies, laws, and 'accepted practices' (p. 5)
- Professional discourses, including morality and belief systems, and formal knowledge and skills taught in social work training
- Practice discourses, including amalgamated formal practice knowledge, practice wisdom and knowledge acquired through experience.

Healy advances law, biomedicine and neo-classical economics as examples of *dominant discourses* because they provide the framework within which activities in health and social welfare, including social work, are conducted. Social workers must be familiar with, implement and respond to the law in a range of areas, including child welfare and protection, adoption, disability and mental health. The biomedical discourse, which was already mentioned above, increasingly impinges on social work practice, as social workers are called on to mediate and intervene in complex medical and ethical disputes between doctors and patients (Healy, 2005).

The discussion of neo-liberal policy in Chapter 2 has underlined the considerable impact of economics and economic policies on the social professions. Within the context of neo-liberalism, New Public Management (NPM) is an emerging discourse in its own right. While she does not include it in her classification of dominant discourses, Healy (2005) argues that NPM may be considered a dominant discourse in aspects of the health and welfare sectors. As a by-product of the 'ascendant neo-liberal paradigm' (Reisch, 2013, p. 67) that has dominated both the economic and social spheres in most capitalist countries, NPM approaches have altered the delivery of services in a range of areas, including welfare provision, health care, social work and tertiary education in many countries. The influence of NPM has extended to community development, significant swathes of which are now directly under the control of the state.

Professional discourses provide what Reisch and Jani (2012, p. 1134) refer to as the 'master narrative' for social work practice, and therefore constitute another set of dominant discourses. These discourses represent the building of a professional identity and an associated *practice discourse*, or sets of theories, knowledge and skills that help to distinguish social work from other professions and areas of work. While the delineation of a distinct niche has been beneficial to social work and to individual social workers, it has given rise to several problems for its practice. In the first place, there has been a dislocation between the original value base of social work and that which it now espouses. This dislocation has happened gradually but steadily until social work has reached the point where its role may be considered as regulatory and sometimes repressive in a society dominated by the market (Parton, 1994).

> ...in recent years, this master narrative has subtly accommodated itself to dominant cultural values – emphasising the individual over the community, equality of opportunity over equity, exper- tise over mutual aid and adaptation over conflict. (Reisch and Jani, 2012, p. 1135)

In conjunction with changing values, shifts in the education of social workers have helped to reproduce these dominant cultural values. Jani, Ortiz, Pierce and Sowbel (2011) give the example of how American social work education has struggled to incorporate a structural analysis of racism, oppression and discrimination into the teaching of diversity, instead giving preference to the achievement of cultural competence which 'others' the service user (Dominelli, 2004a). This 'othering' undermines the possibility of an in-depth understanding and engage- ment between service user and social worker. Mlcek (2013) refers to the whiteness discourse in social work and how this perspective, which is 'individualised into actions of power and privilege within a profes- sional context' (p. 4) needs to be constantly challenged in social work education.

Secondly, Healy and Meagher (2004) use the term 'deprofessionalisa- tion' to refer to several developments associated with managerialism that have threatened professional social work practice. These include the 'frag- mentation and routinisation' (p. 244) of practice and the attendant erosion of professional discretion and creativity, the 'underemployment' (p. 245) of professionally qualified social workers in jobs for which they are over-qualified, and the fragmentation of the social work role through the employment of quasi-professionals to undertake aspects of the role. These developments were explored in detail in Chapter 2.

Discourses in social work: Intersections and divergences

In this chapter, we are particularly interested in exploring the character- istics and inter-relationships between key discourses that impact on both contemporary social work and community development. Ife's Framework of Human Service Delivery (Figure 3.1) is useful in this regard as it identifies the relationship between dominant professional, managerial and market-led discourses and the community discourse, which in turn offers an alternative way of conceptualising contempo- rary social work in theory and practice. In his framework of human service delivery the positioning of the four discourses on two axes illus- trates the principal characteristics of each of these discourses and their

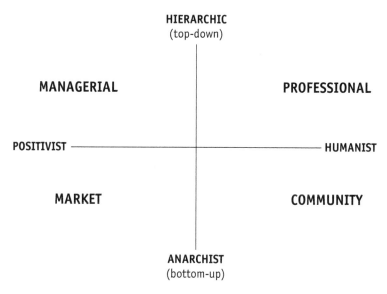

Figure 3.1 Ife's framework of human service delivery
Source: Ife (1997).

relationship to each other. The managerial discourse is hierarchical or top-down and positivist in nature because decisions are made by senior managers and are often based on statistics or evidence-based research. The professional discourse is top-down because it relies on the professional knowledge and judgment of the social worker, but is fundamentally humanist or person-centred in nature. Ife suggests that the professional discourse is the one 'in which traditional social work has been most comfortable, with its emphasis on professional expertise, individualised service, and its combination of humanist values and "top-down" intervention' (1997, p. 56). The market discourse which is positivist and anarchistic or bottom-up also exerts an influence in social work, particularly in the US, but as we have seen in Chapter 2, market-led social work is growing in other countries including the UK, Australia and New Zealand.

In contrast to the managerial, professional and market discourses, the community discourse described by Ife is a critical form of practice that is based on initiative and development from the bottom up. Ife suggests that the community discourse is the natural location for social work practice. This discourse joins the humanist position with an anarchist or bottom-up perspective (Ife, 1997, p. 49); this location is consistent with social work history, knowledge and values such as social justice, equality and empowerment. It is based on an organic 'bottom-up' process that is often at odds with the demands of managerialism, professionalisation and market forces. In contrast to these discourses, it is characterised by the emphasis on 'welfare as social activity, or *participation* in a community context' (ibid., p. 50). All of these values are integral to a humanist, bottom-up and anarchist approach, which emphasises that 'people should be able to articulate their needs and aspirations and should be empowered to act in order to have them met' (ibid., p. 80).

Parton (2009) points out that Ife's framework represented a challenge to the changing policy landscape in the late 1990s, when neo-liberalism undermined both social work and community development in favour of an emphasis on 'managerialism and the market in the way social service departments were organized and operated' (p. 70). In particular, and as we have seen, the dominance of managerialism has adversely affected both social work and community development and represents an ongoing challenge at this juncture in the twenty-first century.

The community discourse is similar to the critical community development approach described in Chapter 1 and developed in this book. Ife suggests that many social workers have seen and continue to see 'social work as an essentially critical practice to bring about a better, fairer and more just society, rather than merely providing professional interventions to individuals and families' (1997, p. 151). Key features of a critical perspective include recognition of injustice and inequality and an emphasis on change (Forde and Lynch, 2014), based on awareness that the personal is political, or that people's experiences can only be understood when placed in the context of the wider social and economic forces that affect all aspects of life. Given this link between the personal and the political, a critical perspective seeks change based on the 'legitimacy of both the individual and structural approaches to empowerment' (Ife, 1997, p. 136). Change can therefore be sought at different levels, individual, organisational and structural. How change may be sought at each of these levels is the subject of the following section on challenging dominant discourses.

Challenging dominant discourses in the social professions

Marston and McDonald (2012, p. 1022) point out that social work 'has been an important project of modernity'. Modernity, or the period that began in the late eighteenth century, is associated with a number of developments or structures, including industrialisation, urbanisation, and advances in scientific and other forms of knowledge (Stones, 2008, p. 7). Developments in knowledge were perceived as reliable, generalisable and universal (Fook, 2012; Parton, 1994). The growth of knowledge and curiosity and of new forms of social surveillance and regulation led to the emergence of distinct professions responsible for specific areas of work. The preoccupation with the 'social' stemmed from 'intersecting and interrelated concerns and anxieties about the family and the community more generally' (Parton, 1994, p. 16). As modernity and the twentieth century progressed, social workers, as the 'primary technologists' (ibid.) of the 'social', were tasked with upholding the institution of the family on behalf of the state, thereby helping to fulfil the twin aims of maintaining social norms and state legitimacy.

Some social theorists argue that since the late twentieth century we have entered the post-modern period (see Fawcett, 2009; Shipman and Powell, 2005), or a period that succeeds modernity and is different in distinct ways. Post-modernity challenges the 'universal science, knowledge and truth' (Parton, 1994, p. 28) of modernity, and instead views reality as fractured, diverse, and based on multiple truths. In a seminal piece the social work writer Nigel Parton (1994) argues that the movement from the structuralism and absolutism of modernity to the more splintered realities of late modernity or post-modernity is perilous, because post-modernity undermines the certainties that were built up under modernity, leaving a legacy of insecurity and doubt. This has implications for social work which, as we have seen, draws on a distinct and established body of knowledge based on 'certain social and psychological truths concerning the individual' (ibid., p. 29). Conversely, Parton acknowledges that the contingent and uncertain nature of post-modernity offers a chink of possibility for greater human agency and opportunities for social workers to 'take hold, in a self-conscious way, of what we do and the way we do it' (p. 30). The flux and instability of the contemporary period demand imaginative, nuanced and localised responses to the situations that social workers face and a recognition that social work practice is a dynamic engagement between the social worker and their environment. Correspondingly, Healy (2005, p. 9) argues that while practice is undoubtedly shaped by over-arching discourses, 'social workers can also actively use and contest the discourses that influence their practice domains'. These ideas are not incompatible with a critical realist practice that emphasises human agency while also recognising that social work is subject to certain 'societal imperatives' (Houston, 2001, p. 857) that both impinge upon and influence social work priorities. This intersection of modern and post-modern ideas offers possibilities for an engaged and responsive social work practice.

What are some of the ways in which social workers can, to quote Parton, 'take hold, in a self-conscious way, of what we do and the way we do it'? How can social workers engage with the critical discourse? Some of these ways do not involve moving outside the sites in which many social workers practice or outside their regular means of working while others involve new and alternative ways of working in response to a range of incipient challenges and threats. We now explore some of these ways of practising and later in the chapter we will explore emerging forms of critical practice.

Challenging discourses: Critical practice at the micro, meso and macro levels

Garrett (2012, p. 13) points out that under New Labour in the UK, public sector social work was portrayed as 'moribund' and incapable of creativity or independence of thought or action. This portrayal served to both discredit the public sector and promote a privatisation agenda in children's services, while overlooking the reality that creativity and discretion are consistent features of practice in the social professions. On a micro or practice level, for instance, Healy (2005; see also Marston and McDonald, 2012; Evans, 2013) points out that social workers have discretion in how they view their relationships with service users, who can be seen for example as 'victims', 'survivors' or as agents who are actively attempting to address the problems they face. Rogowski (2011; Ruch, Turney and Ward, 2010; Ife, 1997) suggests approaching case work in different ways, as an individual, relationship-based process or as a political practice by which the client or service user's experience can be connected with that of others in similar situations. Dominelli (2004a) refers to the development of counter-discourses (p. 38) through exposure of the mismatch between service users' experiences and official accounts of their lives. Levin (2010) presents extensive evidence of the way in which social workers in Norway fulfil a number of roles within the context of case work, and how these roles move considerably beyond the fulfilment of official or professional requirements. These approaches to case work recognise the service user as a citizen capable of acting to address their own situations and realising their own rights (Dominelli, 2004a), and citizenship as a set of 'reciprocal caring actions' (Jordan and Drakeford, 2012, p. 159) rather than a transaction carried out for purely economic purposes.

Also at micro or case level, Harry Ferguson (2008, p. 577) refers to the 'rhythms of practice' and how the physicality and mobility of social workers' practice offer opportunities for 'regular displays of skill, creativity and courage while on the move'; he gives the example of how social workers use their cars as they travel between meetings as sites of practice, supervision and debriefing. Another example of physicality in the course of regular working is social workers' involvement in sporting events aimed at encouraging the integration of refugees in Australia (Marston and McDonald, 2012). Not only do these events contribute to integration and acceptance, they demonstrate social workers' capacity to challenge dominant or influential discourses, in this case the 'discourse of illegality' (ibid., p. 1032) and its negative effect on Australians' attitudes towards refugees.

At the meso or organisational level of practice, social workers can achieve much while adhering to their established ways of working. Advocacy, engagement with other human service workers, representations of issues at meetings and organisation and operation of collective activities for service users and fellow professionals all represent recognised ways in which social workers can engage in critical practice. Crucial to this form of practice is the 'capacity to operate effectively' in 'a large bureaucracy, a community-based agency or a private profit-making enterprise' (Ife, 1997, p. 168). Whatever the ongoing impact of managerialism, social workers can exert agency and thereby effect change in what they do and how they practice (Levin, 2010). Practice Example 3.1 illustrates how social workers in a large bureaucratic organisation used the professional and managerial discourses to engage in critical practice.

Negotiating discourses: Challenging managerialism in a large bureaucracy

The dominant NPM agenda in Irish social work has led to an increasingly bureaucratic social work practice environment with 'high priority placed on tangible outputs' and less regard for 'relationship– and principle-based work' with children and families (Buckley, 2008, p. 23). A social worker who works in a community work setting describes in an interview* how she and her colleagues constantly challenge this dominant discourse in their employing organisation, a large statutory health agency in Ireland. She describes how they use several strategies to address issues with senior management and other decision-makers in the agency. These strategies include attempting to communicate with management by email, speaking up at planning meetings and speaking to managers, decision-makers and local councillors at events organised by the agency. She gives an example of how her line manager 'made a very trenchant contribution' to discussions about proposed cuts to funding of community and voluntary sector groups, and how the cuts were consequently averted.

The social worker acknowledges that change does not always follow the efforts of her colleagues but argues that this does not negate the importance of constantly engaging decision-makers. She also acknowledged the difficulties facing less established social workers in being seen to challenge those in powerful positions, but points out that there is strength in numbers and that if social workers and other workers co-operate in addressing issues they can achieve change.

Source: * Research project carried out by Forde and Lynch in 2009–2010. Fifteen social workers in a range of practice settings in Ireland were interviewed about their experiences of using community development approaches in their practice.

This example from social work practice illustrates the permeability of the boundaries of discourses and demonstrates that particular discourses do not necessarily represent obstacles to critical practice and the achievement of change. The social workers in the large organisation harnessed the professional and managerial discourses to make their voices heard.

They used their professional knowledge and skills to represent their opinions and concerns to their organisation and when necessary they used the management system to address the problem of cutbacks to community groups. While as Ife suggests the community discourse may be the ideal location for critical social work practice, critical practice can be effectively undertaken in any context.

Critical practice at the structural or macro level involves engagement outside social workers' everyday practice settings. Social workers may become involved in their professional associations in order to influence decisions affecting the profession or to lobby for policy change at national level (Ife, 1997; Jones, Johannesen and Dodds, 2004). The success of these endeavours varies from place to place. In South Africa, the liberalisation and globalisation of the post-apartheid economy has widened the gap between rich and poor and had an adverse effect on the situation of the poor and dispossessed, most of whom are black (Sewpaul, 2006). While individual social workers have attempted to challenge these inequalities through individual action and involvement in social movements, the South African social work statutory and professional bodies have been slow to move 'toward social activism, lobbying and advocacy' (Sewpaul, 2006, p. 431; see also Gray and Lombard, 2007). In contrast, and as Case Study 3.1 shows, social workers in Australia have made effective use of their professional associations to challenge regressive policies. In doing so they used the knowledge and influence they acquired through the professional discourse to engage with the influence of the legal discourse.

Healy and Meagher (2004) stress the importance of collective organisation in the face of managerialism and erosion of working conditions. They suggest that there are emerging opportunities for the development of alliances between professional associations representing social service workers and trade unions, two groupings which have traditionally been opposed. 'Broad-based coalitions' (p. 257) between professional associations and unions would enable the representation of the interests of a broad range of workers and service users, and open possibilities for collaboration between these groups.

Negotiating dominant discourses: Experience from Australia

case study 3.1

In 2010 the Australian Association of Social Workers (AASW) successfully campaigned to reverse a decision by the Australian government to withdraw early intervention mental health social work services from patients with severe mental health disorders. Kandie Allen-Kelly, the CEO of the AASW, suggests that the swift and mass mobilisation of social workers after the decision was announced reflected the 'fundamental commitment to social justice, community development, networking, and social action' (2010, p. 247) in the Australian social work curriculum. This example provides evidence that social workers can use the professional discourse to challenge policies that are detrimental to their profession and to those with whom they work. It also illustrates the importance of social work representative bodies in addressing structural issues concerning equality and human rights.

Community workers face similar dilemmas to those described above and they have the capacity to exert similar discretion in the face of change. For instance, the community development writer Marjorie Mayo (2002; see also Shragge, 2013) acknowledges that the professionalisation of community work has wrought considerable changes in the community development landscape but argues that professionalisation is not incompatible with a critical or transformative community development practice. On the contrary, the professional values, knowledge and skills that characterise professionalism are essential to a critical and effective community development practice. For instance, campaigning work cannot be effectively undertaken if the campaigners do not possess professional skills of organisation and communication. In a large-scale survey of community development work in Ireland, Geoghegan and Powell (2006) discovered that while most of the community development organisations which responded to their survey were state-funded and employed professional community development workers, a small but significant proportion of the organisations (14%) engaged in campaigning and protest work in addition to service provision. A survey of UK community development workers in 2001–2003 found that between 30% and 40% of paid workers engaged in more conflictual aspects of campaigning work (Henderson and Glen, 2006). Rather than being antagonistic therefore, the relationship between professionalism and critical practice can be synergistic.

These examples of agency are illustrative of an approach that can function at 'the micro and macro levels simultaneously' (Lorenz, 2006, p. 175), challenging existing arrangements and envisaging other ways of practicing, overseeing and 'administering' practice. This understanding of the agency of social workers is particularly important as we discuss how the community discourse can be used in emerging contexts for practice. This is the subject of the following sections.

Social work in the community: Emerging opportunities for critical practice

The knowledge that discourses can be used and shaped according to circumstances enables us to envisage a dynamic social work practice that engages with and responds to the environment in which it is taking place. For most social workers, the community is the wider environment in which their work is located. As Chapter 1 highlighted, there are different forms of community and social workers engage with all of these.

> Social workers may be said to practise in the community, to work with the community and to work with 'minority communities', such as gypsies and travellers... and communities of need such as the disabled or minority ethnic groups. Social work in deeply divided 'communities' is now beginning to receive academic attention worldwide.... (Mantle and Backwith, 2010, p. 2382)

Ideas about community have influenced social work theory and practice since its earliest incarnations. From the time of the Settlement Movement there has been almost constant engagement between social work and community, but the nature, focus and extent of this engagement has taken different guises over time. This section briefly considers some of the approaches which social workers have used to engage with communities and focuses on their relevance to a critically engaged social work practice. These approaches are community social work, ecosystems and ecological approaches and community development.

While there are discernible connections between *community social work* (CSW) and the community-based endeavours of the Settlement House Movements in the US and England from the nineteenth to the early twentieth centuries, Stepney and Popple (2012) argue that the key characteristics of community social work developed after the publication of the Barclay Report (1982) on social work in England and Wales. Despite differing perspectives amongst members of the Barclay Commission, the Barclay Report emphasised CSW as preventative practice based on the development and support of community networks and partnership between social workers, other professionals and members of the community. While the idea of community social work has continued to garner attention the lack of clarity as to the nature and focus of this approach has persisted. Since Barclay, the literature on CSW has tended to avoid the discussion of how community social work may operate in practice, instead 'preferring to see it as a way of thinking rather than as a blueprint for action' (Teater and Baldwin, 2012, p. 43). Recently a small number of social work writers have attempted to identify the parameters of CSW in order to promote its relevance to practice (Harrison, 2009; Midgley and Livermore, 2005; Stepney and Popple, 2008; Teater and Baldwin, 2012). Teater and Baldwin (2012) suggest that community social workers need a strong theoretical and practical knowledge base, familiarity with their communities and a skill set based on the principles of enabling and empowerment. Stepney and Popple (2008) propose a number of methods of CSW; each is based on the principles of holism, integration and empowerment. Apart from the difficulty of delineating the characteristics of CSW in practice, CSW is curiously apolitical and therefore quite distinct from community work or community development. CSW is typically associated with ideas of self-help, voluntarism and facilitating access to local services and tends to focus on change at the individual level.

> Community work is concerned with tackling injustice and inequality by organising people and promoting policy change at the local level, all of which is likely to find expression in collective action.... On the other hand, CSW is concerned with developing more accessible and effective local services... and attempts to find alternative ways of meeting the needs of individual service users. (Stepney and Popple, 2008, p. 113)

Consideration of the individual within the context of their environment is also the starting point of *ecosystems* or *ecological* approaches The environment may be the community in which the individual lives, the policies that affect them and the delivery of services by agencies used by them (Teater and Baldwin, 2012). Ecosystems approaches are about adaption or achieving a 'better fit' between the individual and their environment. This occurs through a process in which the social worker helps service users 'to become more instrumental in bringing about change to improve their lives' (Henriques and Tuckley, 2012, p. 169). Despite the implication of fault or pathology that this process implies, there is no assumption that the person is responsible for what has happened to them. Systems approaches have been criticised for their complexity and for lacking a critical or structural perspective (Healy, 2005; Payne, 1997); however, emerging models attempt to address this latter deficiency. Stepney and Popple (2008) refer to eco-social models that seek to explain the phenomena that they describe and advance possible solutions. For example, Rigby and Whyte (2013) outline the use of a dynamic ecological framework to analyse and assess the nature and extent of international child trafficking.

As Chapter 1 emphasised, *community development* is a distinct approach in its own right but also an approach which social workers use to engage with communities. In some countries social work and community development have always been strongly connected. Most Australian and South African universities emphasise community development as a core social work method (Allen-Kelly, 2010; Gray and Lombard, 2007). In South Africa social work traditionally played a developmental welfare role, which it has sought to maintain and develop post-apartheid, through, amongst other activities, social workers' involvement in community development and grassroots organisations (Gray and Lombard, 2007). Healy (2012) disputes the prevailing idea that social work is a wholly individualist profession and points out that 'social workers have extensive involvement in community work as researchers and practitioners' (p. 178). Ife (1997) points out that social workers have always undertaken community development practice, through their involvement in social movements such as trade unions and the women's, peace and environmental movements. Their engagement with the environment is the subject of the following section.

Social work and the environment

Social workers and community workers in many places around the globe are increasingly being drawn into a range of activities associated with the effects of global warming, climate change and globalisation on communities. These activities, which are the subject of an established but growing literature (for example Jones, Johannesen and Dodds, 2004; Besthorn and Meyer, 2010; Jones, 2010; Dominelli, 2010b, 2012a, 2012b, 2013; Alston and Besthorn, 2012; Jennings, 2002; Webber and Jones, 2012; Huegler, Lyons and Pawar, 2012; Alston, 2013; Tudor, 2013; Vickers and Dominelli, 2014; Hessle, 2014), are growing in importance as the unfavourable effects of these phenomena hit communities around the globe. The increased regularity with which environmental disasters occur is giving rise to the realisation that governments, professionals and communities need to find consistent, sustainable ways of responding to these events. At a march to highlight the effects of climate change in New York in September 2014, the United Nations Secretary-General Ban Ki-moon referred to climate change as 'a defining issue of our time' (Goldenberg et al., 2014).

Dominelli (2012a, 2013) introduces the idea of 'green social work', or a holistic social work practice based on social justice and human rights principles and concerned with improving the well-being of both human beings and the environment that they inhabit. Green social work seeks to address power relations founded on political social structures that adversely affect environmental eco-systems and human lives (Dominelli, 2012a, 2014). Dominelli describes green social work as a critical perspective and practice that seeks sustainability and challenges unsustainable practices that characterise neo-liberalism:

> Green social work adopts a political stance in that it recognises that power relations shape human interactions and that these are rooted in an ethics of care whereby people care for one another and the environment in sustainable ways to ensure that all living things will survive now and for generations to come. (2013, p. 437)

Green social work necessitates engagement by practitioners in collective work with communities, both local and global, to tackle structural issues and inequalities such as poverty, the effects of industrialisation, environmental degradation and diminishing natural resources (Dominelli, 2012a). As Dominelli (2013, p. 433) notes, 'the differentiated outcomes of environmental degradation and disasters affect poor and marginalised people, poor regions and poor environments the most'.

Alston (2013) and Jones (2010) suggest that the social work profession has tended to overlook the natural environment, preferring instead to focus on ecological approaches concerning individuals, families and communities. The reasons for this are complex but primarily influenced by social work's adherence to a set of modern ideas characterised by certainty and the confidence that human beings have control over their environments (Jones, 2010); this sense of certainty and control has been undermined by the growing number and intensity of natural disasters all over the globe. Green social work differs from ecological approaches because it broadens the scope of practice from engagement with individuals in their social systems to environmental actions that address power relations within socio-geo-political structures that impact on people's lives (Dominelli, 2012a). It facilitates the *agency* of people in the local area, respects their knowledge, and works towards a positive outcome with all stakeholders to protect both people and the natural environment (Dominelli, 2013). Practice on the ground involves providing support to people to enable them to realise their human and environmental rights, mobilising to develop alliances and partnerships that would promote individual and community well-being and health and protect the environment, and empowering local peoples and communities to influence policy and decision makers (Dominelli, 2013).

Involving local people in decision making is crucial and underscores sustainable development based on local knowledge and a bottom-up process where experts and local people can work alongside each other (Dominelli, 2013; Ife, 2013). In this regard, social workers can play a number of different roles: facilitator, coordinator, community mobiliser, negotiator between communities and different levels of government, mediator between conflicting interests and groups and advocate for the rights of local people (Dominelli, 2013, p. 483). Besthorn (2014, p. 21) points out that these roles are familiar to social workers and suggests that they should not 'get bogged down in big plans with infeasible objectives', but instead focus on what is achievable.

> If we ask the question 'what can social work do to eliminate environmental crisis?' we are likely asking the wrong question. The more appropriate question is 'what can social work do to improve the lives of people?'; that is, 'what can social work do to join with those peoples at local levels most impacted by environmental decline and most knowledgeable and prepared to take actions necessary to improve their unique situations?' (Besthorn, 2014, p. 21)

Dominelli's vision for green social work is echoed in the Global Agenda for Social Work and Social Development (2012), which recognises the unequal effects of political, economic and social systems for communities at local, national and global levels. One of the goals of the Global Agenda is to promote sustainable communities and environmentally sustainable development. Actions identified include the promotion of community capacity building in the context of natural disasters, promotion of education and practice that facilitates sustainable responses to disasters, and research into the social work role in environmental and disaster situations.

Case Study 3.2 is an example of the response of social workers following a series of earthquakes in New Zealand. This example highlights the importance of critical social work practice that challenges the causes of social issues and seeks to address them in sustainable ways, through involving communities in finding solutions to the problems that they face. Dominelli (2012a) and Jones, Johannesen and Dodds (2004) provide several other examples of social work responses to the adverse impacts of globalisation, including climate change.

Critical practice in post-earthquake New Zealand

case study 3.2

Tudor (2013) describes the responses of social workers after the series of devastating earthquakes in Christchurch, New Zealand, in 2009 and 2010. Nearly 200 people died following one of the earthquakes and thousands were affected. Tudor points out that as well as damage to homes, services and businesses, the earthquakes had a severe impact on many people's mental health and well-being. She describes how social services and communities responded quickly to the emergency through the establishment of a call centre that connected people to a range of community services, but government has been slow to address the myriad issues that face the people of Christchurch. These issues include lack of government intervention to ensure the honouring of insurance claims by insurance providers.

Tudor points out that one grassroots agency, the Aranui Community Trust, allocated a social worker who was tasked to check on Aranui residents' wellbeing. As well as doing this the social worker moved on to broader areas of work 'with a key focus on reducing isolation and supporting the inclusion of older people in their community' (Tudor, 2013, p. 24); this took a number of forms including the running of a drop-in group for older residents.

Tudor argues that in the context of crises such as the earthquake, social work needs to operate in accordance with its own value base of social justice, by connecting personal troubles with 'broader social and political structures and interventions' (ibid., p. 24), using community development approaches and working in partnership with community groups to identify sustainable solutions to the problems faced by communities.

Questions

1. In your view what types of knowledge and skills would social workers need to use in the situation Tudor describes?

2. In a context like the one Tudor describes what can be achieved by social workers using community development approaches?

3. What can be achieved by social workers working in partnership with community groups?

In conclusion: Policy and practices beyond dominant discourses

Challenging discourses has implications for policy and practice at all levels of human service work, from the individual to the organisational, national and global levels.

In this chapter we have seen that individual social workers are policy actors with the capability to effect change through their behaviour, words and actions. Marston and McDonald (2012, p. 1035) note that small acts by social workers can 'amount to a seismic shift', as the cumulative weight of many of these acts can contribute to significant change.

At organisational level there is scope, and indeed an imperative, for social work managers to exhibit greater flexibility towards the challenges of the practice environment. Lawler and Harlow (2005, p. 1171) argue that organisational and social care managers need to 'eschew "once and for all" solutions', and instead develop imaginative and flexible responses to accelerating social change. These responses need to include learning from policy and practice in other places. This thinking involves moving beyond the limits of dominant discourses like managerialism and exploring the potential of fresh and innovative ways of addressing social issues. As we have seen in this chapter, social workers have the capability and the vision to do this effectively.

At supra-organisational level, engagement with and by professional bodies is a crucial to the development and effectiveness of critical practice. As we have illustrated in this chapter, collective approaches can be most effective in bringing about change.

- A range of discourses shape and influence social work practice; these include the 'dominant discourses' of professionalism and managerialism.

- Discourses are dynamic rather than fixed entities which social workers can both use and challenge in their practice.

- The community discourse offers social workers opportunities for critical practice in existing practice settings and in a range of new and alternative settings.

- Thinking about Ife's framework of human service delivery, where would you locate your practice? Consider both the characteristics of the discourses and inter-relationships between each of them. Is your practice located in one discourse, or in several? For example, is the professional discourse more important in your practice than the managerial one?
- Debate the position of the community discourse in contemporary social work practice.
- What part, if any, does the community discourse play in your practice? Illustrate with an example.
- What are the pressures, tensions and challenges that arise in drawing on different discourses in your practice? How do you address these pressures?

taking it further

- Allen-Kelly, K. (2010) 'Out of the Wilderness – Australian Social Workers Embrace their Campaigning Roots', *Australian Social Work*, 63(3), pp. 245–249.
- Alston, M. and Besthorn, F.H. (2012) 'Environment and Sustainability' in K. Lyons, T. Hokenstad, M. Pawar, N. Huegler and N. Hall (eds) *The Sage Handbook of International Social Work*, London: Sage.
- Dominelli, L. (2012a) *Green Social Work: From Environmental Crises to Environmental Justice*, Bristol: Polity Press.
- Healy, K. (2005) *Social Work Theories in Context: Creating Frameworks for Practice*, Basingstoke: Macmillan.
- Ife, J. (1997) *Rethinking Social Work: Towards Critical Practice*, Frenchs Forest, NSW: Pearson Education.
- Reisch, M. and Jani, J.S. (2012) 'The New Politics of Social Work Practice: Understanding Context to Promote Change', *British Journal of Social Work*, 42, pp. 1132–1150.
- Tudor, R. (2013) 'Social Work in the Quake Zone: Supporting the Sustainable Development of Christchurch's Eastern Communities', *Aotearoa New Zealand Social Work*, 25(2), pp. 18–26.

4 Directions in social work theory

Introduction

There is a rich and diverse theoretical tradition in social work that informs community development practices. In this chapter, we make connections between social work values, theory, practices and a critical form of community development. We seek to make these relationships transparent. Radical or structural social work practice theories and the various tributaries of critical social work connect with collectivist approaches and community development ideas. Guided and informed by our value base and commitment to social justice, we venture into the theoretical domain and interweave purposes, practices, ideas and theories to actively engage with groups and communities. Our exploration expands the conceptual spaces and possibilities for social work in a community context. We offer examples where social workers have incorporated community development ideas in their work within different practice settings. Here, we draw on the social work literature and our own practice as well as our research with social workers who shared their practice frameworks with us.

Making Connections between Values, Theories and Practices

In Chapter 1, we embedded critical and transformational change and social justice goals within the practice of community development and social work. As stated by the International Federation of Social Workers (2014), '*human rights and social justice* serve as the motivation and justification of social work action'. As expressed in Chapter 1, the perspective we adopt is a critical one, and we delve into the diverse strands of critical practice for social work which has resonance for community development. In Chapter 3, we located critical practice ideas within a community discourse (Ife, 1997, 2013). Here we build on these ideas and draw on the theoretical insights of social work writers such as Dominelli (2012a), Ife (2013), Gray and Webb (2008), Mullaly (1997), Healy (2000, 2005, 2012) and Stepney and Popple (2008). Aligned with our belief that theory is not something that is simply 'applied' to practice but an integrated and reciprocal process, we draw out key ideas and explore them in the context of community settings and practices. As Healy (2005) emphasises in her book *Social Work Theories in Context*, theoretical ideas are transformed through their application within specific practice contexts. Social workers are involved in a dynamic and active process of 'theorising' that develops understandings and generates meanings in context (Thompson, 2010). We are referring to the thinking and the doing of social work that Neil Thompson emphasises when he expresses, 'to do social work is to theorise practice (to draw on sets of ideas to make sense of it) and to practice theory (to make use of those ideas in a practical context)' (ibid., p. xvi). This also creates opportunities for the generation of knowledge and new ideas.

The subject of social work theory, models and practice methods has been described as a 'journey into the disputed world' where different theories offer varying and divergent explanations, each founded on particular values and ideologies (Stepney and Ford, 2012, p. xi). Of necessity, we will tread carefully and thoughtfully. Questioning how knowledge is created and how power relations influence processes of knowledge creation is critical for reflexive professional practice (De Cruz, Gillingham and Melendez, 2007). In relation to community development, Beth Reed (2005) cautions that while theorising practice can facilitate the enactment of social justice principles and goals, it can also hinder this process through 'obscuring the forces that perpetuate injustices' and affect our ability to create change (p. 98). She is referring to the frequently hidden or implicit power relationships inherent in different world views and what kind of knowledge is privileged over others. As shown in Chapter 3, the social professions face significant external challenges from contemporary neoliberal and managerial influences, and we may be swayed by external agendas that are not located within a social justice perspective (Ledwith, 2011).

In a practical sense, theories 'help us to analyse issues, situations, and local contexts, and help us raise critical questions about what needs to happen – and how it needs to happen' (Weil and Ohmer, 2013, p. 124). For social workers practicing in a community development context, this process involves dialogue with community and organisations and connecting local knowledge with principles, values and practices of the practitioner (Weil and Ohmer, 2013). As argued in Chapter 3, locating social work practice within the community discourse places the notion of 'change from below' or 'bottom-up practice' as a central concern which challenges taken-for-granted assumptions and top-down perspectives and practices (Ife, 1997, 2013). Thus the ideological and theoretical basis of these ideas become important for practitioners. Conventional understandings of 'expertise' are challenged as well as how we think about and understand theory (Ife, 1997, 2002, 2013; see Healy, 2000, 2005; Weil and Ohmer, 2013). For example, in Paulo Friere's (1997, 2005) model of 'popular education', theorising with groups and communities involves a process of 'shared reflective analysis' (Weil and Ohmer, 2013, p. 128).We explore this model in detail in Chapter 5.

As we asserted in Chapter 1, we are particularly interested in theories of change because of their relevance for community development practice (Ife, 2013; Weil and Ohmer, 2013). Our chapter begins by tracing the ebb and flow of practice theories in social work to illuminate historical sequencing and theoretical junctures in the story of social work. Of course, the junctures central to the project of our book are the emergence of critical perspectives and progressive, collective and emancipatory approaches to practice. These theoretical ideas fit with the critical community development perspective adopted in this book. The chapter proceeds to expand on important ideas from the critical social work tradition and we see that critical social work approaches have incorporated both modernist forms of structural analysis and post-modern ideas 'which emphasise more diverse sources of power and emancipation' (Mendes, 2007, p. 26). We explore how these critical practice ideas are enacted in the contexts of contemporary practices.

The ebb and flow of ideas in social work

When Malcolm Payne wrote 'the current idea and practice of social work is only of its time, our time' in his book *Origins of Social Work* (2005, p. 1), he makes the point that social work activity is shaped by the conditions and contexts within which it is practiced. However, history is ever present, and as Harris argues (2008), there are key 'moments' in the history of welfare that continue to play a part in constructing present practices in the UK. Far from being portrayed as simply a response to individual human needs and problems (Rush and Keenan, 2013; Harris, 2008), a far more complex picture emerges in the story of social work which we explored in Chapters 1 and 2. From a number of intersecting points, social work emerged as both a part of social service delivery but also of social movements seeking change or development of service provision (Payne, 2005). The latter ideas arose from the reformist ideology of the Settlement House Movement in the USA which was led in Chicago by the influential social worker Jane Addams. Her work in *Hull House* endeavoured to 'bridge the gap between middle and working class, the propertied and the poor, the native born and the immigrants' (Fook, 2012, p. 4). It is distinctive because of its shift to neighbourhood, community and wider social change practices with vulnerable and disadvantaged groups (Payne, 2005).

In making connections between social and economic circumstances and individual experience, we discover the beginnings of 'critical' social work in the community context (Fook, 2012; Healy, 2005). Payne (2005) highlights the emergence of group work ideas from the settlement move-ment and processes of informal education, giving the example of *The Inquiry* (see Payne, 2005, pp. 205–206, for a detailed history). This was a group of influential theorists including the educational philosopher John Dewey, as well as social workers Grace Coyle and Ada Sheffield in the US in the 1930s and 1940s. Here, we see groups becoming mechanisms for social change through individual empowerment and democratic social action. Engaging with groups as vehicles for social change is fundamental to contemporary social work and critical community development prac-tices and social workers draw extensively on group work ideas, practices and skills in their work with communities (see McMaster, 2004; Toseland and Rivas, 2011; Weil and Ohmer, 2013; see Healy, 2012).

More 'scientific' approaches such as psychological behavioural and social learning theories emerged in the 1970s in response to more 'inter-pretative' psychoanalytic casework practices. These then merged with individualist therapeutic interventions based on cognitive theories in the 1990s, thereby sustaining the focus on interpersonal helping (Payne, 2005). As noted by Payne, it was only later that the 'democratic ideal' of group work was rekindled through radical Freirean educational ideas of the 1970s merging with feminist ideas in the 1980s focusing on 'consciousness-raising and dialogue within equal, democratic relation-ships' (2005, p. 206).

Two strands of social theories emerged in the 1970s. *Radical theory*, social work's reaction to individualistic and 'social control' dimensions of psychodynamic theory, shifted the focus towards community develop-ment and advocacy and marked the beginnings of social work's involvement in user movements, anti-discriminatory practice and empowerment theory in the 1980s and 1990s (Payne, 2005). Healy (2012) notes that some social work practitioners viewed community develop-ment as an alternative to psychodynamic orientations of practices within professional social work which they considered had neglected issues of oppression and social injustice. Early radical approaches were influenced by Marxist theory, which centred on class in analysing and responding to human oppression (Healy, 2005). This radical tradition in social work was exemplified in the work of Bailey and Brake (1975), Brake and Bailey (1980) and Corrigan and Leonard (1978) in England, Galper (1975) in the USA and Throssell (1975) in Australia.

More recently, Lavalette (2011) reminds us of the backdrop to the radical social work movement in Britain, highlighting three critical junc-tures. Firstly, the expansion of university social work programmes to meet the increased demand for social workers led to the introduction of ideas from the critical social sciences such as Marxist and feminist perspectives which challenged traditional social work theory; secondly, the emergence of a 'radical critique of state directed welfare provision' in Britain (p. 2);

and thirdly, the impetus of social movements in the USA such as the civil rights movement and the anti-war movement as well as social protest in Britain, USA and across Europe (see Lavalette, 2011 for further details). Significantly, the connection between radical social work and community development practice is made in Marjorie Mayo's contribution to the seminal text *Radical Social Work* in 1975.

Community development practice is intertwined with the continuing story of social work. Tracing the historical development of community development in Britain, Marjorie Mayo highlights different models and alternative perspectives from professional/traditional practices that facilitate community initiatives within existing social relations to radical/transformational practices that sought fundamental social change (Mayo, 2009, p. 130). She emphasises the need for practices to be informed by critical theory. More recently, Banks urges us 'to reclaim some of the critical potential' of community development that Marjorie Mayo explored in her 1975 chapter and 'return to communities as sites of struggle, where issues of individual and social justice meet' (Banks, 2011, p. 184). Reflecting on the current contexts of social work practice (such as risk assessments and case management) in the UK, Baldwin argues for community approaches that can enable a more 'radical, anti-authoritarian social work of the future' (2011, p. 187). The impact of managerialism, cutbacks in social welfare provision and retrenchments in both the UK and Ireland have led to the re-emergence of activist social work activity that is more aligned with social work's radical tradition (see Lavalette, 2011; SWAN, 2014). An example of this is the Social Work Action Network (SWAN) that we explore in Chapter 6. We will return to these important ideas from the critical social work tradition and their relevance for community development later in this chapter.

The other strand of social theory was *systems theory* (mostly practised in the USA) based on ecological underpinnings. A systems conceptualisation facilitates understanding of the individual within their environment and specifically, their interactions and transactions with a range of social systems at different levels – the family, immediate social networks, neighbourhood and community systems, institutional or organisational systems and societal/structural systems. Viewing the individual within his/her social system broadens the scope of analysis and extends possibilities for interventions beyond the individual level to community and policy domains. Systems theories such as ecosystems approaches remain highly influential in social work, although these approaches have been criticised for their failure to address power relations, exploitation and structural injustices (Healy, 2005; Ife, 2002). More recently, however, there has been a renewal of interest in ecological approaches underpinned by social justice and human rights perspectives that are linked to social and environmental concerns (Dominelli, 2012a; Ife, 2013). We discussed social work and the environment in Chapter 3.

The turning tide: Anti-oppressive practice

In the 1980s, the tide of radical social work practice theories began to ebb. However, there was a re-envisaging of radical ideas as embodied in anti-racist and anti-discriminatory practice approaches in Britain, 'focusing on a social justice agenda and seeking structural change benefiting socially excluded groups' (Payne, 2005, p. 214). These ideas reframed practices in social work over the 1980s and 1990s (see, for example, Dominelli, 2002; Healy, 2005). The class analysis of the 1970s was widened to encompass other types of oppression such as race and gender (Baines, 2007). Drawing on anti-oppressive practice, social workers engaged with both individuals and communities to achieve change through critical analysis of the underlying causes of oppression. The 'doing' of anti-oppressive social work as a *transformative* and *political* form of practice is emphasised by Donna Baines, who locates these practices in, and across, all practice domains whether 'clinical, community, policy or grassroots levels' (2007, p. 26). Healy situates anti-oppressive practice approaches firmly within the critical social work tradition, which she broadly defines as 'concerned with the analysis and transformation of power relations at *every* level of social work practice' (Healy, 2005, p. 172). She identifies key understandings and actions of anti-oppressive practice as follows: recognition of the structural root causes of problems, an emphasis on *radical* social change, a critical analysis of practice relationships and taking actions to transform these (Healy, 2005, p. 179). Healy argues that this approach is 'on the cusp' of modern and post-modern critical social work as it relies on ideas of critical consciousness-raising and generates a structural analysis of oppression where the 'personal and cultural' is acknowledged (2005, p. 191).

While acknowledging the contested position of anti-oppressive practice within social work, Dominelli (2009) emphasises that egalitarianism, reflexivity and ethical processes are central to building the kinds of relationships that enable social transformation to occur. In relation to some areas of practice such as mental health, anti-oppressive practice has been critiqued as privileging knowledge of the 'expert' practitioner rather than creating spaces for service users' own forms of knowledge (see Wilson and Beresford, 2000). Peter Beresford traces the role of service users from the early conceptions of radical social work and concludes that this has been 'more symbolic than as active partners in its construction' (p. 98); this has limited the emancipatory potential of social work practices. In the context of service user movements in disability and mental health, Collins (2009) argues that social work has remained on the 'outside' rather than working in partnership with these collective movements to achieve social change. We discuss some of these challenges for social work in Chapter 6.

The mechanisms of oppression

Uschi Bay discusses an anti-oppressive and empowerment approach in the context of community development practices in rural and remote Aboriginal communities and settlements in Australia (2009). She argues that understanding 'the specific mechanisms of oppression' (personal, cultural and structural) within diverse community groups is crucial for practitioners as well as analysing power relations that affect people's opportunities and livelihoods (ibid., p. 280). Here, social workers engage with socio-political and historical impacts on community groups who are experiencing marginalisation and multiple oppressions. They seek to use processes that are 'egalitarian, dialogical and participatory' in their work with communities to enable collective analyses of how the community (and sub-groups within it) are located in policy discourses (ibid., p. 279). It is through this work with communities that alternative frameworks are proposed for the construction of problems and solutions. The necessity of practitioner skills in policy analysis, community development processes and the linking of the personal, cultural and structural analysis of oppression is highlighted (ibid., p. 279).

According to Baines (2007), 'anti-oppressive practice is a set of politicised practices that continually evolve to analyse and address constantly changing social conditions and challenges' (p. 20). The gains, complexities and challenges of engendering meaningful social change through anti-oppressive practices by social workers within the public services are highlighted in research conducted by Strier and Binyamin (2013). These authors highlight the negative impact of neo-liberal policies and neo-managerial ideologies and increasing privatisation on the welfare state in the Israeli context. Their case study is interesting because it depicts the shift from an individualistic discourse on poverty towards collective and emancipatory practices involving a range of community development initiatives. Adopting a structural analysis of poverty, Family Aid Centres (FAC) were a combined initiative of municipal public social services that employ social workers and a private foundation that provided services for people experiencing poverty and social exclusion. FACs sought to resource and mobilise the community, involve client groups in policy practice projects, build alliances and partnerships at the community level and develop creative interventions that incorporated personal, community and policy advocacy. The services promoted non-hierarchical and democratic processes that facilitated client participation in decision-making and egalitarian relationships.

Using a case study methodology and drawing on multiple sources of data such as external evaluations, documents, participative observations, focus groups and interviews with a range of stakeholders, a number of advantages of the FAC approach were identified. In addition to a higher level of satisfaction with client–worker relationships, there was a greater recognition of community development and development of community projects and programmes. Training and mobilisation of community activists, advocacy in relation to issues such as housing rights, food security and the welfare of single mothers, and recognising and valuing the role of social workers in the area of poverty were identified as achievements. These findings illustrate the relevance of anti-oppressive social work practice approaches for community development and working alongside communities to enact collective and emancipatory social change.

The research findings also reveal significant challenges. Firstly there were problems in 'transforming public social services into more democratic organisational settings' (Strier and Binyamin, 2013, p. 13). While steering committees were created as mechanisms for client participation at an organisational level and also for involvement in community projects, implementing these and preventing tokenism emerged as issues. The authors concluded, 'the system was unable to incorporate genuine client participation as part of its organisational culture' (p. 13). The authors also express, 'ultimately clients remained sceptical about the ability of improved services to better their situation' (p. 13), which suggested to them that the frame of reference needed to include wider political, social and economic policy concerns. Furthermore, the 'oppressive institutional context' of public social services (budget constraints, caseloads and working conditions) was seen to restrict the opportunities for change. Despite these considerable challenges, it is encouraging that the authors conclude 'public social services may offer a significant platform for launching alternative professional messages, for creating subversive organisational microclimates, for forging islands of counter culture, for exposing professionals and clients to alternative visions of social problems, to a search for shared solutions within a highly regulated and controlling organisational milieu' (p. 15). Writing in the Irish context, Michael Rush and Marie Keenan (2013) highlight the pressing need for more case examples to illustrate anti-oppressive practice *in action* within contemporary social care systems to elucidate social change practices. Re-envisaging anti-oppressive social work, Rush and Keenan (2013) argue that public policy advocacy is an essential strand of anti-oppressive practice if we are to alter or transform existing social relations and resist or oppose the ideologies of current welfare regimes.

Continuing in the radical social work tradition and drawing on an anti-oppressive practice framework, other critical practice theories emerge. Structural social work sought to transform the social order through a process of dialogue and consciousness-raising about the sources of oppression as well as taking actions at both micro and macro levels of practice (Mullaly, 1997). Healy proposes that the utility of theories should be judged within specific practice contexts and in relation to how they assist practitioners to realise particular purpose and value bases (2005, p. 11). Here we see clear connections to critical community development practice.

Structural social work: Transforming the social order?

Structural social work adopts a collectivist perspective in responding to oppressive practices drawing on Marxist ideas of transformative activity (see Healy, 2000, for a more detailed discussion), Paulo Friere's pedagogy concerning *conscientisation* and feminist analyses (Mullaly, 1997). These derivations resonate with the community development approach explored in this book (see Chapter 5). Hick and Murray (2008, p. 91) delineate key understandings that characterise Structural social work:

- a problematisation of dominant social and economic structures through pursuit of a 'conflict' or 'change' perspective
- a focus on multiple, intersecting forms of oppression produced and reinforced by structures
- an emphasis on the dialectical nature of the interaction between individuals and macro-level structures.

It is evident that the theoretical ideas that are so important to community development such as critical consciousness-raising and dialogic practices (see Chapter 5) are embedded in the history, theory and practice of social workers. It has been argued that Structural social work is a potentially integrative approach that can transcend distinctions such as 'direct interventions', 'community development' or 'policy analysis' as well as divisions such as working 'within' or 'against' the system (see Hick and Murray, 2008, p. 96). We will explore these juxtapositions further in Chapter 6.

An integrative structural framework holds particular resonance for social work practitioners seeking to achieve social justice goals within a range of diverse practice contexts. For example, Goldsworthy (2002, p. 327), writing about her work within a small church-based agency in Victoria, Australia, describes the 'community development continuum' which integrates modes of practice. She incorporates 'empowering casework, community building and social action' within a practice framework that addresses issues at multiple levels simultaneously. She argues that dichotomies between approaches are 'incongruous with the realities of practice' and have impacted negatively on disadvantaged communities (p. 327). George and Marlowe (cited in Hick and Murray, 2008) report on multiple practices within a structural approach adopted by a grassroots organisation in rural India including legal action, social care to empower service users, resource generation projects and organisational networks to address poverty and violence while challenging the caste system of 'untouchability'. These examples highlight the value and potential of integrative theoretical frameworks and understandings such as Structural social work which can enable practitioners to work towards progressive and emancipatory social change.

Post-modern orientations in social work theory

Continuing on our historical journey, we see the development of radical social work in theory, and in practice (Payne, 2005; see Mendes, 2005, 2009 for an Australian overview). Informed by structural and radical theories, practices offered a critical analysis of oppression and social divisions and a 'reform agenda' (Payne, 2005, p. 215). These drew upon critical social science theories such as feminist, post-structural and post-modernist theories which broke away from positivist and scientific analyses to social constructionism that embedded social understandings in their cultural and historic contexts (ibid.). While feminist perspectives are diverse, they centre on 'a theoretical understanding of the position of women and frameworks for action to improve this' (Orme, 2008, p. 65).

The focus on 'deconstruction' or the dismantling of taken-for-granted assumptions and established frameworks characterises 'post-modernism' (Fawcett, 2009). Ife links post-modernism to bottom-up practices as it 'assists with the articulation of change from below' (2013, p. 155). In this regard, he notes that 'critical theory emphasises the importance of under-standing people's reality (or realities) and of taking action to bring about change through the dismantling of structures of power and domination as well as the deconstruction and reconstruction of discursive power and social relations, and through opening up possibilities for people to take action to meet their self-defined needs' (p. 155). He argues that post-modern feminism (an approach that seeks to alter structures or discourses of power and oppression, and addresses dominant patriarchal systems and structures) offers an analysis that fits with this bottom-up perspective (Ife, 2013). As expressed by Ife, 'community work can become a genuine dialogue about power, about knowledge, about wisdom, and about change, and can seek to empower local community members to validate and use their own experience, knowledge, expertise and skills to work towards change' (p. 157). We see that Ife's version of post-modernist prac-tice is linked to social justice and a human rights perspective.

Healy notes the increasing influence of post-modern theories on the profession of social work in Australia since the 1990s and their applica-tion to community and policy practice as well as casework (Healy, 2005; see also Fook, 2012). However, due to the focus on relativism and the multiple understandings fostered by post-modernism, it has been critiqued as 'disconnected' from an ethical position and social justice stance (Fawcett, 2009; Healy, 2005; Ife, 2013; Stepney and Popple, 2008).

As Reed states, 'many "truths" are possible, which vary depending on the vantage point of the observer and the particular circumstances' (2005, p. 88). This has led critical social workers to draw on both modernist forms of structural analysis and post-modern ideas that emphasise diverse and multiple perspectives (Mendes, 2007).

Critical realist practices

The continuing relevance of *critical* post-modern orientations for social work is highlighted by Fawcett (2009) on the basis of 'its commitment to construct-ive critique, theoretically nuanced practice and the need for social workers to continually differentiate between acceptable and unacceptable social prac-tices in a variety of complex contextual situations' (p. 128). While Stepney and Popple (2008) explore the potential of Critical Post-modern Practice for a 'critical community-based social work', like us they lean towards another configuration of critical practice ideas, *Critical Realist Practice*.

A central tenet of the critical realist philosophy based on the work of Roy Bhaskar (1978) is that there are *real, unseen* mechanisms in the natural and social world which contribute to shaping social events and people's lives (Houston, 2010b). As argued by Stepney and Popple (2008), 'critical realism seeks to be sensitive to the multiple realities of subjective experience but views these within the context of dominant social structures' (p. 162). This contrasts with the relativism inherent in post-modern prac-tices where there is an emphasis on multiple perspectives and understandings and *all* knowledge is considered as relative so that one perspective is not privileged or dominant (Fawcett, 2009). In this regard, Houston argues post-modernism constructionism cannot fully address human distress because it 'subjectivises the impact of the *real* social world' (p. 858). Critical realist practice is aligned with a 'bottom-up' approach that starts with the community and explores 'causal mechanisms' and structures that lead to oppression and injustice (Stepney and Popple, 2008). As a meta-theory, crit-ical realism can encompass a range of theoretical approaches and practice methods which immediately broaden the repertoire and scope of practices with the purposes of transformation and social change. As Stepney and Popple (2008) note, participatory methods are favoured, 'drawing upon a variety of knowledge, practice wisdom and theory, set in the context of relevant policy and community resources' (p. 163).

Houston (2001) argues that a critical realist perspective has particular rele-vance for social work. For similar reasons, we argue that it is particularly relevant to our version of critical community development. Firstly, it is a transformational approach. It seeks to uncover the components or *structures* underlying the experiences of people in their daily lives and in doing so, challenges these when they result in human oppression (Houston, 2001).

As observed by Houston, 'it is only by understanding the deep causes of oppression that we can develop ways of dismantling it' (Houston, 2010b, p. 76). Secondly, it offers a meta-theory to understand these causal mechanisms. A wide range of pertinent explanatory theories can be considered. On this basis, we can develop hypotheses about the operation of complex causal mechanisms at different levels. This includes our thinking and actions as part of the system and our own role as change agents (Gorski, 2013) Thirdly, the focus on structures enables a deeper exploration of the root causes of oppression and through processes of consciousness-raising, people are empowered to enact meaningful change. In this way, oppressive structural mechanisms are exposed (for example, the adverse effects of a neo-liberal economy on people's lives) and the conditions for emancipatory mechanisms can be activated (Houston, 2010b, p. 76).

In our Irish research we found that practitioners were drawing on critical ideas and enacting them in their practices in community development contexts. The practitioner in the example below articulates her understandings of critical practice and the link to collective action which connects with critical realist ideas. Here, critical practice is intrinsically connected to critical thought and analysis.

Practitioner perspective: Values, theories and practices

I believe that critical practice should lead to some kind of collective action. I think how the practice is analysed depends on how the social work intervention gets constructed ... I really believe that if that is from a social analysis, it really determines the intervention and it will determine, I think, social workers building those alliances, building the networks, building solidarity and really constructing a piece of social work that has social justice as its basis and that can move from seeing the problem as being an individual pathological problem to being one grounded really in a more sociological definition of the problem.

I think this is a great example of critical practice; I remember it from the time I was a student. It was a referral that was made to the social work department about a family where there was a twelve-year-old child babysitting a young child. It was used as an example of how the social worker really analysed the problem and the roll out of the intervention. Rather than seeing it as you have to engage a fifteen- or sixteen-year-old to do your babysitting, that there was real deep analysis about what was going on in this family and what it led to was that there were huge issues around domestic violence, you know, and it was because of the domestic violence that had led to a separation that had led to a drop in income, that had led to a mother having to go out to work, to not being able to afford a babysitter and having a twelve-year-old and a young child. So I think very much the critical thinking and practice that went on was a really positive

practice example 4.1

response and it was, again, about how the problem was constructed and how the intervention was constructed which determined the response.

Source: Research project carried out by Forde and Lynch in 2009–2010. Fifteen social workers in a range of practice settings in Ireland were interviewed about their experiences of using community development approaches in their practice.

This example highlights practice understandings that acknowledge the deeper structural causes of injustice as well as the value of alliances and networks (Fook, 2012; Ife, 1997; Stepney and Ford, 2012). Specifically, Ife urges social workers to engage with 'potential allies' in working towards social change (1997, p. 203). As illustrated in the second practice example below, change or transformation is a central concern to this practitioner underpinned by the belief that 'change can happen'. This motivates and sustains critical practices.

Practitioner perspective: Values, theories and practices

practice example 4.2

The main approach for me is that I believe that community work and community development are ultimately about change and that *change can happen*.... I think it is about naming poverty and about naming the issues. So I would be influenced by any approach that will *name* the injustice and *name* the issues and *name* poverty and *name* the reality of what happens in people's lives....

I would be influenced by a participatory approach and by that, I mean of being able to include people and being able to hear people's voices and being able to believe – and I suppose it is part of the human development approach as well – that everybody has potential, that no matter how big or how small the contribution might be that people have something to say....

I would be hugely influenced by an approach that questions underlying assumptions. That does not take things as they are presented but would kind of critically look at and critically analyse what really is going on here – so any approaches that would do that. A collective action approach would appeal hugely to me and I would be very influenced by it. I have been and I hope I have been able to incorporate some of that into the work because I believe very strongly in the collective and in solidarity and, you know, building those networks in terms of none of us can do it on our own, we all need each other. I adopt an approach that is within the framework of human rights and whether it is in terms of our own constitution (Irish) or whether it is in terms of whatever be it the UN Convention on the Rights of the Child or whatever the Declaration of Human Rights but that it is done within some kind of framework around rights as opposed to needs. So those are the kind of the approaches that I would take, those that influence my practice. These are the kind of values that I would work from or that I would try to adhere to and I think there is always the value of equality and I think in particular for women, you know. I just think that it is so important that we are able to analyse in the work that we do the position of women really in this or the position of women within the family or within the community and that we can work from the value of equality as well and equality for all but also from the gender perspective.

Source: Research project carried out by Forde and Lynch in 2009–2010. Fifteen social workers in a range of practice settings in Ireland were interviewed about their experiences of using community development approaches in their practice.

Questions

1. Expand on and discuss the theoretical perspectives that the practitioner identifies as influential to her practice. How do her ideas fit with a critical realist perspective as discussed in this book?
2. Discuss how she integrates theoretical ideas into her practice framework and the compatibility of these perspectives.
3. Do these ideas hold resonance for you in your own practice? Think about and share in groups what values and theoretical approaches are influential for your own practice.

Of crucial significance to community development is the concept of 'change from below' or bottom-up practices (Ife, 2013; Ledwith, 2011). According to Ife, this entails the reframing of theoretical understandings so that 'they relate to the lived experience of people in the community, and are grounded in their reality' (2013, p. 157). For us, these ideas connect with a critical realist perspective. For the social work practitioner, the process involves starting from where the community is and valuing local knowledge, skills, culture and resources (Ife, 2013). This way of working also necessitates a critically reflexive and reflective approach as illustrated in the practice example below.

Practitioner perspective: Values, theories and practices

practice example 4.3

We are not the experts and even as a social worker I would say you know we aren't the experts. It is like acknowledging that people can identify their own needs and their own solutions and OK you might have certain skills that you can share, certain knowledge you can share but at the end of the day individuals and communities are the experts in their own situation and can, maybe with some support and resources, be helped to find their own solutions.

So I think the challenge for social workers is to really analyse what I am doing, which will provide some analysis then of *how* they practice. You know to step back and really think what is it that I am doing here? What is it that I am about? What is it that I am trying to do as a social worker?

Source: Research project carried out by Forde and Lynch in 2009–2010. Fifteen social workers in a range of practice settings in Ireland were interviewed about their experiences of using community development approaches in their practice.

Questions

1. Consider what 'change from below' means in the context of your own practice.
2. What theoretical insights might inform this approach to practice in a community context?
3. What skills are important for this approach to practice?

Complexities of power in practice

Healy (2005) highlights the importance of post-structural theories in illuminating the complexities of local power *in practice* in combination with broader structural analyses of modern critical social work (p. 206). Michel Foucault's work has been highly influential in opening up possibilities for reflexive and emancipatory social work practices through stimulating understandings of how power relations are *created, sustained and challenged* in local contexts (see Healy, 2000, pp. 43–45, for a detailed discussion of Foucault and critical post-structural theory; see Gray and Webb, 2008 for a detailed critique). Post-structuralism emphasises the role and influence of language on power, knowledge and identity (Agger, 1991 cited in Healy, 2005). Therefore, language becomes 'a key site of political struggle' (Healy, 2005, p. 198). In Chapter 3, we explored the concept of 'discourse' (that is, the language and social practices that we use to understand the social world) and discussed the major discourses that mould understandings and practices in contemporary contexts. We showed how social workers and community workers can challenge dominant discourses and create new opportunities for critical and creative practices in the community development context.

Healy has argued that post-structuralism (that is, where meaning is constructed through discourses) can lead to more diverse forms of activism linked to consciousness-raising and collective action (2000). Foucault views power as *exercised* rather than possessed, as *productive* rather than principally oppressive, and as *coming from the bottom-up* (Sawicki, 1991, p. 21, cited in Healy, 2000). However, Joseph (2010) questions the radical and emancipatory potential of Foucault's analysis 'if it does not have a developed conception of the underlying structures that agents must transform' (p. 183). He argues that the transformational potential of Foucault's work can only be attained within a *critical realist* ontology which seeks to acquire knowledge about the components or *structures* underlying the experiences of people so that these can be targeted and challenged when they result in oppression and injustice (Houston, 2001).

Advocacy, empowerment and human rights

Following on from the work of Foucault, Payne (2005) notes another related juncture in the origins of social work when he highlights anti-discriminatory practice ideas and ethnic and cultural sensitivity in social work. The significance for international social work is emphasised. The discourse of 'international social work' has varied and contested meanings connected to processes of globalisation and impacts on localised practices (Harrison and Melville, 2010; Dominelli, 2012b). As stated by Dominelli (2012b, p. 40), 'globalisation and indigenisation present opportunities and challenges for practitioners attempting empowering, locality-specific and culturally relevant practices'.

The resurgence of interest in advocacy and empowerment approaches with minority populations and groups experiencing oppression in American social work was exemplified by the work of Solomon (1976) and Lee (1994). Significantly, Payne notes that advocacy practices were less individualistically orientated but took the form of 'lobbying for social reforms in a practice akin to community work' (2005, p. 215). Mendes' review of social work in Australia (2005) refers to Lopez' history of multi-culturalism (2000) that illuminates the role of Australian social workers in resisting assimilationist policies and advancing migrant welfare. Immigration and the movement of peoples globally are concerns of social work, and as noted by Harrison and Melville (2010), social workers practise 'at the interface between migration and welfare' and advocate for the rights of peoples who are excluded on the basis of culture, race, ethnicity, religion and language (p. 57). However, Segal and Heck (2012) argue for a stronger community development emphasis and make the point that immigrant and refugee issues tend to be addressed at the individual level and often in relation to existing policy implementation rather than social change practices.

In Australia, social work has engaged with a historical legacy of colonisation of Indigenous Australians and 'particularly the collaboration of social workers with what has become known as the Stolen Generation of Aboriginal children' (Mendes, 2005, p. 123). The Stolen Generation refers to the high numbers of Aboriginal and Torres Strait Islander children who were forcibly removed from their families from the nineteenth century until the 1970s 'to assimilate them into European society and culture' (Bennett, 2013, p. 10). Recently, the collection of work *Our Voices:*

Aboriginal and Torres Strait Islander Social Work (2013), explores this historical and socio-cultural context and sets out contemporary Australian Indigenous social work practices drawing on the work of Indigenous practitioners. This work is strongly connected to community and collectivist understandings of social work underpinned by social justice and human rights. Community development in this context necessitates 'an understanding of Aboriginal and Torres Strait Islander experience of colonising practices, including removal, separation, assimilation and the phenomenon of multifaceted resultant trauma' (Menzies and Gilbert, 2013, p. 69). Indigenous rights and voice are at the centre of social work practice with Indigenous communities (Briskman, 2014). As Ife argues, postcolonial perspectives are significant for community development practice in enabling the voices of peoples who have been oppressed to be heard and to challenge 'the perpetuation of structures and discourses of colonialism' (2013, p. 152). This highlights the need for Indigenous practice models that address decolonisation (see Muller, 2014).

A number of critical issues emerge in developing an understanding of 'decolonisation'. Firstly, it is complex process that is personal, social and political (Laenui, 2007), where the 'internalised and subtle perpetuation of colonisation' must be challenged at a personal level before structural change can occur (Muller, 2014, p. 54). Secondly, acknowledging the significance of history is an important part of the decolonisation process (Zubrzycki and Crawford, 2013). This requires that non-Indigenous workers assume responsibility to gain knowledge about the history and continuing 'acts of colonisation' in the communities in which they work and the implications for practices. Thirdly, as Muller argues (2014), the issues connected to colonisation and decolonisation are relevant for both non-Indigenous peoples as well as Indigenous peoples. This requires 'the settler society' to collaborate in the decolonisation process with Indigenous peoples (ibid., p. 64). Drawing on the work of Hawaiian theorist and activist, Poka Laenui (2007), Muller presents a framework for decolonisation encompassing six overlapping stages: Rediscovery and Recovery (this involves reconnecting with traditional practices and languages and Country and kin); Mourning (the expression of anger and sense of injustice); Healing and Forgiveness: Reclaiming Wellbeing and Harmony (engaging in reflection, cultural and spiritual processes); Dreaming (strengthening philosophy and knowledge); Commitment (a commitment to social action and participation); and Action: Decolonising Knowledge (rediscovering Indigenous knowledge and to 'understand theory and research from our own perspectives and for our own purposes') (Tuhiwai-Smith, 2001 cited in Muller, 2014, p. 64). See Muller (2014) for a detailed discussion of each of these stages.

As embodied in definitions of social work by the International Federation of Social Workers (2014), human rights and social justice are core concepts and driving principles of social work actions. This practice framework is common to both social work and community development (Ife and Fiske, 2006). While rights discourses inform social work in different practice contexts here they guide collective and critical community action as illustrated in Practice Example 4.4, in which a social worker describes the development of a rights-based approach to poor housing conditions.

Urban regeneration in the Irish context is the backdrop to our final practice example below. During a period of rapid social and economic growth (known as the 'Celtic Tiger') in Ireland significant social and environmental 'regeneration' activities occurred in some of the disadvantaged and socially marginalised inner city communities (Share, 2010). Social partnership is a historical and distinctive approach to governance in the Irish context, which has impacted on areas of local authority housing and regeneration programmes (see Share, 2010, pp. 186–187). As Share describes (2010), the period of rapid economic development in Ireland was 'fuelled by a construction industry bubble'. This was followed by an equally rapid collapse in the construction and allied sectors (p. 185) which impacted significantly on the sustainability of social partnership and urban regeneration activity.

practice example 4.4

A practitioner's account: Human rights and critical practice strategies

O'Donohue Gardens* is a local authority flats complex with 276 housing units. It is an area that had been neglected by successive governments. It was an area that the Celtic Tiger certainly didn't visit. It had been left to rack and ruin, it ran into terrible decay and as a result there were a lot of social problems on the estate. Now it was also earmarked as one of the regeneration projects that would come under the public private partnership and at that time there were three projects in the city. People were promised the world – they were promised new houses, new gardens, new shops, community resource centre, health facilities, parks, you name it – it was all part of the bigger plan as part of the regeneration.

In May 2008, it all came to an abrupt end when the public private partnership with the development company collapsed and with it collapsed the hopes and dreams of every family in the three estates. Again, I think it was just such a huge blow to people after so many years and I can't begin to describe the devastation for people who had been promised a home and all they wanted was a home with a key to their front door, with a garden, with a play area for their children .... So I think it was absolutely hugely devastating to people and just a huge blow to a community that had already received quite a lot of blows along the way.

Again, the challenge was how to respond to that and we did respond and we developed alliances with the other two communities, so between the three communities we took to the streets and we decided to protest and we decided to protest in many different ways. We took to the streets and we developed a response that we called, 'We are not going away' within the context of human rights. That people had a right to a home and to everything that goes with that home and by the collapse of the public private partnership and by the dismantling of this community in O'Donohue Gardens possibly for further private developments along the way that this was a violation of people's human rights. We documented the process as well and we developed our banners that, I think, named very clearly what was going on. We did it visually linking in with the whole notion of documenting the protest and using the visual which can be very powerful and we also linked it in to the 60th anniversary of the Universal Declaration of Human Rights.

So the challenge is to try to support local people to respond somehow to that and to have a say in this and I think that is really difficult when people are living in conditions like that. Where there is sewerage coming up from toilets, where there are pipes bursting, where there is no water, where there is graffiti written on walls and it is just a horrible environment for people to live in and it is wrong. It is so wrong. When we began to develop that protest that people in the estate came out, the people themselves came out. Some of the marches to City Hall, they were extraordinary, it was quite extraordinary to see people coming out because it is a long way from the estate to City Hall and it was a walk, you know, and thankfully it never rained when we were walking. But it was quite, I think it was quite extraordinary for people even to begin to question, you know, themselves.

I think that the responses are varied and there are responses from, I suppose, agencies and from people who don't like to see the issues being named and feel that the campaign is very antagonistic, you know. We would say that the campaign is very real and we would say that the campaign is very necessary and we would say the campaign is…really telling the story of how things are and the reality for people's lives.

* Pseudonym. Real name has been changed.

Source: Research project carried out by Forde and Lynch in 2009–2010. Fifteen social workers in a range of practice settings in Ireland were interviewed about their experiences of using community development approaches in their practice.

Questions

1. What critical practice strategies can you identify in this practice example?
2. Discuss the critical ideas and understandings that you consider are informing these strategies.

3. What values and principles do you think were influential for the practitioner in this context?
4. Explore how the approach resonates with/does not resonate with your personal and professional value base as a practitioner. Why is this?

This example illustrates critical consciousness-raising processes leading to collective action. As we can see from the practice example, consciousness raising occurs within a 'dialogical relationship', where issues are defined, connections are made between the personal and political and action can be initiated (Ife, 1997). The practitioner narrative vividly highlights processes of community development as a form of critical practice that is value-based, participatory and seeks social change. The perspective shows how a human rights framework can inform and underpin practice with communities who are experiencing disadvantage. As noted by Harrison and Melville (2010), 'rights discourses represent political tools available to social work activists in their quest for social change' (p. 153). As defined by Jim Ife, the concept of 'empowerment' is closely aligned with social justice and seeks 'to increase the power of the disadvantaged' (2013, p. 63). Social work practices involve resisting oppression or collusive forms of power but also proactively constructing forms of power together with, and on behalf of others (Tew, 2006). Michele Share foresaw a return to 'traditional modes of community activism and mobilisation' (2010, p. 208) in the Irish context. 'Tenants First' movements emerged within disadvantaged urban communities across Dublin to secure the rights of tenants in the public housing system.

In conclusion: Critical realist practices – a way forward?

In this chapter, we traced the development of theoretical ideas in social work and the diverse strands of critical practice that have resonance for social work and community development. Our explorations show that theoretical ideas such as critical consciousness-raising, collectivist and dialogic practices are embedded in the history, theory and practice of social workers. In our Irish research we found that practitioners were drawing on critical ideas and enacting them in their practices in community development contexts. We argue that a critical realist perspective is particularly relevant to our version of critical community development. Critical realism can encompass a range of theoretical approaches and practice methods and offers a way forward to broaden the repertoire and scope of social work practices with the purposes of transformation and social change.

■ Radical or structural social work practice theories and the various tributaries of critical social work connect with collectivist approaches and community development ideas.

■ Critical realist practice is aligned with a 'bottom-up' approach that starts with the community and explores causal mechanisms and structures that lead to oppression and injustice.

■ The focus on structures enables a deep exploration of the root causes of oppression. Through processes of consciousness-raising, people are empowered to enact meaningful change.

■ In our Irish research we found that practitioners were drawing on critical ideas and enacting them in their practices in community development contexts.

■ Human rights discourses inform social work in different practice contexts and guide collective and critical community action.

Identify a community issue or population experiencing disadvantage. Drawing on one of the critical practice perspectives/ideas discussed in the chapter, consider how it might inform your understanding and actions. Interrogate your approach using the questions below:

■ How does your approach challenge the status quo or an environment that may be unjust?
■ What assumptions does your approach make about social justice?
■ How are your practices connected to your own personal and professional values as a practitioner?
■ How do you know that your practice contributes to change for social justice? What sources of 'evidence' are important?
■ How could you extend collective action beyond the local community to develop national, international or global alliances?
■ Reflect on the usefulness of Questions 1–3 to facilitate the exploration of hidden or implicit power relationships in your own practice.

Source: Adapted from Reed (2005) and Ledwith (2011).

taking it further

- Bay, U. (2009) 'Framing Critical Social Work Practices with Rural and Remote Communities' in J. Allan, L. Briskman and B. Pease (eds) *Critical Social Work: Theories and Practices for a Socially Just World*, Sydney, NSW: Allen and Unwin.
- Bennett, S., Green, S., Gilbert, S. and Bessarab, D. (2013 eds) *Our Voices: Aboriginal and Torres Strait Islander Social Work*, South Yarra: Palgrave MacMillan.
- Fordo, C. and Lynch, D. (2014) 'Critical Practice for Challenging Times: Social Workers' Engagement with Community Work', *British Journal of Social Work*, 44(8),pp. 2078–2094.
- Gorski, P. (2013) 'What is Critical Realism? And Why Should You Care?', *Contemporary Sociology: A Journal of Reviews*, 42, pp. 658–669.
- Gray, M. and Webb, S. (2008) 'Critical Social Work' in M. Gray and S. Webb (eds) *Social Work Theories and Methods*, London: Sage Publications.
- Healy, K. (2005) *Social Work Theories in Context*, Basingstoke: Palgrave MacMillan.
- Houston, S. (2001) 'Beyond Social Constructionism: Critical Realism and Social Work', *British Journal of Social Work*, 31, pp. 845–861.
- Lavalette, M. (2011) *Radical Social Work Today: Social Work at the Crossroads*, Bristol: The Policy Press.
- Stepney, P. and Popple, K. (2008) *Social Work and the Community: A Critical Context for Practice*, Basingstoke: Palgrave MacMillan.
- Weil, M. and Ohmer, M.L. (2013) 'Applying Practice Theories in Community Work' in M. Weil (ed) *The Handbook of Community Practice*, Second Edition, Thousand Oaks, CA: Sage Publications.

Websites

- International Federation of Social Workers (2014), available online at http://www.ifsw.org [Accessed 24 September 2014].

5 Making connections in principle and practice

Introduction

Chapter 1 pointed out the value-based nature of social work and community development and the similarities between the core values and principles that inform the two disciplines. In this chapter we resume this discussion and specifically explore the relationship between social work and community development in practice. We begin with an overview of the key junctures in community development practice in the twentieth century and consider some of the intersections between community development and social work. This analysis includes examples of participative and empowering community development from the Global South. The chapter proceeds to critically analyse the community development process, its broad scope and critical or transformational potential. It considers the connections between community development and social work practice, and assesses the opportunities and challenges that community development approaches offer social workers to engage in critical practice.

Community development: Origins, continuity and change

As we saw in Chapter 1 community development is not a singular or unified discipline. Like social work it has a complex history and has been consistently subject to diverse influences that vary according to place and time. This section picks out the key elements in the evolution of community development and looks at how community development has been shaped by its context. The section also explores some of the connections between community development and social work over the last century.

Community development as grassroots movement

Grassroots or organic community development draws its impetus from the actions of individuals or groups who seek to effect change within or beyond a community. This 'bottom-up' activity has a long-standing history in many places. Ife (2013; see also Brueggemann, 2013) suggests that community centres, which preceded the Settlement Movement of the late nineteenth century in Britain and the US, have always provided a focal point in communities. The first community centres were churches and other places of worship 'where people could meet, discuss important matters, interact socially and engage in organised community activities' (Ife, 2013, p. 218). Community centres have continued to be a significant feature of community development activity, although they take different forms and serve a range of different purposes, both real and symbolic (Thornham and Parry, 2015). Other forms of grassroots community development also have long-standing histories. Mayo (1994, p. 137) refers to Britain's 'tradition of working-class self-help', manifested in the work of trade unions, friendly societies and community organisations. In their study of community in Britain, Crow and Allan (1994) point to the extensive formal and informal community networks that exist in both rural and urban parts of the country. In Ireland, civil society and community activity flourished in the years after independence in 1922 (Forde, 2009). A network of parish councils which was developed by the rural organisation Muintir na Tíre from the 1930s was eventually superseded in the 1970s by community councils, community co-operatives and local development agencies (LDAs) (Forde, 2009), which sought to bring economic investment to depressed rural areas (Varley and Curtin, 2002).

Grassroots community development also has a long history in mainland Europe, where it is generally referred to as social pedagogy, a philosophy and set of activities that are common in the Nordic countries and other parts of northern Europe (Eriksson, 2011, 2013). Both individual and collective in focus, social pedagogy is carried out by professional social pedagogues, including social workers, who work with 'individuals and groups in need of support and help' (ibid., p. 407). Like community development, social pedagogy has a tradition as a grassroots initiative and as an intervention. Eriksson describes how in the 1970s Swedish social workers' engagement in local development work was based on 'strong elements of class struggle and class analysis' (ibid., p. 413). A contemporary example of a grassroots initiative is a disability group which is seeking to increase the influence in society of people with disabilities, while a Swedish folk high school which is located in a disadvantaged area and which teaches migrant women 'the tools to become active citizens' (ibid., p. 404) exemplifies the intervention approach to social pedagogy.

Intermittent radicalism has been a feature of community development activity, emerging from the grassroots of communities affected by poverty, oppression or discrimination. Ledwith (2007, pp. 284–285) points out that 'community development has always had a radical agenda ... inspired by a vision of social and environmental justice'. Action or inaction of the local or central state often provoked a reaction from community groups;

this would sometimes be followed by a response from the state. Labour organising in the US originated in the nineteenth century and led to the achievement of workers' rights, which were successfully defended in the 1930s through widespread strike action (Brueggemann, 2013). At the same time, community organising approaches were being used to address a range of issues through collective organising and activism. These approaches are a form of community development that aims to prepare 'people within local organizations and institutions to build power and take responsibility for solving the problems in their own communities' (Bunyan, 2010, p. 111; see also Bunyan, 2012). The most famous US organiser was Saul Alinsky whose Back of the Yards movement mobilised large numbers of local people to take control of the running of their own communities. Social workers became involved in a range of community organising activities in marginalised areas of the US (Brueggemann, 2013). In England, the poor living conditions of public housing tenants in the twentieth century led to a succession of rent strikes by tenants (Wood, 1994); slum clearances and relocation of tenants to New Towns were accompanied by interventions such as the employment of development workers in order to revive 'a sense of community' (Gilchrist and Taylor, 2011, p. 28) amongst the dislocated tenants.

A global upsurge in radicalism in the 1960s and 1970s was spurred by a confluence of issues, including racial discrimination, second wave feminism and anti-war sentiment in the context of the Vietnam War (Craig et al., 2011). Activists used a range of community development approaches. For example, Taylor (1997; also Bollens, 2000) describes how popular movements used community development approaches in their efforts to act as a countervailing force and a voice for the dispossessed during apartheid in South Africa. The Aboriginal land rights movement in Australia in the 1960s adopted community development approaches to assert 'collective control of resources and a practical autonomy' (Kenny, 1996, p. 107). In the US black communities used community development to begin to gain control of and develop their communities during and after the height of the civil rights movement; the result was the widespread establishment of community development corporations (CDCs) (Brueggemann, 2013), which continue to function in the US.

Community development as intervention

Like grassroots community development, community development as an intervention has a long-standing history. Amongst the most significant interventions were the community development programmes instituted by colonial powers in Asian and African countries prior to the achievement of independence. France, Great Britain and the US all introduced variants of community development programmes from the early to the middle years of the twentieth century. Reasons for the establishment of the programmes included economic benefit to the coloniser, administration and control, and prevention against the spread of communism (Mayo, 1974). Atampugre (1998, p. 356) writes, for example, about French efforts to establish co-operatives in cotton-producing areas of West Africa, but contends that the co-ops 'had more to do with administering the area than improving cultivation'. Marjorie Mayo argues that community development was the chosen approach because it offered a 'less troublesome' (p. 77) alternative to force in ensuring compliance and facilitating trade and exports. Post-independence, the unequal relationship between the former colonies and countries in the Global North was maintained through the imposition of structural adjustment policies, loans and Western 'expertise', including forms of participation that reinforced rather than challenged power differentials (Craig, 2010; Francis, 2001; Perold et al., 2013).

Mayo (1974) draws parallels between the use of community development under colonialism and its employment by governments in their own countries in the second half of the twentieth century. From the 1960s, governments sought to compensate for the 'rolling back' of the state and the contraction of welfare states by introducing large-scale interventions such as the War on Poverty in the US (established in 1964), the Urban Programmes and area-based Community Development Programme (CDP) in Britain (established in 1968 and 1969 respectively), and the Australian Assistance Plan (established in 1973). Large numbers of community workers were employed on these programmes. At supra-national level, the European Community established the First Anti-Poverty Programme (1975–1980), which aimed to identify solutions to poverty and disadvantage through learning from the work of anti-poverty projects at local level in a number of countries (Room, 1995). Local projects employed community workers and drew on community development approaches. Two further Anti-Poverty Programmes ran in 1986–1989 and 1990–1994. While the War on Poverty had an economic focus from the start, the CDP and Urban Programmes in Britain did not, and subsequently radicalised as workers developed a Marxist critique that emphasised that responsibility for the disadvantage of neighbourhoods lay with the state, not the communities themselves. This critique focused on

> the state as the instrument of capitalism, highlighting the flight of financial capital from these areas and describing how state subsidy, for example in housing policy, favoured the middle classes – a critique paralleled in the US. (Gilchrist and Taylor, 2011, p. 51; see also Community Development Project Interproject Editorial Team, 1977)

Radicalisation of the CDP led to its early closure by the Labour Government in the late 1970s (Dominelli, 2004a; Popple, 2000).

The 'turn' to community-based solutions described here and in Chapter 2 has brought community development centre-stage while simultaneously claiming it as an intervention or 'tool' of the state. This has had significant implications for the focus and practice of community development work. Not only has it become the 'vehicle' for the delivery of government policy (Popple, 2000, 2007), but like social workers, community workers have increasingly been tasked with 'encouraging the helpless to help themselves' (Shaw and Martin, 2000, p. 407; see also Miller and Ahmad, 1997) by working to channel people experiencing poverty and unemployed people into a range of self-help programmes. Geoghegan and Powell (2006) cite the example of community employment (CE) schemes in Ireland; these schemes are used to provide long-term unemployed people with employment in a range of areas, including in the voluntary and community sectors. They describe these schemes as a type of secondary labour market that furnishes cheap, temporary jobs while reducing the numbers of unemployed.

From the 1970s employment in state-funded projects and in local government led to the professionalisation of community development in the UK, Ireland and Australia (Craig, 1989; Fitzpatrick, 1997; Kenny, 1996; Miller and Ahmad, 1997; Whelan, 1989). Kenny (1996) describes the ambivalence with which some Australian community development workers viewed professionalisation, because of fears that professionalisation would erode 'critical activism' (p. 107) and generate a divide between paid workers and communities. Similar reservations have been expressed in the UK (Miller and Ahmad, 1997) and Ireland (Whelan, 1989). Ingrid Burkett (2011b) acknowledges the advantages of professionalisation, including the development of academic and professional standing, but identifies an inherent tension between the 'professional and popular' (p. 577) projects of community development. She argues that professional community development should be about 'development *by* people' and '*with* people', and needs to guard against practice that is '*for* people', or 'done *to* people' (ibid., her italics).

'Community': An enduring site of change and resistance

While on the one hand ideas of 'community' have been commandeered by governments to offer a set of alternatives to the retreating welfare state, community has also remained a site of resistance to neo-liberalism and a conduit through which responses to the neo-liberal hegemony are formulated. Theorists and practitioners who promote community as a site of resistance point to examples of how local action or action that commences with a grouping of people with similar interests can effect significant change in localities and in the wider society. Case Study 5.1 about London Citizens provides an example of how community action at city level has been effective in highlighting and addressing both economic and social needs at both urban and societal level.

Challenging neo-liberalism: London Citizens

Community organising approaches, which have their roots in the US, have begun to gain a foothold in the UK in the last twenty years. As we have seen, community organising is an inherently critical activity that presses for change at the macro or societal level, based on the idea that power can be built and used by collectives.

Bunyan (2010) cites the example of London Citizens, a broad-based coalition of voluntary and community organisations, youth groups, schools and churches. Since 2000 London Citizens have undertaken two high-profile campaigns. The first of these was the 'living wage' campaign, which commenced in 2001 and sought to address poverty by challenging low wages in large private and public organisations in London. The campaign achieved significant improvements in pay, terms of employment and conditions of workers in a range of organisations. The second campaign, 'Strangers into Citizens', mobilised member organisations of London Citizens and others including politicians and political activists to push for full legal rights for undocumented migrants who were long-term resident in the UK. In 2007 a rally in London organised by 'Strangers into Citizens' was attended by over 10,000 people.

The work of London Citizens offers an intermediate level (Bunyan, 2010) between the experience of the individual and the macro level of society and state. The intermediate or meso-level 'is critical in terms of connecting people beyond the local and opening up the arena of public and political activity' (Bunyan, 2010, p. 123). This level of engagement facilitates the linking of the personal and the political, or making the links between people's experiences of poverty and inequality and what is happening in the wider society.

Bunyan notes that while London Citizens has faced a number of challenges, including difficulties in building and sustaining a resource and power base, and justifying the need for an oppositional stance at a time when partnership and co-operative approaches are being pushed by government, the organisation has survived and is now part of Citizens UK, a national coalition of community organising groups.

Questions

1. Drawing on the example of London Citizens, and your own experience if applicable, discuss the value of community organising as a practice approach.
2. What kinds of challenges and tensions do such broad-based coalitions face in the contemporary neo-liberal climate?

3. How can these alliances extend beyond the local context to develop the impetus for change at a national or international level?
4. What place, if any, do you see for social workers within organisations/coalitions like London Citizens?

Burkett (2011a) argues that some of the key principles associated with neo-liberalism can be re-imagined in ways that 'offer a broader and more progressive vision for community organizations' (p. 119) than neo-liberalism envisages. In this way, as well as referring to economic self-sufficiency, the principle of 'self-reliance' may refer to political and intellectual independence, which together foster independent and creative thought and action. Similarly, 'entrepreneurship', a central tenet of neo-liberalism, may be re-envisaged as 'social innovation', or a spectrum of forms of innovation that encompass a range of marketplaces, economic, social and service-oriented. Jennings (2002), Bertotti et al. (2011) and Eversole (2013) describe a number of social enterprises that were established in and by local communities in response to disadvantage and the withdrawal of public services in England and Australia. These enterprises seek to serve both social and economic purposes. For instance, a number of community banks were established in rural parts of Australia in response to the closure of bank branches in these places. Jennings (2002) describes the development of a community bank in the shire of Kulin in Western Australia. The community bank was established by members of the community using money pledged by local people. The community bank is just one of a number of initiatives established by the Kulin community since 1994; these include a community newspaper, a multi-purpose health service, provision of housing for older and younger people and the Kulin bush races, which bring in significant revenue that is ploughed back into other community projects. Jennings emphasises that the Kulin initiatives exemplify community development in practice. 'Through participation, community members gain control over the economic life of their communities within a self-help framework to identify needs, reach collective decision-making, and take action' (Jennings, 2002, p. 312). The initiatives in Kulin exemplify the capacity of self-help and grassroots action to address economic needs and, by extension, social needs.

Directions in community development in Latin America: Challenge and innovation

The Global South provides a rich source of examples of community action in the face of political upheaval, oppression and economic hardship. While in Western countries politics has not tended to be a preoccupation of community development, in many parts of the Global South community development and the political sphere have been closely intertwined (Pearce, Howard and Bronstein, 2010). This is particularly the case in Latin America, where important and diverse influences on community development have included Marxism, political advocacy by the Catholic Church, and liberation theology and its encouragement of 'civic engagement by all persons in society, especially the socially excluded' (Reisch, Ife and Weil, 2013, p. 78). The fraught nature of politics in Latin America, which has a history of colonialism and intermittent dictatorship, 'has politicised the poor, and fostered self-organisation in the absence of a welfare safety net' (Pearce, 2010, p. 18). In its turn this self-organisation has been characterised by a high degree of creativity and innovation 'which has caught the imagination of many parts of the world' (Pearce, Howard and Bronstein, 2010, p. 266).

Much of the innovation in Latin America has originated in Brazil, where community or popular education and experiments in municipal participatory budgeting have influenced and encouraged similar forms of experiment, both small- and large-scale, in other parts of the world (Fung and Olin Wright, 2003; Hope and Timmel, 1984). Paolo Freire's ideas about education were tested in Brazil before finding a global audience. In his seminal work *Pedagogy of the Oppressed* (1997) Freire questioned the dominant 'banking' form of education, which relies on the transmission of knowledge from teacher to learner, and underlined the importance of the experience and knowledge of the learner. Central to Freire's model of education is 'conscientisation', or consciousness-raising, a dialogical process that leads to a critical analysis of one's existing situation, and from there to a consideration of ways in which that situation may be changed. Conscientisation is a gradual process that builds from dialogue and reflection to eventual action. It is concerned with connecting the 'personal with the political', or linking people's personal situations with wider social processes that impact their lives, and enabling the realisation that in their turn people can act on these processes to effect change. Conscientisation is explored in more detail later in this chapter.

Research Box 5.1 provides an example of how community development work by Indigenous people in Mexico has provided them with economic, social and political opportunities. It illustrates the outcomes of conscientisation by demonstrating how the people of Chiapas have taken control of their economic and social well-being and asserted their rights as an Indigenous group, and how women have attained confidence and independence through participation in economic activity.

Community development in Mexico: Seeking the *good life*

Giovannini (2014) describes the concept of *buen vivir*, or 'good living', a Latin American approach to development that emphasises Indigenous identity and ways of life and the relationship between humans and their natural environment. Giovannini identifies three unique characteristics of *buen vivir*: it is generated by peoples who have been marginalised historically; these peoples understand well-being in communal or collective terms, and they understand that the natural environment is the subject of rights claims.

Giovannini explores the development of thirteen community enterprises established by the Mayan people of Chiapas State in Mexico. The enterprises engage in a range of activities, primarily ecotourism, agriculture and handicrafts. Their goals are in five areas: social, cultural, economic, political and environmental. For instance, political goals include connections with social movements and the pursuit of autonomy from the central state, which has acted in ways that are contrary to the identity and rights claims of the Indigenous people. These community enterprises, which function autonomously at local level, 'have become instruments for reinforcing the protection of indigenous cultures and territories' (Giovannini, 2014, p. 13).

The community enterprises promote *buen vivir* by championing Indigenous culture and identity, drawing on natural resources and encouraging people's participation in the public sphere (Giovannini, 2014). Giovannini points out that 'the need for participation in the public sphere was advocated especially by women, who found in their organizations an opportunity to slowly change their lives by becoming active outside their homes' (ibid., p. 11). Broadening participation is achieved through women's participation in all of the enterprises, some of which are exclusively run by women. Through their participation women acquire a voice and power in contexts which were traditionally patriarchal; 'community enterprises promote genuine forms of participation that increase women's control over their everyday lives at both the social and political levels' (ibid., p. 13). This provides a connection between the personal and the political whereby women's everyday experiences are translated into collective action.

The example of *buen vivir* described in Box 5.1 illustrates three key aspects of community development. In the first place, values are central to a community development approach. These values may differ according to context and what is valued in one place may be very different from that which is emphasised somewhere else or by a different group. Second, effective community development practice develops from the ground up, as communities identify their own needs and seek to address them. Finally, community development is a holistic and iterative process that builds from personal empowerment into a collective and powerful movement for change. This process is explored in more detail in the following section.

The community development process: Synergies with social work

This section will identify and explore the elements of the community development process, which may be envisaged as a cycle. It will discuss the connections between the community development cycle and social work practice and in doing so identify the potential for a social work practice based on a community development approach.

The cycle of community development

One of the distinguishing features of community development is that it is a cyclical process. Its cyclical nature may be distinguished from a linear approach, which has a beginning, middle and end. While beginnings and endings occur in community development, it is more common for one action to prompt another, thereby maintaining the cyclical nature of the work, and specifically sustaining a process of engagement and learning that builds over time and with growing experience. Hope and Timmel (1984) refer to the community development process as a 'commitment cycle', or a process that begins with reflection on or evaluation of the situation, followed by identification of who will be involved and planning for action, decisions about goals and objectives, implementation of the planned activity, and reflection to see how the work is going, to see if any adjustments need to be made to activities, and to consider what should happen next.

This cyclical process of engagement may remain small-scale and local in scope or it may build 'steadily outwards, from issue to project, from project to alliances/networks, gathering momentum towards movements for change' (Ledwith and Springett, 2010, p. 16; see also Ledwith, 2005). This illustrates the transformational nature of community development; it seeks change rather than stasis. For instance, a rural women's group with which one of the authors worked started by undertaking personal development training, which was followed by a series of initiatives, including the generation of linkages with other women's groups and the annual celebration of International Women's Day. The group's work culminated in securing funding for the purchase of radio equipment which was used to facilitate broadcasting to other women on the local radio station.

Ledwith and Springett (2010) argue that practice that is holistic or 'interconnected' (p. 193) contrasts with the neo-liberal worldview with its 'top-down, vertical perspective' that prizes 'relations of superiority and inferiority' (p. 189) rather than interrelationships and the interdependence of the world and everything in it. Like community development, social work practice is process-driven and relationship-based but the dominance of neo-liberalism has made it more difficult for social workers and other human service workers to maintain a focus on the process-based nature of the work that they do. While the challenges of managerialism and accountability and the growing complexity of the social work environment have curtailed the opportunities for person-centred work, we have seen that this approach to practice still exists and there are opportunities for re-envisaging this approach in the current landscape of practice. Green and McDermott (2010) and Fook (2012) suggest a re-imagining of systems approaches, so that social workers acknowledge the growing complexity of the systems that surround them, grasp the 'inseparability of person and environment' (p. 2428) and learn to work 'with evolving systems' (ibid.) including the local and the global, and the social, cultural and economic systems that impinge on people's lives. Green social work is an example of practice that takes changing systems – environmental, social and cultural – into account when working with communities and service users. The example in Practice Example 5.1 below also illustrates how systems thinking can influence practice.

Reflection

Reflection is the starting point of the community development cycle. The cycle begins with reflection on the current situation, and then proceeds to action, followed by reflection on the action undertaken and on what will happen next. It is an iterative and reflexive process that enables a group to move forward and back from reflection and evaluation to action and back again. Reflection and evaluation are essential elements of the process. Reflection enables the consideration and questioning of the reality of a situation or problem and leads to the development of ideas about how it may be addressed. Through *critical reflection*, individuals and groups undergo conscientisation or develop a critical consciousness whereby they develop a realisation of the root

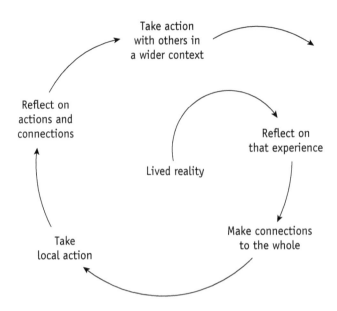

Figure 5.1 Spiral of learning and action

Source: Ledwith and Springett (2010)

causes of the problems like poverty and disadvantage, oppression and discrimination (Freire, 1997; Ledwith and Springett, 2010).

Ledwith and Springett (2010) envisage conscientisation as a spiral (see Figure 5.1). Like the cycle of community development, the spiral is cyclical or iterative in nature. Its starting point is the lived realities of people's lives. When people are facilitated to reflect on their lives, they start to make connections to 'the whole', or to the world around them and how this impinges on their lives and well-being. In turn, these connections may lead to the identification of actions that can be undertaken at local level. Ledwith (2005) gives an example of how conscientisation occurs in practice. She refers to a group of people who come together because of a concern for the need for safer play facilities for the children in their area. In order to focus the group on the problem, the community development worker presents a set of slides of the existing play areas. The slides help the group to see the existing play facilities in a different way.

> Everyday experience is too familiar to be questioned. Taking the reality and capturing it in another form enables people to begin the process of questioning. (Ledwith, 2005, p. 99)

Once the members of the group start asking questions the worker responds with further questions in order to engage them in a critical dialogue.

Why? Where? How? Who? What? In whose interests? Why are those swings rusty and broken? Why are broken bottles lying around? Why is it so dangerous? Why is it open to the road? Successive questions probe deeper towards the source of the problem. (ibid., p. 99)

When the cause of the problem has been identified, the group can then plan ways to resolve it. In this case, if the local authority is responsible for the play area, the group can develop a strategy for approaching the decision-making body to raise the issue.

Once actions at the local level have been attempted, they may lead to the generation of links with others who share similar issues or concerns, at local, national or international level. Using the example of a community garden, Ledwith and Springett (2010) discuss the significance of action in the wider context.

So, while a community garden will not solve all the issues faced by a community... it does have the potential to begin the process of change by connecting people with each other and with nature. However, for the process to be truly transformative, that is, to create the positive feedback talked about in systems theory, the act needs to be connected to other acts of participation, such as LETS, farmers' markets, credit unions, allotments, cooperative shops and other projects that contribute to a movement that integrates human well-being with environmental well-being. (p. 193)

Reflection is a core dimension of social work practice and there is an extensive social work literature on the nature and purpose of reflection. While Brookfield (2009) argues that reflection is crucial to social work practice, he points out that 'reflection' and 'critical reflection' are sometimes conflated, thereby undermining the specificity of critical reflection. Similarly, critical reflection takes different forms and is therefore a contested concept (ibid.). Brookfield argues that critical reflection has a twin purpose, which is linked to conscientisation. The first is to externalise power relations through public acknowledgement of the social worker's power, and the second is to continually seek to challenge hegemonic ideas and practices, by critically reflecting on their own ideas, assumptions and ways of working. For example, Morley and MacFarlane (2010, p. 53) argue that social workers in the field of mental health need to challenge hegemonic ideas about the causes of mental illness by engaging in 'critical questioning around taken for granted assumptions' and work towards the development of 'critical discourses which represent alternatives to the medical model of mental health'. The practice examples in Chapter 7 and in the next section of this chapter also illustrate how social workers critically reflect on their work by making connections between service users' experiences and hegemonic ideas and practices.

Participation

As we saw in Chapter 1, participation is an integral element of the community development process. Without participation, community development cannot occur. Participation is a factor at all stages of the process, from the identification of an issue through to reflection on what happens after action has been taken. In terms of encouraging participation in practice, Gunn (2006; see also Beresford and Croft, 1993) identifies a number of ways in which participation and collective action can be achieved; these include imaginative ways of contacting and engaging people, development of accessible structures and processes, and building rewards into the process. Hawtin and Percy-Smith (2007) and the social work writers Teater and Baldwin (2012) discuss the usefulness of community profiling; community profiling is a community development tool that involves conducting a profile of a community to identify its needs and resources so as to plan for meeting these needs. A distinguishing feature of community profiling is the participation of the community in the profiling process. Members of the community initiate the profiling, and participate in all stages, from planning to gathering data to deciding on the plan of action that stems from the profiling. The Centre for Social Justice and Community Action at the University of Durham has developed toolkits for participatory research (links are provided below).

Participation is also a feature of social work practice. It has gained in importance in recent years with the growing emphasis on service user perspectives and participation in social services including social work (Adams, 2008), and on anti-oppressive practice (Dominelli, 2012b). Davies et al. (2014) and Adams (2008) make the important distinction between bottom-up participation, in which service users claim a voice, and top-down participation or state-sanctioned service user participation, such as advisory groups and forums of service users. In their study of the experiences of people who used the Australian mental health service, Davies et al. (2014) point out that service users are dissatisfied with formal and structured types of participation like service user committees and panels; instead they have rich and diverse conceptions of participation that reflect an emphasis on social justice aims, including a concern with seeking 'an equitable balance of power, respect, financial security and recognition' (p. 123). They argue that these social justice goals should be the real test of participation, not whether people are given opportunities to participate.

Education

Another core element of the community development process is education. In Chapter 1 we identified the role of community development workers and social workers as educators who facilitate empowerment through enabling individuals and communities to develop autonomous voices and to challenge hegemonic power relations locally, nationally and globally. Education usually occurs informally, through discussion and dialogue or through practising in particular ways. Ledwith and Springett (2010), Ingamells et al. (2010) and Westoby and Kaplan (2014) refer to the importance of dialogue and story-telling in community development practice. This approach has its roots in the work of Paolo Freire and is concerned with conscientisation or consciousness-raising and the generation of action. Lathouras (2010) identifies the three principles of dialogue as seeing through others' eyes, building relationships and precipitating action; she points out that this approach 'requires a shift in thinking from the practitioner doing something *for* or *to* people, to doing something *with* people' (p. 14). This approach challenges professionals, particularly social workers, who are used to often unequal relationships with service users. For social workers and community development workers, education is a reciprocal process and involves learning from communities and service users as well as imparting knowledge, skills and experience.

Story-telling can happen in different ways. For example, Grant-Smith and Matthews (2015) discuss the use of public art in the form of murals to tell the story of Shandon, a historic part of Cork, Ireland's second city. They describe how the murals 'told a story of Shandon's cultural past and validated the history, lived-in experience and memories of the contributors' (p. 143). Cardboard Citizens in the UK (http://cardboardcitizens.org.uk/) use theatre workshops, training and performances to tell the stories of people who have experienced homelessness. In particular, they use theatre of the oppressed (Boal, 1979), a form of theatre 'developed from a lived experience of discrimination' (Ledwith and Springett, 2010, p. 120), such as homelessness, racism or sexism. Theatre of the Oppressed seeks empowerment and change through interaction between the players and the audience; on their second viewing of a performance, the audience, or 'spect-actors', can intervene to address the dilemma or problem that a protagonist faces and change its outcome, thereby offering opportunities for action to the protagonist.

Practice Example 5.1 illustrates the community development process in operation by providing an example of the process based on the experience of a social worker who works in a community development setting.

Community development with the Roma community in Dublin

The Roma are a minority ethnic group, often colloquially referred to as Gypsies or Travellers, who live in tightly-knit groupings in many European countries, the US and Latin America. In Europe the Roma have historically been subject to racial stereotyping and labelling and have consequently suffered considerable stigmatisation, discrimination and exclusion, both personal and structural (NASC, 2013), problems which continue to manifest in the 'host' countries where Roma people live. In 2013 there were an estimated 40,000 Roma living in Ireland (ibid., 2013). These include Irish Travellers and a smaller number of Roma people, most of whom originated in Romania or Bulgaria. This case study focuses on work with the latter group, of whom there are about 5,000 in Ireland.

Humphries (2008, p. 73) suggests that 'strategic action' can follow collective processes of critical reflection and dialogue that question 'the motives and outcomes of current arrangements'. A practitioner in a statutory agency describes* how her agency facilitated a meeting of professionals to discuss the difficulties experienced by the Roma community in an area of Dublin. The meeting was precipitated by a concern that the needs of the Roma were not being met, despite the existence of a range of services. It was agreed that a community development approach would be used in order to build a relationship with the Roma community. When it emerged that the Roma had little understanding of the services of which they could avail the initial meeting was followed by a series of information-sharing meetings that involved both professionals from several disciplines and members of the Roma. The social worker describes the process:

> within the social work department there was a definite feeling that we weren't meeting the need of this community, the same referrals kept coming back in and a lot of these families then were sitting on waiting lists because there was a real kind of – people didn't really know where to go next.

> So engagement started to happen with other agencies in the area and they all had the same issue – that they didn't feel that they were meeting the needs of the Roma community within the Dublin 24 area so the (agency) called a meeting of professionals together and we discussed this issue and a few ideas came up and one was to look at a community development approach to meeting the needs and understanding the needs of Roma people.

> So the primary care social worker and myself and a community development worker from the partnership got together and looked at the issue in more detail and really realised that we didn't understand the needs of this community, specifically within the area – we had an idea from research and reading what some of the needs might be but we didn't really know what their needs were. What we did know was the needs of the agencies but the actual Roma people's needs were missing. So we set about trying to engage slowly with the Roma community.... So, it actually worked really well because the primary care social worker was engaged with one family and she slowly spoke to them and they began to engage other families and I think, for me, that was community work. It was kind of going in there, not jumping in with two feet, but just slowly approaching the community, seeing what they thought of the idea and starting to

talk to other families. We invited the families to come and meet with us and we actually brought in two cultural mediators from the Roma community to mediate and interpret. We were linked with (names agency) who already had done a number of projects with Roma people and we actually just sat down and looked at 'What are your needs?'; 'What are the needs that need to be met today?'; 'What are the bigger needs, what are the issues that are facing them on a daily basis?'

That was our first point of call and really what came back from that was that there were really low levels of information coming in to the community, for example around immigration, around social welfare benefits, around school. So we sat down and looked at that and devised a plan of five meetings, information sharing meetings where we invited agencies in, we invited the Roma community to attend and I think it is very much the start of a process and that is where we are now. We have just finished our five information meetings and are looking at what can we do next to begin to engage and empower this community.

We wanted to make sure that we were empowering or beginning to empower this community to have a voice in Irish society... to empower the women within the community because we were aware that really there was a very patriarchal system – and there is – we also knew that we couldn't change that overnight but we wanted to ensure that we were all the time thinking about empowering the group but also the women in the group.

Source: * Research project carried out by Forde and Lynch in 2009–2010. Fifteen social workers in a range of practice settings in Ireland were interviewed about their experiences of using community development approaches in their practice.

In conclusion: The social work cycle?

The example in Practice Example 5.1 demonstrates how social workers can use the community development cycle effectively in their work with vulnerable groups and communities, and how the community development process can be used to seek social justice goals.

In particular, at a time when social work and community development are being constrained by neo-liberalism, by reductionist ideas of community and by a restrictive funding landscape this example of social work epitomises the enduring importance of 'a broader paradigm of community development work that is responsive to people, contexts and the specifics of issues emerging over time' (Lenette and Ingamells, 2014, pp. 13–14; Ryder, 2013). Lenette and Ingamells argue that this broad approach

> requires getting to know the people, the specifics of life experiences, settlement challenges and changing relations to their environment as well as the work of mobilizing various parts of the community to open up and respond. (2014, p. 13)

This approach has much in common with 'indigenisation', or practice that learns about and values the culture, knowledge, experiences and practices of Indigenous peoples (Bennett et al., 2011; Dominelli, 2012a, 2012b; Ife, 2013). This form of community development is, by nature, time-consuming, labour intensive and inherently cyclical. New waves of migrants to many countries in the Global North necessitate continual re-engagement in this work, or what Westoby (2010, p. 70) refers to as 'systematic ways of re-engaging constantly, rebuilding relationships, rechallenging assumptions'. In addition to a commitment from individual social workers and community development workers, this requires an organisational commitment so that social workers are supported to work in 'culturally respectful, courageous, and hopeful' (Bennett et al., 2011, p. 34) ways.

- Notwithstanding the increasing encroachment of the state into community development activity, a critical, challenging and creative seam of community development activity has survived and thrived.

- Community development is a cyclical and iterative process that involves reflection, action and participation; the elements of this process have much in common with core aspects of social work practice.

- Similarities between the community development process and social work practice enable the construction of a critical social work practice that draws extensively and effectively on community development ideas.

stop and think

- Discuss the relevance of the following concepts and ideas for your own practice with groups and communities: self-help and grassroots actions or activities; 'community' as a site for resistance and change; 'community' as a site for challenge and innovation.
- Consider the meaning of the following elements of the community development process in the context of your own practice with individuals, groups or communities: critical reflection in action; participation; education.
- Consider a community issue that you feel passionately about in your work with a group or community experiencing disadvantage and discuss how you would use the community development process in working with this group.

- Davies, K., Gray, M. and Webb, S.A. (2014) 'Putting the Parity into Service-user Participation: An Integrated Model of Social Justice', *International Journal of Social Welfare*, 23, pp. 119–127.
- Gamble, D. and Weil, M. (2010) *Community Practice Skills: Local to Global Practice*, New York: Colombia University Press.
- Giovannini, M. (2014) 'Indigenous Community Enterprises in Chiapas: A Vehicle for *Buen Vivir?*' *Community Development Journal*, DOI:10.1093/cdj/bsu019.
- Ife, J. (2013) *Community Development in an Uncertain World: Vision, Analysis and Practice*, Cambridge: Cambridge University Press.
- Kenny, S., Fanany, I. and Rahayu, S. (2012) 'Community Development in Indonesia: Westernization or Doing it Their Way?' *Community Development Journal*, 48(2), pp. 280–297.
- Ledwith, M. and Springett, J. (2010) *Participatory Practice: Community-based Action for Transformative Change*, Bristol: The Policy Press.
- Lenette, C. and Ingamells, A. (2014) 'Mind the Gap! The Growing Chasm between Funding-driven Agencies, and Social and Community Knowledge and Practice', *Community Development Journal*, DOI:10.1093/cdj/bsu024.

Online Resources

- Centre for Social Justice and Community Action and National Coordinating Centre for Public Engagement (2012) *Community-based Participatory Research: A Guide to Ethical Principles and practice*, Durham University: Authors, available online at www.dur.ac.uk/resources/beacon/CBPREthicsGuidewebNovember2012.pdf [Accessed 4 March 2015].
- Pain, R., Whitman, G., Milledge, D. and Lune Rivers Trust (no date) *Participatory Action Research Toolkit: An Introduction to Using PAR as an Approach to Learning, Research and Action*, available online at www.dur.ac.uk/resources/beacon/PARtoolkit.pdf [Accessed 4 March 2015].

6 Creative activism in social work practice

Introduction

In this chapter we focus on the ways in which social workers can effect social change through critical or 'creative' activism within and outside the workplace. We show that activism is connected to the activist or radical tradition addressed in Chapter 4. While we are interested in capturing the broad landscape of political practices, we are also interested in social change practices that are more nuanced and strategically woven into the fabric of day-to-day practices. Here, we open up spaces to explore both the overt and covert forms of resistance running above, along and below the changing landscapes of policy and practices in contemporary environments.

From our own research, we are aware of the creativity and innovation inherent in activist practices. We conceptualise a form of activism that is distinguished by a creativity that is both responsive and adaptable to diverse and shifting situations (Forde and Lynch, 2014). This inspired our reference to 'creative activism' in the chapter title and we highlight different forms and facets of activist practices.

In this chapter, we explore how contemporary conceptions may facilitate different forms of activism in the challenging, structured and sometimes restricted environments in which many workers function. We consider contemporary expositions and analyses of social work activism in different countries and contexts (for example, Reisch and Andrews, 2002; Ferguson and Lavalette, 2005; Sewpaul, 2006; Mendes, 2007; Lavalette, 2011). Analyses of activism draw on expansive ideas of citizenship, including the concept of 'justice-orientated' citizen (Westheimer and Kahne, 2004) and contextualised, post-structural, flexible, nuanced or 'creative' approaches to activism emerge (De Wan, 2010; Ferguson and Woodward, 2009; Martin, Hanson and Fontaine, 2007). We show that it is not uncommon for contemporary activists to use a mix of 'insider' and 'outsider' approaches in seeking to influence their own and external agencies (Baker et al., 2004; De Wan, 2010; Mayo, 2005; Mullaly, 1997).

Our chapter critically analyses a variety of approaches to social work activism, including public advocacy and engagement with the state (Gal and Weiss-Gal, 2013; Mendes, 2007). We discuss new and emerging 'fronts' of social work activism, including collective right-based approaches that have been articulated by social work writers and practitioners in a range of practice contexts (Ife, 2010; Ife and Fiske, 2006; Lundy and Van Wormer, 2007; Ramon and Maglajlic, 2012; also Cornwall, Robins and Von Lieres, 2011). Activism is explored in the context of practice where managerialism is the dominant discourse, particularly the 'management-dominated, highly regulated statutory sector of social work' (Mantle and Backwith, 2010, p. 2384; see also Buckley, 2008; Collins, 2009; Shevellar, 2011).

Social workers as activists

To locate activism within social work, we turn to the different traditions or approaches to social work that are identified in the literature. For example, James Midgley (2001) identifies three traditions: the remedial, the developmental and the activist, while Michael Lavalette and Vassilios Ioakimidis (2011) posit two: 'official' social work and 'popular' social work. For Midgley (2001), debates about the orientation, commitments and function of social work are accentuated in the international practice context, particularly in relation to developing countries of the Global South. He differentiates between 'remedial social work' that is orientated towards individualised therapeutic interventions and 'developmental' forms which respond to human need through mobilising and organising local communities. He links the latter to community approaches that address issues such as poverty, literacy and health. In contrast, a distinctive form of social work practice that is identified by Midgley is 'activist social work' that challenges social inequalities, oppression and injustice and seeks to promote liberation. Historically, this is connected to the activist or radical social work tradition addressed in Chapter 4 and linked to the major social movements of the 1960s and early 1970s such as the women's movement, the civil rights movement, the gay movement and workers' rights.

In distinguishing between 'official' and 'popular' social work, Lavalette and Ioakimidis (2011) link the latter to 'a range of campaigning, political social work and welfare initiatives' (p. 140). They argue that 'popular' social work in Britain and Europe has been less visible in the official history of the profession. While stating that 'official' social work is not homogenous, Lavalette and Ioakimidis (2011) contend that it 'may be any combination of regulated, qualified, state recognised social work' (p. 139). On the other hand, 'popular social work' is defined as 'activities of a range of individuals and groups who address aspects of trauma, inequality and oppression, in ways that are non-hierarchical, mutually supportive and based on notions of solidarity' (Lavalette, 2013, p. 113). These activities are located alongside or at times directly opposed to 'professional', 'state' or 'bourgeois' social work (p. 113). This is a potentially useful conceptualisation of practices, particularly in the Irish and UK context where the majority of social workers are employed by the State (Lynch and Burns, 2008).

Moving to a community development context, there are frameworks that are useful to conceptualise activist positions and understandings for social workers engaged in community development practice. For example, Jim Ife (2013) advances perspectives to view social problems or issues as follows: individual; institutional reformist; structural; and post-structural. He argues that locating problems at the individual level leads to therapeutic interventions and 'control' functions while the institutional reformist perspective focuses on reorganising institutions and gaining more services and resources. However, a more 'radical' approach, the structural perspective, focuses on structural change to address structural disadvantage or oppression such as liberation movements. Finally, the post-structural orientation refers to multiple understandings and analysis of discourse, particularly discourses of power. Ife locates traditional social policy strategies within the first two perspectives, and community development based on social justice ideas within the latter two.

The debate between the 'reformist' and 'revolutionary' approaches among activist social workers is articulated by Healy (2000). She points out that, while recognising the necessity of fundamental social change, social workers from the 'reformist tradition' work with oppressed peoples within the existing structures to achieve change. On the other hand, Healy notes that activist social workers from the 'revolutionary tradition' work towards the overall transformation of society and argue that the reformist approach may perpetuate oppressions. We agree with Healy's argument that both approaches are based on core characteristics that include the structural analysis of social problems, focus on oppressions, egalitarian practice processes, strategies that challenge oppressive structures, and the social work role as facilitator of the 'voices' of oppressed and marginalised peoples (Healy, 2000). Significantly, Webb (2010) connects both 'the politics of *redistribution* and *recognition*' to social justice activism in social work (p. 2376). He argues for an approach that embraces 'an ethics of recognition' (in relation to cultural injustice and suffering) and 'an ethics of redistribution' (in relation to addressing economic injustice). Similarly, Marston and McDonald (2012) argue that social workers as political change agents must work to address both economic and cultural injustices. They illustrate their point by arguing that 'constructing people as *unlawful* (that is, in the case of refugees, and use of language such as "illegals" or "queue-jumpers") puts them on the side of a moral binary that works against their claims to be recognised as a person with rights' (p. 11). This then limits access to material resources. Social workers can work alongside communities to reframe these identities in the public domain (Marston and McDonald, 2012).

The constraints and possibilities for activist practices in relation to the goal of the *redistribution* of power are discussed comprehensively by Healy (see Healy, 2000, pp. 30–36). She argues that there may be limited opportunity for engaging in activist activity 'within the system'. However, some authors have identified a range of 'insider' approaches (see, for example, Mullaly, 1997; Ife, 1997). For example, working towards democratic processes from *within* the agency, challenging constructions of social problems and oppressive policies, and ethically informed practices 'to defend the service user from the agency' are key strategies outlined by Mullaly (1997, p. 183). In Chapter 3 we provide several examples where practitioners challenge dominant discourses in their everyday practices within different work settings. Drawing on Paulo Friere's (1997) model of education, practitioners can embed consciousness-raising into everyday practices through problem-posing and 'reframing' of social problems with individuals, groups and communities with whom they work (see Ife, 1997; see also Mullaly, 1997). This process is explored in detail in Chapter 3. This places issues or problems within a broader political context and opens up possibilities for people to take action to effect change.

However, activist activities may extend beyond the workplace through coalition building with radical change organisations such as unions and advocacy groups (Healy, 2000). Similarly, Ife (1997) emphasises a political role for social workers in relation to developing alliances with other groups such as trade unions, political parties and human rights groups to achieve social justice goals. Working outside of the workplace entails a range of practices which could involve contributing to the development of 'community controlled' services and programmes outside the mainstream, engaging with social movements and coalitions for structural change, involvement with trade unions and membership of professional associations (Mullaly, 1997). Contemporary activists may use a mix of 'insider' and 'outsider' approaches in seeking to influence their own and external agencies (Baker et al., 2004; De Wan, 2010; Mayo, 2005; Mullaly, 1997). For example, a range of both 'insider' and 'outsider' strategies is employed by social work practitioner activists working with immigrants and asylum seekers (Fraser and Briskman, 2005; Mynott, 2005). An example of an 'outsider' perspective is building solidarity between organisations created by asylum seekers and welfare organisations 'to alter the balance of forces within a profession or a particular workplace in favour of those who seek to resist acting as immigration officers' (Mynott, 2005, p. 140).

'Creative activism' within and beyond the workplace

In our own research in Ireland, practitioner accounts of critical practice resonated with the literature on new and emerging forms of activism. Drawing on the voices of practitioners in our study, we conceptualised a form of activism that was distinguished by a creativity that is responsive and adaptable to diverse and shifting situations (Forde and Lynch, 2014). Some of the activism that practitioners were engaged in was connected to the socio-economic crisis in Ireland. For example, a practitioner in a community work context referred to the 'relentless campaign' in which she and her co-workers were involved to highlight the effects of cutbacks on the voluntary and community sector (Forde and Lynch, 2014). A mix of 'insider' and 'outsider' approaches in seeking to influence their own and external agencies emerged in practitioner accounts. For example, one practitioner employed in a statutory service spoke of working 'behind the scenes' to support a state-funded youth service to mount a campaign to protest against funding cuts. She articulated the tension between 'working for the state when the issues are against the state' (Forde and Lynch, 2014, p. 10). Another practitioner working in a large voluntary agency discussed working within the system 'very quietly and as politically as we can' to promote change. For us, this resonated with the concept of 'a more humble' political agency where the everyday actions between workers and citizens can become sites for meaningful change (Marston and McDonald, 2012, p. 14). We noted that this was consistent with the idea of activism as a collective activity that emanates from the everyday experience of individuals who connect with others to seek to 'alter power relations within existing social networks' (Martin, Hanson and Fontaine, 2007; see also Crossley and Ibrahim, 2012). Despite small beginnings, these action networks have the potential to evolve into formal social movements (Martin, Hanson and Fontaine, 2007, p. 82).

The experiences of the social workers in our study emphasised the flexibility of contemporary activism, which offered 'creative alternatives for activists and organisations suddenly struck by cuts in their state funding and forced to find new ways to make themselves heard' (De Wan, 2010, p. 530 cited in Forde and Lynch, 2014). Marston and McDonald (2012) provide the example of social workers within organisations learning to become 'bilingual' by strategically employing managerial language to funders but using 'a more explicit social justice discourse' with the people and communities with whom they work (p. 13).

Our study also highlighted another facet of activism. Some practitioners' involvement in activism was sporadic or intermittent rather than sustained (Forde and Lynch, 2014). For example, one practitioner told us that she had been involved in activism for many years but recently her personal family commitments had to take precedence. We argue that individualism and 'conflicting life-choices' (Gane, 2001, p. 269) in late modernity can lead to constant tensions between personal and professional demands and 'fighting the cause' (Collins, 2009). Episodic activism enables practitioners to seize opportunities when they arise, but does not require constant commitment (Forde and Lynch, 2014). We contend that these examples of activism exhibit more contextualised, flexible, nuanced or 'creative' approaches to activism.

Some of the accounts in our research resonated with the broader literature on policy practices and shifted the focus to the local organisational level 'as a site of policy activism' (Marston and McDonald, 2012, p. 3). In the next section we explore these possibilities and ideas in the international context.

Social workers as social policy activists

'Policy practice' or the involvement of social workers in social policy formation, implementation and change is an area of social work activism that has received attention in the literature (Gal and Weiss-Gal, 2013; Levin, Goor and Tayri, 2013; Marston and McDonald, 2012). Agency Advocacy (AA) is described by Levin, Goor and Tayri (2013) as 'meso-level social policy practice' which encompasses agency policies, local programmes and direct practices (p. 522). These activities may also involve building coalitions to increase marginalised groups and communities' access to resources. Levin, Goor and Tayri note that social workers may not engage with policy practices at the agency level as these are perceived as 'macro-level' activities and, therefore, outside of day-to-day practice. We agree with these authors when they argue that 'meso-level changes in organisational policies, climates and behaviours will, in time, seep into micro-level encounters' (p. 537). Rather than a linear process, they suggest multiple circles of influence that drive change processes both inwards and outwards and that AA can provide a focal point for both meso-level and macro-level policies. This idea of multi-directional change processes resonates with our own conceptualisation of activism where small-scale change activities can reverberate well beyond the immediate level of the agency. These iterative processes connect with the community development cycle that we discuss in Chapter 5.

In Chapter 1 we made the point that social work is an international occupation with different manifestations in different places, depending on local conditions, policies, and welfare systems. A cross-national study that compared eight countries (Australia, England, Israel, Italy, Russia, Spain, Sweden and the USA) drawing on available research data and academic and professional articles and reports found that social workers' engagement in policy practice was limited (Gal and Weiss-Gal, 2013). However, what is interesting is that these researchers noted several differences in the level and type of policy involvement that emerged across countries. A number of 'routes' that social workers took to influence policy processes were identified as: membership and participation in activities organised by their professional representative bodies such as the National Association of Social Workers (NASW), policy practice by academics through media, access to policy-makers and research activities, membership of advocacy organisations, social movements and social welfare providers, and direct policy practice within their workplaces ('the insider route'). Gal and Weiss-Gal (2013) present a conceptual framework comprising of three inter-related dimensions (opportunity, facilitation and motivation) to explore social workers' engagement in policy practice (see *Research Box 6.1*). Interestingly, the authors note that neither the extent of social problems encountered by social workers nor the particular political circumstances or context appeared to exert a specific influence on whether they engaged in policy practice or not.

Research Box 6.1

Policy practice engagement

The Policy Practice Engagement (PPE) Conceptual Framework draws on the dimensions of opportunity, facilitation and motivation to explore social workers' engagement in policy practice. Each of these three elements of the framework is presented below.

Opportunity

The first dimension of the PPE framework is opportunity. It is posited that opportunity and the level of access to political bodies and institutions influences whether social workers become involved in policy practice and this also shapes the type of policy activities undertaken. The cross-national study found that in the USA, legislative lobbying is a significant activity and occurs mostly through the professional social work association at national and state level, advocacy bodies and coalitions. However, in other countries social work representation was by means of parliamentary committees (Israel) or formal consultation processes (UK). The authors also identified a number of 'alternative activities' such as social action through various representative organisations, advocacy organisations and court appeals as well as the use of mass media and policy analyses (Gal and Weiss-Gal, 2013, p. 10).

Facilitation

The second dimension of the PPE framework is organisational or workplace culture that may facilitate or restrict policy practice. This refers to the prevailing values and practice approaches of the organisation and the provision of support and resources that might enable policy practice. The cross-national study found that in Spain and Israel, the 'insider route' is more common for social workers working within local government agencies and state services than in countries such as Sweden, USA, Russia and England. The 'insider route' is direct engagement within the workplace context. The authors note that, in the Swedish context, most social workers are employed in local government providing direct services to individuals and families with very limited involvement in policy formulation. In the UK, the limited role of state-employed social workers in policy practice is linked to the implementation of New Public Management (NPM) principles within social service provision. Gal and Weiss-Gal note that where such limitations on direct policy practices exist, social workers may have to resort to more 'circuitous routes' such as policy practice *by proxy* (that is, through professional social work bodies or associations) or via 'recruitment networks' (direct participation in activities initiated by social work organisations). In relation to social workers employed in non-government agencies, Gal and Weiss-Gal discuss a range of factors that may impact on the extent to which social workers engage in policy practices such as the goals of the organisation, size, funding sources and type of leadership. They note that social workers may undertake advocacy roles as members or employees of these organisations. They also discuss the 'civil society route' where social workers are engaged in advocacy activities within or in conjunction with advocacy organisations, social movements and social welfare providers (p. 4).

Motivation

The third dimension relates to the motivation of the individual social worker. Gal and Weiss-Gal highlight a number of external motivations including 'whether engagement in policy practice is a legitimate and desirable component in social work practices or is regarded as deviant, unprofessional and the domain of members of other professions' (Gal and Weiss-Gal, 2013, pp. 12–13). An interesting finding was that there was greater engagement by individual social workers in policy practice when their professional organisations (such as the Australian Association of Social Workers) were more involved or where policy practices were more *embedded* within the professional discourse (USA, Israel and Spain). Critical perspectives and structural analyses of individual problems in social work education were also noted as factors related to professional socialisation that contributed to individual external motivation for engaging in policy practice. Their study found that in countries such as USA, Israel, Spain and Australia where social workers were more involved in policy practice, applied social policy was more integrated into the social work curriculum. Finally, it was noted that internal motivation such as interest, but also individual traits and values, played a role in social workers' engagement in policy practice.

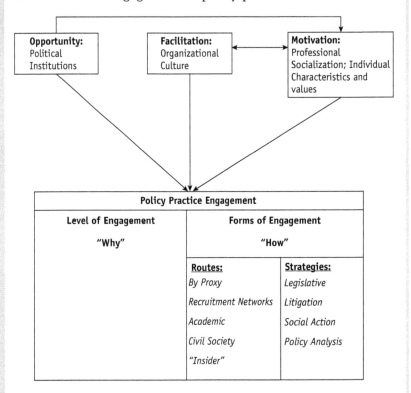

Figure 6.1 Policy practice engagement (PPE) conceptual framework
Source: Gal and Weiss-Gal (2013)

Questions

1. How important do you consider policy practice to your professional activities as a social worker? What do you think has influenced this position?

2. Consider your own organisation or workplace. Identify any organisational factors or characteristics that would facilitate your engagement in policy practice. What are the barriers to engaging in policy practice within your work context?
3. Consider the political institutions in your own country and the level of access you have to these institutions as a social worker. Based on your analysis, what kinds of approaches or 'routes' do you think would be most conducive to policy practice?

We now turn to explore broader conceptualisations of social work activism in the international context. We draw on some of the research that explores the link between social work and social activism specifically.

Conceptualising activism in research and practice: International perspectives

The international literature discusses a broad range of activist activities undertaken by social workers (Andrews and Reisch, 2002; Fraser and Briskman, 2005; Forde and Lynch, 2014; Mendes, 2005, 2007; Mynott, 2005). In an Australian study, in-depth interviews were conducted with ten Victorian social workers who were involved in social and political activism (Mendes, 2007), indicating that a number of factors may be important in promoting social workers' engagement in these activities. Notably, all of the study participants worked in senior or management positions within non-government or semi-independent agencies in urban settings. The findings suggested that personal background, experiences and beliefs were influential factors in driving their social justice activism. It emerged that all the employing organisations were supportive of the activist activities. These findings fit with the 'motivation' and 'facilitation' dimensions of the PPE Framework described earlier. Other factors that were noted included engagement with wider social and political movements that extended beyond professional social work affiliations. Based on the findings, Mendes emphasises the role of social work education and professional social work associations to promote the connection between social work and social action.

Similarly, other authors, such as Mimi Abramovitz (1998) in the USA, have argued for greater visibility of social work's activist tradition through teaching the history of social activism and social reform to social work students to 'ensure that their profession remains a site for political struggle' (p. 524). This is particularly pertinent in the current policy and practice context outlined in Chapter 2. Drawing on the work of Jacques Rancieres, a French philosopher, Paul Michael Garrett (2013) argues that social work tends to be situated within 'police orders' rather than 'a vehicle for transformational politics' in the current neoliberal policy context (p. 14). 'Police' refers to the network of relationships and practices that sustain the existing social order and dominant perceptions of the world. This is broadly conceived to include government agencies such as health and social services as well as management systems such as the economy and social policy formulations. Societal structures (such as law and politics) are 'a function of the police order and serve to legitimate existing distributions of power and identity and to guarantee the existing hierarchical disposition of specific groups' (James 2012, p. 124, cited in Garrett, 2013). In opposition to this police order is 'politics' which rejects this social hierarchy, strives for 'active' equality (both as a beginning point and as an ongoing process) and enables previously inaudible 'voices' to be heard (Garrett, 2013). While acknowledging 'political' activities outside of social work such as social movements and various service user movements and the 'subversive' acts of individual activists within and linked to social work, Garrett (2013) uses these ideas to stimulate more radical thinking and activism within the profession, and in social work education.

In the USA context, Andrews and Reisch's (2002) large national study of self-identified 'radical' social workers concluded that some practitioners were attempting 'to translate their radical vision into practice on a daily basis' (p. 27). However, many participants acknowledged that radical ideas had little influence on practice, theory or social policies and they were pessimistic about the future of radicalism in social work. Of particular interest to us is the finding that for many study participants, radical social work was viewed as synonymous with 'grassroots community-based practice aimed at the transformation of society and its members' (p. 15). Some participants linked community practice with activities addressing 'the harmful actions of corporations and governments' (ibid., p. 15). While practices were connected to a range of issues such as homelessness, civil rights and hunger, many of these activities were undertaken outside of traditional social work organisations or were not specifically identified as social work practice.

In South Africa, Vishanthie Sewpaul (2006) observes that while some social workers have been active in challenging economic, health and welfare policies, this has been on an individual basis or as a member of a progressive civil society organisation. She concludes that 'social work as a whole has not moved towards social activism, lobbying and advocacy' (p. 431). The role of social work 'in bridging the gap between the global and the local' is emphasised. Sewpaul is referring to the necessity for social workers to engage with 'global structural forces' connected to the problems of poverty, exclusion and oppression that impact on communities with whom they work (p. 430). This is exemplified by the approach taken in South Africa by the Treatment Action Campaign (TAC). This campaign 'mobilised local communities and networked globally to bring pressure on multi-national drug companies and the South African government to make treatment accessible to HIV+ men, women and children' (Sewpaul, 2006, p. 431). Currently TAC leads campaigns addressing a range of community health issues in South Africa (Treatment Action Campaign, 2014). Sewpaul envisages a social work that contributes to an alternative world order underpinned by redistributive justice drawing on the example of the Campaign against Neo-liberalism, where South African activists developed THEMBA ('There Must Be an Alternative') meaning 'hope' in the isiZulu language (Bond, 2005 cited in Sewpaul, 2006).

Activism, citizenship and community development

Contemporary analyses of activism draw on expansive ideas of citizenship including the concept of the *justice oriented citizen* (Westheimer and Kahne, 2004). Seeking to address social problems in society, the *justice oriented citizen* 'critically assesses social, political and economic structures to see beyond surface causes; seeks out and addresses areas of injustice; and knows about democratic social movements and how to effect systemic change' (p. 240). This notion of citizenship resonates with our own conceptualisation and forms of activism that we will now explore in the context of community development practices.

In their essay, *What Counts as Activism?*, Martin, Hanson and Fontaine (2007) expand on the notion of activism to encompass a range of activities and actions that are small-scale in geographic terms, but create profound social change, particularly in women's lives and within their communities. These ideas fit with the notion of the *justice oriented citizen* who, in seeking to find solutions to social problems and improve society, challenges established systems and structures that 'reproduce patterns of injustice over time' (Westheimer and Kahne, 2004, p. 240). Drawing on a study on gender and entrepreneurship, these feminist geographers explore these social change processes from 'everyday actions by individuals that foster new social networks or power dynamics' to 'political action that transforms a community, develops a formal organisation, or extends in scale to reach social networks beyond the initial embeddedness of the instigating activist' (Martin, Hanson and Fontaine, 2007, p. 79). In this way, these actions may culminate in 'new formal political networks or social movements' (ibid., p. 80). They illustrate this form of activism with the story of Connie Mbowane, the principal of a primary school in a community experiencing poverty and disadvantage in South Africa. Connie was providing schooling in a single building to over one thousand children each day 'by juggling the hours that learners and teachers from the different institutions could spend there' (ibid., p. 89). Most of the children's parents were unemployed but she mobilised the unemployed men and women in the community to set up a vegetable garden to feed the children and provide financial support for both the school and community. She encouraged men and women in the community suffering from HIV/AIDS to work in the garden and to grow and eat the organic vegetables (ibid., p. 89). Martin, Hanson and Fontaine (2007) emphasise their conception of activism as 'women's place-based activism' where social location and connections enable actions for broader social change (p. 91).

These accounts expand ideas of citizenship and highlight the potential of small-scale actions within communities to facilitate wider scale social change. However, turning to community development and conceptions of citizenship within contemporary practice contexts, Tina Lathouras (2013) found few examples of 'citizen-led structural politicking' or what she terms 'avenues for citizenship' with a 'socially transformative essence, that of democratic equality' despite the connection made by practitioners between community development and 'citizenship-making' (pp. 15–16). In her research with community development practitioners across two Australian states, she noted 'a paucity of stories told of practice driven by and involving communities that goes beyond the local level' (p. 16). She suggests that this may be due to community members as well as practitioners becoming 'depoliticized' as a consequence of current governance arrangements within the neo-liberal practice context and the 'top-down' orientation of practices and service delivery systems. She did, however, identify practice examples of what she terms 'practitioner-led structural politicking'. This work mostly involved advocacy for social policy reforms through established networks within the sector with links to local communities and practitioner-led social action to build infrastructure to support work at the local level. Shaw (2011) highlights a significant future challenge for community development as 'how people can learn to be engaged – and, where necessary *to dissent* – as actors in democratic politics in a context in which they are positioned as passive consumers, problematic objects of policy or resources for the diminishing welfare state' (p. 128). Nevertheless, Griffiths, Connor, Robertson and Phelan's (2013) analysis of a community action campaign to prevent the closure of a public swimming pool in a regional Australian city of Newcastle demonstrates how the dominant discourse of neo-liberalism (with the emphasis on cost savings and 'cost recovery') was countered by the development of an alternative discourse that was located in the needs and assets of the local community. A range of activist strategies (such as campaigning) were adopted underpinned by a social justice discourse that positioned the pool 'as a public good/public asset that was directly contributing to wider social justice goals in the city' (p. 287). Like the Govanhill Pool example in Chapter 1, the Newcastle campaign exemplifies the conflict community development or community action approach.

We draw on some further examples where processes of civic participation lead to concerted actions for social change. Joyce Mandell's case study (2010) of Lawrence Community Works (LCW) in Lawrence, Massachusetts, provides an example of civic engagement processes leading to public action. Using a community-building approach to community organising, her analysis connects conceptions of social capital and social change by showing how neighbourhood networking events such as 'picnics' can build civic participation and empowerment when linked with leadership education and training and opportunities for civic engagement and public action. As one LCW organiser expressed (ibid., p. 274):

> Our Marxist credentials here are quite intact but when I first started organising, I couldn't talk to people about being oppressed or exploitation or power. People just wanted to talk about their kids or the alleyways. You just go where the people are. It's not about the campaign or the 'win'. It's about really being interested in who people are! Or why do it!

This was the beginning point for a range of activist activities undertaken by the network members such as conducting resident surveys, testifying at the Massachusetts State House to support affordable housing legislation and lobbying the US Congress.

Another example is the account of a neighbourhood planning process to establish a local community garden in an Australian suburb, which became a community-building process and then evolved into community mobilisation and social action when the local council opposed the community garden (MacLeod and Byrne, 2012). Community development practice was conceptualised as 'a spectrum, with gentle, non-conflictual, inclusive developmental processes on one end of the spectrum (community building) and mobilising residents to confront abuses of corporate and state power in the localities in which they live at the other end (community organising)' (p. 36). As we discussed in Chapter 5, community organising is 'a process of assisting communities join together to identify and solve problems' and is often distinguished as either 'conflict or consensus orientated' (Ohmer and Brooks, 2013, p. 1). Ohmer and Brooks argue that each of these orientations is distinct however they can be combined to 'address community issues and concerns strategically' (p. 2) as illustrated in MacLeod and Byrne's account.

'Shifting forms of citizenship': The struggle for rights and recognition

Cornwall, Robins and Von Lieres (2011) argue that 'shifting forms of everyday citizenship' present challenges for activism in the future (p. 20). Linking notions of citizenship, human rights and activism, they contend that contemporary citizenship is sometimes defined in terms of 'what is lacking' such as an absence of rights, entitlement, care or dignity.

However, they argue that it is 'much more diffuse' and linked to the subjective experience of belonging, recognition, inclusion and respect (p. 20). They suggest that broad and universal perspectives on human rights 'offer too limited a frame through which to understand the particularities of people's struggles for rights and recognition' (Nyamu-Musembi, 2005 cited in Cornwall, Robins and Von Lieres, 2011, p. 20). Drawing on case studies from the Citizenship Development Research Centre at the University of Sussex in England, these authors highlight the diversity of conceptions of citizenship and demonstrate the dynamic, variable and creative ways in which people articulate, define and enact rights. These ideas of citizenship connect with our conceptualisations of creative, diverse and emerging forms of activism in contemporary contexts.

Context shapes how citizenship is practised although influences such as Indigenous values relating to culture and protest and conceptions of citizenship inherent in political and developmental processes may not always be visible (Cornwall, Robins and Von Lieres, 2011). To illustrate this, these authors draw on examples of activism from the Global South such as in 'post-revolutionary' South Africa where non-violent street protest is part of public culture at national level whereas in several post-colonial countries public protest is viewed as a threat to the legitimacy of the state and to law and order. In Chiapas in Mexico, Indigenous people painted a mural to express their own perception of rights, self-determination and cultural values thus articulating a 'politics of difference'. This was a local strategy for indigenising aspirations and democratic values in opposition to 'governmental impositions' (Cortez, 2005 cited in Cornwall, Robins and Von Lieres, 2011, p. 15).

Social movements that are orientated towards cultural and political identity can play a significant role in changing institutional practices as well as having broader impacts on social policy (Martin, 2001; see Cuthbert and Quartly, 2012). Drawing on the example of women's self-help movements, and specific analysis of the post-partum depression movement in the USA (see Taylor and Van Willigen, 1996), Greg Martin (2001) argues that new social movements (NSMs) that are mainly 'cultural, symbolic and geared towards a politics of identity' can be influential in changing social policy (p. 379). This women's movement addressed gender relations, collective identity, practices in institutions and also impacted on social policy. The South African land and AIDS treatment movements have highlighted another significant role for NSMs in providing the groundwork for 'new, middle-level institutions' that can represent the needs of marginalised people to the state (Cornwall, Robins and Von Lieres, 2011, p. 24).

Definitions of social movements emphasise that they are *not* organisations but organised arrangements between a range of different actors (which may include formal organisations) engaged in political actions to promote or resist change in society (Marx and McAdam, 1994; Della Porta and Diani, 2006; see Thompson, 2002 for a discussion of the development of NSMs and the relationship to social work). NSMs have a broader focus than the more 'traditional' economic concerns of social movements and address a range of political and social issues (Thompson, 2002).

Ife argues that social work has a significant role to play in social movements in relation to 'developing an oppositional politics and to legitimise the voices of the marginalised' (1997, p. 186). By 'oppositional politics' he means exploring alternatives to the existing social order to achieve social justice goals as exemplified in the new social movements which provide the means for the voices of excluded groups to be heard. He argues that social workers can bring a range of skills to social movements, such as skills in public advocacy and community development. However, as Thompson (2002) notes 'the interrelationships between various social movements and social work have been complex and varied' (p. 716).

Engaging with social movements poses a number of challenges for social workers. Collins (2009) questions whether these activities should be undertaken 'outside social work', that is, can social workers engage 'as social workers' in social movements such as anti-capitalist and anti-war movements? (p. 248). In addition to limitations of time and energy, there are recurring questions about 'what lies within the sphere, the scope of social work and what lies outside of it' (p. 348). In exploring the relationship between social movements, social justice and social work, Thompson (2002) pinpoints the 'fundamental tensions between social work as a force for social regulation and as a force for social development and emancipation' (p. 711). There are ongoing debates about 'what social work is or ought to be' in England where competing conceptions of social work are articulated as 'aspirational' (taught at university and more aligned with creative and critical practices) and 'statutory social work' (a more narrow and restrictive approach experienced by social work students on field placement) (Higgins, Popple and Crichton, 2014, p. 14).

As Collins points out, the power of the professional role (that is, the discourses of professional social workers) can distance 'the professionals' from people's movements (2009, p. 346). However, he argues that at the very least, social workers can learn much from these movements. They remind us to be 'continually aware of the broad structural location of social work, and its role in both acting to maintain the existing capitalist order, while at the same time fighting against its worst features' (p. 348).

Voss and Williams (2012) note the rise of locally based social movements in contrast to mass mobilisation and national protest as a response to changing relations between the state, economy and civil society. These movements such as the landless workers movement in Brazil (these workers were fighting for the right to use/own unproductive land) are characterised by local level organising, citizen participation as decision makers in matters that affect them and the ability 'to tap into global networks' (ibid., p. 360). These authors argue that these movements are creating new spaces 'to contest market domination and state indifference' (p. 360). This opens up new opportunities for social workers to engage with these emerging social movements at the local community level to build capacity and support democratic processes to challenge injustice and achieve social change.

New and emerging forms of social work activism

We now turn to new and emerging fronts of social work activism in the contemporary policy and practice environment. Maria Pentaraki (2013) writes about continuing neo-liberal re-structuring, mounting inequalities and social spending cuts in Greece in the face of the public debt crisis. She highlights the activist role of social workers in working with communities and taking actions to 'delegitimise the necessity of social spending cuts as well as the hegemony of neo-liberalism' (p. 706). Placing the Greek situation in a wider context, that is, within neo-liberal 'global restructuring' and the democratic 'transformation of society' (p. 701), she urges actions on two 'fronts'. The starting point is for members of the Professional Association of Social Workers (PASW) in Greece to critically reflect on the underlying agendas of neo-liberalism and engage other social workers, service users and members of the community in critical intellectual activity. She argues that this will build capacity for engagement in collective action for countering hegemonic ideas and strengthening egalitarian and democratic processes. A second front is at a practical level although underpinned by theory ('social work praxis'). Here, she envisages a range of community work approaches, methods and activities such as group work, social networking, collaborative partnerships between service providers (statutory, voluntary, service-user led organisations, groups and community members), interventions at multiple levels, collective action and structural analysis of social problems.

She makes the point that social workers need to move beyond traditional approaches to address the impacts of austerity and adopt more militant tactics such as becoming active in anti-austerity campaigns and other social movements at local, national and international levels (Pentaraki, 2013). What is useful in the account is the multi-layered and expansive vision for activist practices within and across different 'fronts' encompassing critical intellectual activity, wide-scale networking and capacity building and 'bottom up' community development practices underpinned by democratic and egalitarian principles.

As highlighted by Lundy and Van Wormer (2007), a social change and human rights framework is critical for social work as a global profession concerned with economic, social and civil rights. This is particularly relevant in contemporary contexts of economic globalisation, cuts to social welfare and increasing economic and social inequities. Other contemporary human rights concerns are growing militarisation and armed conflict (Lundy and Van Wormer, 2007).

Brooks (2013) argues for social workers to engage in political activism in preventing and responding to all forms of torture, inhuman and degrading treatment, particularly in relation to the 'War on Terror' in the aftermath of the September 11 terrorist attacks in the USA. She urges social workers to participate in political advocacy at the global level and contest perspectives that 'help to maintain and legitimise torture' (p. 9). This form of political activism focuses on challenging violent and oppressive structures.

Social Work Responses to Militarism and Violence

case study 6.1

Change strategies that can be used by social workers to challenge militarism and violence are elucidated by Brooks (2013). She draws on Tim Gee's Idea Counterpoint theory (2011, cited in Brooks, 2013) which posits that (counter) power is exercised through challenging dominant narratives, setting up resistance and seeking alternative channels for communication. In this way, the need to infringe human rights to prevent attacks of terror, or notions of acceptability in relation to inflicting torture on certain groups, is challenged and articulated to develop alternative ways of thinking and countering the abuses of power. She argues that this can occur through networking and multi-disciplinary collaborations. Another means of communicating these ideas is through the use of social media such as Twitter and Facebook which Brooks describes as 'powerful tools for activists' (p. 10). She argues that these strategies contribute to 'challenging the narrative around terrorism and torture' which helps to counter the perpetuation of political violence, establishes space for healing for survivors of torture and trauma and engenders 'a rights respecting community' (ibid., p. 10).

Brooks refers to the use of social media as a tool for activists to communicate ideas. Drawing on the example of an online professional community, the SWForum in Hong Kong, Leung, Lam, Yau and Chu (2010) discuss how information and communication technologies (ICTs) can be used for social work activism by creating a space for alternative discourses on social policy via fostering a collective identity among participants through online sharing. We discuss this example in Chapter 7. At the organisational level, Breuer, Landman and Farquhar (2014) make the point that the internet has broadened the 'repertoire' of collective action for social movements and grassroots organisations (p. 2). Digital networks provide opportunities for 'decentralised campaigning based on parallel activities of independent individuals' (p. 2). These authors highlight the significant 'multiplier effects' as users of social media platforms such as Twitter, YouTube and Facebook, 'share information across their networks, expanding the reach and impact of information' (p. 2). The use of social networking in the context of social work activism is an area for further research.

Ramon and Maglajlic (2012) make the point that human rights issues such as the impact of political conflict and displacement of peoples have been largely absent from social work in international forums, research and education. They highlight a new and emerging front for social work activism when they argue for a deeper structural analysis linked to human rights at a global and local level as problems in this context 'require an identified and internalised political role for our profession' (p. 10).

Socially just and rights-based social development policies are another domain for social work activism at the local, regional and global levels. Social workers may work with a range of government and non-government agencies including the United Nations. Desai and Solas (2012) discuss social work's commitment to actions to alleviate poverty and social exclusion in the world within a social development paradigm based on 'people-centred ideologies' (p. 4). Social workers can engage in social justice activism in a number of ways, including 'recognising, exposing and challenging hidden agendas', forging global and regional links and partnerships and engaging in advocacy for socially just, sustainable and right-based social development policies (Desai and Solas, 2012, p. 11).

In exploring the 'green shoots of a new, engaged social work practice' driven by social justice concerns, Ferguson and Lavalette (2005, p. 207) consider the implications of the anti-capitalist movement or global justice movement for social work. They argue that the social work value base of social justice, human rights, empowerment and liberation is congruent with these movements and can underpin the emergence of more radical practices and potential interconnections as practitioners become increasingly disillusioned with marketisation and managerialism within social work. These authors emphasise the intellectual work that is required to critically analyse the effects of neo-liberalism on social work. They envisage a number of approaches such as the strengthening of social work representation, the proliferation of national and international practitioner networks, and re-engagement with service user movements (such as disability and mental health users' movements) to enable a return to more radical practice approaches. Ultimately, they argue that it entails re-engaging with collective approaches and the value of community development.

According to Ife, human rights 'remain a legitimate stance from which to critique power' (2013, p. 78). Ife and Fiske (2006) emphasise the importance of social workers as 'human rights workers' in the context of community development practice (for a detailed discussion, see Ife, 2010, 2013). They are referring to a 'bottom up' approach whereby the meanings of rights are defined through community processes and collective action is undertaken with communities and others to realise these rights. However, actions are underpinned by, and reflect values enshrined in, human rights legislation and United Nations (UN) conventions. In Chapter 4, we showed how rights discourses inform collective actions in a community development context (see Practice Example 4.4). In Chapter 1, we argued that local action has become more important in the face of globalisation. However, it is also necessary for social workers to engage in actions at the international level to find solutions to very complex human problems (Hokenstad, 2012). Social workers may practice in international contexts with organisations such as the UN and international non-government organisations in response to global issues such as civil conflict, human trafficking, migration and disasters (Hokenstad, 2012).

In the context of human rights campaigns, social workers have been actively involved with non-government agencies (NGOs) and civil society political and advocacy organisations (Harrison and Melville, 2010). Bernadette McMenamin is an Australian social worker who has documented the experience of ECPAT (End Child Prostitution in Asian Tourism) which is a global children's rights movement to combat the commercial sexual exploitation of children.

ECPAT/Childwise

case study 6.2

McMenamin (2003) describes the establishment of ECPAT/Childwise which is a rights-based global network established to address the issue of the sexual exploitation of children. Underpinned by the principles of the Convention on the Rights of the Child, it was initiated by a number of Asian based NGOs who launched an international campaign to End Child Prostitution in Asian Tourism (ECPAT) through raising international awareness of the problem, building an active grassroots global network and working with governments and communities to implement laws and policies to stop child sex exploitation. ECPAT has supported the formation of national grassroots campaigns across the world including Australia, Europe, New Zealand, USA, Latin America and Africa. Such groups have successfully lobbied their governments to introduce extra-territorial child sex tourism laws which permit the prosecution of their nationals for child sex crimes (outside their countries) and successful prosecutions have ensued, particularly in Australia. Several Asian countries have introduced or strengthened local child protection laws as a consequence of ECPAT campaigns. Other initiatives have been undertaken in these countries to combat the international child sex trade including special policing units, hotlines, bilateral training and joint police investigations. Collaborations with the international travel and tourism industry (including government authorities and industry bodies) have yielded a range of solutions to address child sexual exploitation in tourism (see for example, Child Wise Australia on www.childwise.net).

Source: McMenamin, B. (2003) 'Global Actions to Prevent Child Exploitation: The ECPAT Experience' in W. Weeks, L. Hoatson and J. Dixon (eds) *Community Practices in Australia,* Frenchs Forest: Pearson Education Australia.

Other authors document the establishment of social action and campaigning networks within different countries at local and national levels (Butcher, Banks, Henderson and Robertson, 2007; Lavalette, 2011). An example is the Asylum Seekers' Network (ASN) that was formed across a large British city to bring together asylum seekers, refugees (asylum seekers who had been granted asylum) and activists to forge solidarity, defend asylum seekers' rights and oppose deportation (Butcher, Banks, Henderson and Robertson, 2007). Another contemporary example is the UK-based campaigning network called the Social Work Action Network (SWAN) which has affiliated networks in Ireland, Canada and Hong Kong.

case study 6.3

The social work action network (SWAN)

SWAN emerged from a series of actions in response to 'the growing crisis in social work' beginning with a *social work manifesto* (Jones et al., 2004) followed by meetings across the UK in 2004/2005 (Lavalette, 2011, p. 9). The network of social work practitioners, academics, students and service users was officially established in 2006 at the end of a social work conference: 'Social work: A profession worth fighting for?'

SWAN aims

> to challenge the impact of cuts and neoliberalism on social work, social care and the welfare state. It is committed to anti-racist and anti-oppressive practice, to service user engagement and involvement, to strong links with relevant trade unions, and to participation in all those movements which hold within them a glimpse of a better future and a more humane world. (Lavalette, 2011, p. 10)

To this end, it organises annual conferences to debate issues affecting social work, social care and the welfare state and the network has expanded across the UK (groups have formed in Birmingham, Brighton, Bristol and the South West, Coventry, Edinburgh, Glasgow, Lancashire, Liverpool, London, Manchester, the North East, the West Midlands, Yorkshire and Wales). As an 'action network' SWAN has organised a number of campaigns in defence of asylum seekers, expressing solidarity with social workers involved in the case of Baby P in the face of very negative media coverage, and developing a Mental Health Charter in response to the crisis in mental health services in the UK. It is associated with several activist organisations and campaigns in the UK such as the national Right to Work Campaign.

Sources: Lavalette, M. (2011) *Radical Social Work Today: Social Work at the Crossroads*, Bristol: The Policy Press.
SWAN – Social Work Action Network (2014), available online at www.socialworkfuture.org [Accessed 24 September 2014].

In conclusion: New fronts for creative activism?

We have argued that social workers can engage in creative and innovative forms of activism within changing landscapes of policy and practice in contemporary environments. In this chapter, we have conceptualised a form of activism that is distinguished by a creativity that is both responsive and adaptable to diverse and shifting situations. We emphasise the flexibility of contemporary activism and the need for approaches that are attuned to diffuse meanings of citizenship which encompass people's struggles for rights, social inclusion and cultural recognition within different contexts. Herein is the challenge for activism in the future. What emerges is a type of activism that opens up spaces for improvisation. It is contextualised, post-structural, flexible, sometimes nuanced and 'creative'. It involves the use of a mix of 'insider' and 'outsider' approaches in seeking to pursue social change at the level of the organisation and beyond. In our research, we identified a form of activism that was sporadic rather than sustained. As we discuss in the chapter, episodic activism enables practitioners to seize opportunities when they arise, but does not require constant commitment. Constant tensions between personal and professional demands can impact on practitioners' capacity to engage in activism in a sustained way. This brings both challenges and possibilities as we venture towards new and emerging fronts of social work activism linked to wider global issues, social justice and human rights.

- Social workers are social justice activists who engage in different forms of activism in a range of contexts.

- Contemporary forms of activism are adaptive and responsive to diverse and shifting situations, particularly in the challenging, structured and sometimes restricted environments in which many workers function.

- We conceptualise a form of activism that is post-modern, flexible, nuanced and distinguished by 'creativity'.

- New and emerging fronts of social work activism are linked to contemporary global issues, social justice and human rights.

- What does 'activism' mean for you? Have you observed or engaged in activism in your personal life, work experience, voluntary work or on placement?
- If so, what forms of activism have you observed or engaged in? What values underpinned these activities?
- The use of social media such as Twitter and Facebook are described as 'powerful tools for activists' in contemporary contexts. Discuss.
- What are some of the gains and challenges of engaging in activism as a practitioner? Consider these within different organisations or workplaces such as statutory social work (child protection or probation) or working within a non-government agency in the community.

taking it further

- Brooks, A. (2013) 'Torture and Terror Post-9/11: The Role of Social Work in Responding to Torture', *International Social Work*, doi: 10.1177/0020872813487932.
- Forde, C. and Lynch, D. (2014) *'Critical Practice for Challenging Times: Social Workers' Engagement with Community Work'*, *British Journal of Social Work*, 44(8), pp. 2078–2094.
- Gal, J. and Weiss-Gal, I. (2013) 'The "Why" and "How" of Policy Practice: An Eight Country Comparison', *British Journal of Social Work Advance Access*, doi: 10.1093/bjsw/bct179.
- Ife, J. (2010) *Human Rights from Below: Achieving Rights through Community Development*, Cambridge: Cambridge University Press.
- Mandell, J. (2010) 'Picnics, Participation and Power: Linking Community Building to Social Change', *Community Development*, 41(2), pp. 269–282.
- Marston, G. and McDonald, C. (2012) 'Getting Beyond "Heroic Agency" in Conceptualising Social Workers as Policy Actors in the Twenty-first Century', *British Journal of Social Work Advance Access*, doi: 10.1093/bjsw/bcs062.
- Martin, D., Hanson, S. and Fontaine, D. (2007) 'What Counts as Activism? The Role of Individuals in Creating Change', *Women's Studies Quarterly*, 35(3/4), pp. 78–94.

Online Resources

- Child Wise Australia (2014), available online at www.childwise.net_ [Accessed 24 September 2014].
- SWAN – Social Work Action Network (2014), available online at www.socialworkfuture.org [Accessed 24 September 2014].
- Treatment Action Campaign (2014), available online at www.tac.org.za [Accessed 24 September 2014].

7 Scaffolding critical practice in the community development context

Introduction

Chapter 6 illuminated the practices of practitioners working within challenging circumstances to achieve social change. Different forms of activism emerged which ranged from episodic to more sustained activities. In this chapter we pose the question, 'How can we support each other as practitioners and stay centred, creative, critical and effective in our work with communities?' Here, we include broader organisational practices, processes and approaches that have the potential to scaffold practices in a critical community development context. We draw on our own ideas as well as a number of interesting and innovative collective approaches to reflection and action involving groups and communities that have been articulated in the social work and community development literature.

In Chapter 4, we outlined the critical practice perspective that we adopt in this book. We were drawn to the framework of critical realism as it enables a deeper exploration of the 'causes' of injustice. Aligned with this perspective is the process of conscientisation or critical consciousness-raising that we discussed in Chapter 5 as intrinsic to community development, and the means through which people are empowered to enact change. In this chapter, we return to these ideas and draw on the concept of critical consciousness-raising as pivotal to our exploration of scaffolding practices and processes. Here, we reiterate that community development is a cyclical and iterative process that involves reflection, action and participation.

Integrating 'scaffolding' into everyday practices can pose challenges. We focus on models of critical community practice that encompass 'scaffolding' such as critical consciousness-raising and reflective processes (Butcher, Banks, Henderson and Robertson, 2007; Stepney and Popple, 2008). The importance of critical thinking (Fook and Gardner, 2007; Morley and MacFarlane, 2010), evaluation, 'reflection in action' and space for reflection on practice (Houston, Skehill, Pinkerton and Campbell, 2005) is emphasised. We explore the value of practice frameworks for social workers and other human service workers (Westoby and Ingamells, 2011; see also Weyers, 2011), and discuss how the elements of 'communities of practice' (Wenger, McDermott and Snyder, 2002) might support and facilitate critical consciousness-raising at a collective level. Practitioner research has a vital role in the generation of knowledge and can provide 'a vehicle for the frontline practitioner to have a voice in their own right' (Hardwick and Worsley, 2011, p. 135). We explore the possibilities of transformational research (Mertens, 2009) and participatory action research (Shdaimah, Stahl and Schram, 2011) for social workers and outline some of the research projects undertaken by practitioners. We are particularly interested in research as a tool for advocacy and social change.

'Critical consciousness': Facilitating and scaffolding critical community practices

As we have shown in Chapter 5, reflection and evaluation are intrinsic elements of the community development process undertaken with groups and communities. We have previously argued that, through critical reflection, individuals and groups undergo conscientisation or develop a critical consciousness whereby they develop a realisation of the root causes of problems such as poverty, disadvantage and oppression. Paolo Freire (1997) referred to this realization as 'conscientisation', or the development of a critical consciousness that questions what may previously have been accepted or taken for granted. We highlighted Brookfield's argument (2009) that critical reflection in social work can act to externalise power relations through public acknowledgement of the social worker's power, and challenge hegemonic ideas and practices by critical reflection on the social worker's own ideas, assumptions and ways of working.

Critical consciousness based on Paulo Friere's model of problem-posing is central to Butcher et al.'s model of critical community practice (2007). We include their model here as it integrates critical theoretical analyses (underpinned by a structural analysis of oppression and injustice) with reflective professional practice. This approach encompasses critical thinking, use of theory and reflection on practice. We argue that it is potentially a valuable framework for developing and scaffolding critical community development.

The model is wide-ranging as it addresses the domains of practice, management and policy. While it does not specifically address social workers in the community, it offers a framework for critical action (that is, both 'bottom-up' and 'top-down' actions taken by a number of actors such as politicians, policy makers, organisational managers and 'community' professionals, grassroots community organisations and groups) based on critical theorising, reflection and a commitment to social justice through empowering and transformative practice (Butcher et al., 2007,

p. 1). Of particular interest to us is the central role of critical consciousness and processes such as supervision, practitioner dialogue and reflective
writing highlighted by these authors. These can scaffold practices, particularly when practitioners are engaged in social activism.

Within the model and at the practitioner level, Sarah Banks (2007)
identifies *values clarification* as important for supporting and developing
the process of critical consciousness, including self-awareness and reflexivity in critical community practice. Value commitments or more
specifically 'critical consciousness' is defined as practitioners 'being aware
of themselves, their own values, the values of the agency for which they
work, the political context of the work and the influence that these have
on the work that they do' (ibid., p. 140). Banks points out a wide range of
activities such as training, supervision, mentoring, peer debate and
support, reflective writing, reading and practitioner research that are the
usual processes of professional development. However, she expands on
these ideas to consider what they might look like in the context of a
critical community practice framework. Her question becomes, 'What
would supervision look like in the context of professional development
for critical community practice?' For example, a specific question could be,
'What might it be like to have *emancipatory practice* as an agenda item?'
(Phillipson, 2002, p. 250, cited in Banks, 2007). Banks proposes episodic
critical reflection and reflexivity undertaken with supportive colleagues
(or 'a critical friend' which could be a colleague or peer) which can assist
with sustaining a 'critical edge to the work' or team or group supervision
that could elicit a wider range of perspectives on a specific practice issue
(p. 148). These ideas about practitioner dialogue and debate resonate with
our later examples of 'communities of practice' that can facilitate engagement in a shared learning process.

Similarly, practising critical reflection in community work is explicitly
addressed by Jan Fook and Fiona Gardner (2007) as a process of uncover-
ing the assumptions and values of the practitioner as well as those of the
employing organisation or funding body. This enables value conflicts or
difference in expectations to be identified, which is particularly relevant
in the contemporary neo-liberal practice environment explored in
Chapter 2. The authors specify a number of reflective processes such as:
using critical reflection as a framework for practice, the use of critical
incidents with communities for practitioners themselves to elicit
'possible directions for change' (p. 179), and the use of journals or art to
explore issues at the individual level or collectively with communities.
They suggest that these writings could be collated and published to
provide 'a variety of perspectives on a community's history and diversity'
(p. 181). A set of critically reflective questions is proposed that could be a
regular aspect of meetings or used for project development. We include
them here.

Suggested Questions:

1. *What is happening here?*
2. *What are the different perspectives about this incident/issue?*
3. *What voices are not being heard?*
4. *Where are people coming from? What are the assumptions and values being expressed?*
5. *How do the community's perceptions reflect those of the broader social structure? How are dominant discourses being expressed?*
6. *What are the variety of views about how to move forward?*

Source: Fook and Gardner (2007, p. 181)

Drawing on the format of a critical incident, Stepney and Popple (2008) outline a process that begins with describing a critical incident or community-based problem from practice. Secondly, the 'incident' is located within its broader theoretical, policy and community context, and thirdly the dominant discourses of key stakeholders (such as service users, community members and managers) are identified. The final stage is 'to reflect and re-theorise, to unpack the stories and causal mechanisms that uphold dominant discourses' (ibid., p. 172). This also involves identifying 'the flow of power' and considering how this could be changed to empower 'subordinate groups to achieve greater social justice', ultimately resulting in purposeful actions. These include emancipatory strategies, community-based initiatives for change and research evaluation (ibid., p. 172). This provides a useful structure to interrogate and scaffold critical practice. We now turn to discuss other ideas, concepts and 'structures' that might enable processes of critical reflection within everyday critical community development practices.

'Critical consciousness': Practice frameworks and communities of practice

In reality, and as discussed in Chapters 4 and 5, social work and community development are diverse, contextualised and negotiated fields, and workers are likely to draw on a range of reference points to scaffold their practice. Practice frameworks can provide a structure to organise thinking and frame actions as well as providing a language to articulate the work and sustain critical awareness (or 'consciousness') in relation to practices, contexts and dilemmas (Kelly, unpublished, cited in Westoby and Ingamells, 2011, p. 3). In the social work context, Healy (2005) notes that frameworks for practice are an 'amalgam of formal knowledge and skills and informal "on-the-job" knowledge and skills developed by social workers in practice' (p. 6). Thus, the formal professional knowledge base is supplemented by 'practice wisdom' and 'acquired knowledge' (p. 5). Westoby and Ingamells (2011) highlight the 'personal dimension' of practice frameworks where knowledge and practices are brought into alignment with the practitioner's worldview, their range of experiences and 'their awareness of reoccurring practice dilemmas and their understanding of the contexts of practice' (p. 2).

The findings of a small Australian study conducted by Westoby and Ingamells (2011) are interesting as they throw light on the value of engaging in a collective process to create 'personal practice frameworks'. Interviews were conducted with nineteen practitioners who had completed a university community development course at some stage over the past twenty years about the value and uses of their practice frameworks within their workplace. All of the practitioners interviewed could articulate their frameworks and many were facilitating others to develop frameworks. Some were writing and publishing from their current frameworks. Westoby and Ingamells write about opening up 'space' on the community development course where students can engage in a facilitated process to create their own practice frameworks. For the students, this process involves community development readings, dialogue with peers and facilitators, and reflection on their own practices, experiences, values and worldviews. Westoby and Ingamells (2011) argue that the process of constructing and articulating a practice framework is 'itself an active engagement in a community of practice, rather than, or as well as, an intellectual or introspective personal journey' (p. 1). As educators, they suggest a number of ways that course participants can explore and compare personal frameworks. They suggest 'narrative questioning' in small groups, comparisons of how different personal frameworks respond to particular practice dilemmas and dialogue across frameworks within communities of practice (ibid., p. 11).

In our own Irish research, social work practitioners articulated processes that resonated with the development of a practice framework for their community development practice.

Practitioner perspective: Values, theory and practices

practice example 7.1

This is an extract from an interview from our research on social workers' engagement with community development in the Irish context. As you read the practice example, note how the practitioner weaves her specific project and practice context, values, theoretical understandings, worldview, professional development and personal life experience into a framework for her practice – illustrating integration of values, theory and practices. It can be seen how a 'critical consciousness' shapes her approach.

We are an anti-poverty social inclusion project... so understanding some of the structural inequalities that exist and the belief of working with people to build capacity and that people have their own solutions. These are the ideas that I am working from, and my value base around inclusion, participation, respect. Working as a social worker, I have a very strong value base and it is something that I think is present all the time and influences our practice. Sometimes we might kind of, we don't always have it, it is not there written on your forehead or whatever but you know it is influencing what we are doing. I think the value base and work from an *anti-oppressive, anti-discriminatory perspective* has a huge influence. It has a huge influence in looking at where we think poverty comes from... it is not an individual problem or a focus on the individual, blame on the individual, it is looking at wider structural perspectives. I am coming from that, that influences me, my political kind of ideas and views which have, I suppose, been developed right throughout my career, through my childhood, through my family background and everything else, you know.

Source: Research project carried out by Forde and Lynch in 2009–2010. Fifteen social workers in a range of practice settings in Ireland were interviewed about their experiences of using community development approaches in their practice.

In a study conducted by Weyers (2011), practitioner frameworks that were critical and analytical, value based and process orientated emerged as important for effective community development practice. Building partnerships and coalitions were also identified as 'habits' or characteristics of effective practitioners. The integration of critical analysis and networking activities is beautifully captured in our own research by a social work practitioner who was working in a community work setting:

I would be hugely influenced by an approach that questions underlying assumptions. That does not take things as they are presented but would kind of critically look at and critically analyse what really is going on here... a collective action approach would appeal hugely to me and I would be very influenced by it. I hope I have been able to incorporate some of that into the work because I believe very strongly in the collective and in solidarity and, you know, building those networks in terms of none of us can do it on our own, *we all need each other.*

Weyers's findings are interesting as they offer some ideas for scaffolding practice. He analysed articles published over a ten-year period in four peer reviewed social work and community development journals to explore the question, 'What makes community development practitioners effective?' Eighty-five studies across nineteen different countries or territories were included. Drawing on grounded theory techniques, he developed a model based on the analysis of community practitioners' behaviours or 'habits' (a construct encompassing dimensions of knowledge, skills and motivation) in relation to effective community development interventions. Practitioner 'habits' were clustered around four different levels: the intra-personal and personal, organisational, inter-organisational or cross-institutional/agency and community/society. This expands our discussion to the broader organisational context and processes and approaches that can scaffold critical community development. We therefore elucidate Weyers's (2011) findings in the research box below and pose some reflective questions for students and practitioners.

Eight core 'Habits' for effective practice

Intra-personal/Personal Level

- Practitioners strive to understand their position within the broader context (professional, organisational, community, cultural and political). They are able to negotiate the tensions, contradictions and expectations within and between these different contexts. These practitioners were able to 'internalise' and enact the principles and values underpinning their work.
- Take opportunities to improve and develop both knowledge and skills. They were critically aware and could initiate action (self-empowering as well as empowering others).
- Undertake self-renewal activities – self-reflection, maintaining support networks and self-care.

Organisation level

- Foster facilitative and supportive relationships within all levels of the employing organisation. However, it was pointed out that this involved seeking support from within the organisation before seeking the support of external sources.

Inter-organisational or cross-organisational/agency

- Build and use partnerships and coalitions. Some of these 'habits' included utilising research and opportunities for shared learning underpinned by values and common purpose.

- Use management and planning as 'empowerment tools' (Weyers, 2011, p. 93). For example, using planning and management meetings as a vehicle for facilitating stakeholder participation and rights.

Community/societal level

- Engage in collective problem-posing and 'conscientisation' at the community level to effect social change.
- Facilitate ownership of the process by the community so that members become active partners in making decisions that affect their lives.

Source: Weyers, M. (2011) 'The Habits of Highly Effective Community Development Practitioners', *Development Southern Africa*, 28(1), pp. 87–98.

Reflective Questions

1. Select one of the 'habits' identified above at the *organisational or inter-organisation/agency level* that resonates for you in your current practice or placement context. How can this habit scaffold or support practices working with communities who are experiencing disadvantage?
2. Select one of the 'habits' at an *intra-personal/personal/professional level*. How can this habit scaffold or support effective practices working with communities who are experiencing disadvantage?
3. How might these 'habits' work together in a synergistic way to scaffold social change practices in your current practice context? Are they particularly tailored to a community development context or can they apply to other contexts of practice?

Weyers locates the utilisation of research and opportunities for shared learning underpinned by values and common purpose at the inter-organisational or cross-organisational level. We now turn to explore processes and mechanisms for relationship-building and shared learning both within and outside of the organisational context. 'Communities of Practice' (Wenger et al., 2002) are interesting in this regard, as this particular form of engagement and learning has been linked more recently to critical community-based education and training in the community development context (Westoby and Shevellar, 2012; Shevellar, Sherwin and Mackay, 2012).

The term 'communities of practice' emerged from the work of Jean Lave and Etienne Wenger (1998). Communities of practice may be defined as 'groups of people who *share a concern or passion* for something they do and learn how to do it better as they interact regularly' (Wenger, 2006, p. 1). Wenger (2006) identifies three essential elements of a community of practice:

- The *domain*: a shared area of interest that defines the identity of the group.
- The *community*: relationship building and interactions such as joint activities and discussions, helping each other as well as sharing information.
- The *practice*: practitioners 'developing a shared repertoire of resources such as experiences, stories, tools and ways of addressing recurring problems' (p. 2).

According to Wenger (2006, cited in Caniglia and Bourke, 2012) 'communities of practice' can evolve organically from existing networks and draw on both inside perspectives (understandings of issues that come from within the community) and outside perspectives (engaging with new ideas from other communities) (that is, 'open a dialogue' between these viewpoints). Participation can occur at a number of different levels (core members versus peripheral members) in an informal context or in more public 'spaces' (including online opportunities). Stimulating innovation and creativity as well as building established patterns for participation and communication enables these communities to develop as illustrated in the Australian case study below.

UnitingCare

case study 7.1

In their resource, a 'Toolkit for Developing Place-based Responses to Disadvantage', Caniglia and Bourke (2012) describe the development of a *Community of Practice* as a means of capacity building across large organisations such as UnitingCare in Queensland, Australia to foster collaboration and develop responses to highly complex social issues linked to geographical or place-based disadvantage. UnitingCare is a church-based, non-profit health and community service provider which operates in over 400 geographic localities across the state of Queensland. At a national level, it contributes to social policy development and advocacy. Through its research, education and advocacy unit, the Centre for Social Justice, a range of resources including this 'toolkit' was developed to support community development practitioners and their organisations working with poverty and disadvantage in particular areas (referred to as 'place-based' disadvantage).

The UnitingCare *Community of Practice* sought to support staff at all levels across the organisation to: share information and resources, exchange and reflect on experiences and case studies, facilitate opportunities for coordination and collaboration, document good practice, seek innovative solutions to 'entrenched problems', sustain effective practice, and build organisational knowledge and capacity (Caniglia and Bourke, 2012, p. 68).

Building a well-defined structure for the community of practice within the organisation and developing a culture of learning that encourages 'reflective questioning' in informal as well as formal interactions such as supervision is emphasised (p. 74). While acknowledging varying forms and levels of participation, specific roles and responsibilities in developing and enacting the community of practice are identified such as 'mentor', 'coordinator', 'core group', 'leaders', 'regular participants', 'peripheral participants' and supportive 'outsiders'. A number of informal activities and varied opportunities for engagement that are identified in the resource include: regular core group meetings to lead the community of practice as well as regular meetings to discuss agency or area based practices, external and in-house training, visits to other services or agencies, the community of practice being included as a standing agenda item at staff/team meetings, focused discussions and debates, strategic partnerships across services, informal lunches, blogs and web-based social networking. Finally, the resource details the need for a clear delineation of 'the strengths, skills and training' that will facilitate coordinated service delivery, strategic development and creative practice. The use of technology is advocated to support collaboration and learning such as online discussion groups, a document repository and a directory of skills or current projects.

Source: Caniglia, F. and Bourke, P. (2012) *Toolkit for Developing Place-based Responses to Disadvantage*, Queensland: UnitingCare Social Justice.

Here we see how communities of practice can provide structures and mechanisms for inter-professional working and collaboration between and within organisations. Clearly, there are significant challenges associated with implementing a community of practice across all levels of an organisation. Nevertheless, organisational support can facilitate the evolution of multiple 'communities of practice' that can sustain practitioners in their day-to-day work. As noted by Orme and Powell (2007), a shift from learning organisations to learning communities enables change that 'will permeate interactions between members of an organisation at all levels, rather than fulfil a solely managerialist agenda' (p. 1000). Communities of practice have the potential to offer spaces and learning conditions to scaffold critical consciousness in working to address highly complex social issues linked to significant geographic or place-based disadvantage. However, as highlighted by Gilchrist (2009), strategic networks can inadvertently preserve privilege and perpetuate inequalities and social exclusion. She argues that professional dominance can be problematic, particularly in circumstances where the change process is prescribed by external factors such as funding or performance criteria. Professionals need to be aware of their power, role and influence in such networks (Gilchrist, 2009). As articulated by Collins (2009), 'professional social work is faced with the real challenge of participation and partnership – a challenge to paternalistic/maternalistic elitism and exclusive knowledge, moving on to a commitment to action, involving users as important stakeholders in providing, developing and evaluating services' (p. 345).

Caniglia and Bourke (2012) identify some key reflective questions throughout their 'toolkit' for organisations and practitioners. We adapt and build on some of these below.

Reflective Questions

1. In what ways do you think that a *community of practice*, as described by Caniglia and Bourke in their 'toolkit', might benefit groups and communities experiencing poverty and geographical (or 'place-based') disadvantage?
2. As a future social work or community work practitioner, how do you think that a *community of practice* could support your work with groups and communities who are experiencing disadvantage?
3. What role do you think *communities of practice* can play in providing the conditions for supporting processes of critical consciousness in day-to-day practices?
4. What are some of the 'dangers' or limitations of this approach in practice?
5. In small groups, discuss the different roles and activities that might be involved in developing a *community of practice*. How do you think you could contribute?

Scaffolding practices: Social workers' engagement with collective activities

Different forms of collective activities have the potential to support and scaffold the practices of practitioners in their work. As noted by Collins (2009), there are a number of ways social workers engage in 'collectives'. He explores both the opportunities and limitations of a range of collective activities such as groups of practitioners coming together to support each other within or across their organisations; the 'protective' function of membership of work-based trade unions and professional associations in the face of victimisation; and learning from the knowledge and experience of collective service user movements at local, regional, national and international levels (pp. 340–347). While he argues that 'collectives' offer mutual support for social workers in very practical ways and open up opportunities for significant learning, he notes that active engagement in a range of these activities may be limited due to professional and personal commitments. He asserts that 'social workers have always faced, and will always face, a struggle to deal with contradictions and tensions in their work' (p. 349).

Social workers seeking organisational change require 'external reference points' for their practices (Healy, 2005, p. 239). Healy articulates a role for 'change-orientated collectives' such as advocacy groups (that is, citizen advocacy groups), industrial unions to protect rights and professional associations that uphold our social work identity and humanist value base (p. 240). However, Mullaly cautions against social work associations becoming 'self-serving, status quo organisations' (1997, p. 199). To counter this possibility, he envisages a social action committee comprised of members of the association that is well supported by the membership and the executive in conducting analyses of policies and programmes, legislation, government actions and corporate interests 'to preserve the social conscience of social work' (p. 199). The involvement of social workers in international associations such as the International Federation of Social Workers (IFSW) as a means of ongoing engagement in human rights discourse and actions (Ife, 1997) is another 'external critical reference point' for social workers.

A new front for social participation and professional solidarity is the emergence of online professional communities. An example of this is SWForum (http://swforum.socialnet.org.hk) which was established in 1999 to promote professional exchange among social workers in Hong Kong (Leung, Lam, Yau and Chu, 2010, p. 54), particularly in relation to social welfare policy developments. Leung et al. (2010) highlight the contribution of the forum to the development of critical awareness among social workers, providing 'multifaceted understandings of the issues' and fostering a collective identity (p. 61).

The role of peer support emerged in our earlier discussion of critical reflection and we return briefly to it here. In a Canadian study that explored critical reflection among 'activist-facilitators' working in international development, it was found that the most common way that participants discussed applying critical reflection was through co-facilitation with peers or collaborative mechanisms 'built into their practice which often included informal time together' (Hansen, 2013, p. 85). The researcher noted that when critical reflection was evident, study participants were able to give examples of facilitation practices 'that challenged dominant hierarchies and forms of knowledge' (ibid., p. 85). However, they also found that participants were 'embroiled in *quick fix* approaches' and 'techno-rational responses to critical reflection' such as 'what worked and what did not' (ibid., p. 85). Major challenges to the use of critical reflection in practice were identified as 'institutional obstacles' related to limited time and the lack of value placed on critical reflective processes. Practitioners were under pressure from organisations and funders 'to produce outputs rather that reflect on process' (p. 82). The researcher poses questions about how activists in development can use critical reflection to unsettle institutional norms and hierarchical conditions. She suggests that practitioners use methods such as narratives or case studies to document knowledge drawing on their experience of feminist and critical pedagogies.

Building critical consciousness in interaction with peers and communities is a strong theme in the social work and community development literature as well as in relation to university teaching and learning practices (see Collins, 2009; Kaplan, 2002; Ledwith, 2011; Wint and Sewpaul, 2008). Allan Kaplan highlights collaborative learning processes involving critical reflection whereby peers take turns 'to mentor and be mentored so long as the relationship and shifting roles are structured and conscious' (2002, p. 162). Another dimension of peer support from within and outside the agency is identified by Mullaly (1997), namely as a means of protecting ourselves, 'not just from agency reprisal but also from burnout' (p. 186).

Scaffolding practices: Social workers as researchers for social change

In her book, *Social Work Research for Social Justice*, Beth Humphries (2008) highlights the political nature of research and illustrates both quantitative and qualitative approaches that can be used in working towards social justice goals within diverse practice settings. Questions that arise are, 'Who benefits from the research?' and, 'To what extent are the interests of people who are marginalised addressed in the research?' As Shdaimah, Stahl and Schram (2011, p. 1) note, 'For social work researchers to participate effectively in social change initiatives, they must think carefully about how to combine research and advocacy.' They remind us that research can be 'a tool for reinforcing the status quo as much as a tool for social change' (ibid., p. 1). Furthermore, Healy urges caution and reflexivity in 'the acts of making social work processes visible' in the context of critical practice research in the postmodern era of increased surveillance and governmentality (2000, p. 146). She argues for social workers themselves to undertake or at least be involved in externally driven research to counter this potential.

In the community context, Donna Mertens posits a transformative research paradigm by arguing that 'if we ground research and evaluation in assumptions that prioritise the furtherance of social justice and human rights, then we will utilise community involvement and research methodologies that will lead to a greater realisation of social change' (2009, p. 3). These key assumptions highlight the ethical responsibility for researchers and evaluators to understand the communities in which they are working so that they can challenge social processes that facilitate the status quo and a recognition of power (that is, what version of reality is privileged over another) (ibid., p. 49). In terms of methodology, Mertens argues that researchers can select quantitative or qualitative or mixed methods, however the research problem should be defined in interaction with communities, methods should be sensitive to cultural factors, power issues should be explicitly addressed and oppression and discrimination identified. This underlines the importance of critical reflection and the process of critical consciousness (discussed earlier) when undertaking research with communities. Mertens formulates some questions (based on Kret, 2006, cited in Mertens, 2009) that assist in raising reciprocal awareness and that may be posed in working with communities. These include, 'What are the important priorities for the community that researchers/evaluators may need to understand and work with?' (question for the community) and, 'What questions should you (as researcher) ask yourself before beginning a study with groups and communities who are marginalised?' and, 'What impact will the research/evaluation have on the community?' (questions for the researcher, p. 92).

A cyclic and iterative research model based on the transformative paradigm is advanced by Mertens. This depicts a dynamic and ongoing relationship between the researcher and community members whereby each cycle of inquiry feeds into the next one. We include Mertens's questions (2009, p. 138) here as they facilitate a critically reflective research process:

- What are your experiences in involving communities in social action, in research or evaluation, or in some other contexts?
- What challenges did you experience or do you imagine you would experience bringing community members into the research or evaluation process?
- What are the implications of taking a participatory approach (research by, for and with the community) versus a partnership approach?
- How can the capacities of community members be enhanced to facilitate their involvement in the research or evaluation?

In this context, we focus on research as a relational process and one that can foster new types of relationships (Denzin and Lincoln, 2003, p. 597; Shdaimah, Stahl and Schram, 2011). The researcher 'becomes an active participant in forging generative, communicative relationships, in building on-going dialogues and expanding the domain of civic deliberation' (Denzin and Lincoln, 2003, p. 598). The goal of research becomes 'one of inciting dialogue that undergoes continuous change as it moves through an extended network' (ibid., p. 603).

We now turn to some examples of research conducted by social workers, focusing on research methodologies that foster these new kinds of relationships in seeking to realise social change. In their book, *Change Research: A Case Study on Collaborative Methods for Social Workers and Advocates*, Shdaimah, Stahl and Schram (2011) discuss their experiences as social work researchers in conducting research with clients and community groups based on a Participatory Action Research (PAR) framework that led to major changes in social policy. This research was carried out in collaboration with activists from an affordable-housing coalition who were leading a campaign to address the issues of low-income home ownership and repair in Philadelphia, USA. The authors report that the campaign for affordable housing drew on the findings of the PAR and ultimately contributed to the creation of Philadelphia's Affordable Housing Trust Fund. This work highlights both collaborative research and the recursive connections between research and advocacy. Based on their experiences, the authors argue that collaborative, community-based PAR is potentially a means of pursuing a 'radical incrementalist practice that achieves small, short-run political gains that can contribute to making possible more significant political transformations in the future' (p. 14). They argue that the campaign was successful (in part) because it was underpinned by credible research. The data illuminated the nature of the problem experienced by specific communities and informed approaches and ideas to address it. They therefore assert that research can be a tool 'to challenge assumptions about underlying problems and proposed solutions' (p. 26). They emphasise that social work involvement in collaborative research 'can help promote a more reflective practice' that is critically engaged and outside of day-to-day social work practices (p. 27). Here we see PAR as an approach that seeks social change or improvements through engaging with people most affected (Humphries, 2008). However, Humphries also cautions that participatory approaches 'can be compatible with top-down planning systems' (2008, p. 70). In Ireland, a community participatory methodology was used to engage service-users as both participants and co-researchers in all stages of a project that investigated the experience of drug problems in communities in Dublin (Loughran and McCann, 2013). Despite the community participatory approach, the authors note that ultimately 'control' of the research remained with the funders.

Methodological approaches that are particularly suited to emancipatory forms of social work research are articulated in the literature. For example, Lenette, Cox and Brough (2013) describe the use of Digital Storytelling (DST) as a participatory, dialogic and iterative process that has the potential to facilitate and enable people who are marginalised to tell their stories (using digital media), build inductive knowledge for social work practice and become a tool for social advocacy. In pursuit of a practice culture in social work that values research activity, Oliver (2012) advocates for an approach that combines grounded theory and critical realism. Drawing on the emancipatory goals of critical realism (as we outlined in Chapter 4), he argues that 'it offers to produce knowledge that is relevant to practitioners by grounding findings in the experiences of those it seeks to inform' (p. 384).

Practitioner research: Developing theory and knowledge for practices with communities

Practitioner research has a vital role in the generation of knowledge. Arguing that practitioner-led research (PLR) is nearly invisible, Hardwick and Worsley (2011) in the UK highlight the numerous advantages of social work practitioners engaging in research. These include their access to practice knowledge through their 'situated perspective'; unique positioning at interface of service-users, carers, organisations and policy; transferability of their knowledge across settings; localised knowledge that potentially can inform social change; and opportunity to have a 'voice' in their own right (p. 135). These UK authors argue for the development of sustainable infrastructure at organisational, funding and policy levels to facilitate practitioner research; the need for practitioners to examine and reflect on their interventions involving communities and policy issues; and opening up possibilities to engage in small-scale research at the local level that generates knowledge for social change. Other UK authors have noted 'a circle of resistance' to social work research perpetuated by systemic issues linked to the policy and practice contexts of social workers (Orme and Powell, 2007, p. 1005).

However, in Australia, a number of capacity building initiatives to engage practitioners in research within health and welfare settings are reported, such as dedicated research positions, academic-practice partnerships and practice research models where research is included in a practitioner's workload (see Harvey et al., 2013). A survey conducted with 103 social workers employed in health settings in Northern Queensland found that most of these practitioners had little or no experience in identifying a research topic or formulating a research question; engaging with qualitative and quantitative research methods; and research-related writing skills (Harvey et al., 2013). Despite this, there was a high level of practitioner interest in undertaking research. Lack of time and resources as well as a lack of research confidence were identified as constraining factors, so it was recommended that funding opportunities, training and mentoring activities would build research capacity within these settings.

Fook (2001) highlights the important role of the reflective practitioner-researcher. In writing about critical community-based practice, Stepney and Popple (2008) point out the commonalities between critical reflection as a framework for research and action-research. They argue, 'both have a commitment to social justice and span the divide between objective and subjective accounts that value experience and action as much as insight' (p. 170). As expressed by Humphries (2008), 'action research speaks to the practical and change-orientated nature of social work' (p. 69).

In explicating the contested term, 'practice research', Pain concludes that it is 'all research that is directly related to practice, and may be conducted by researchers, practitioners and/or service users' (2011, p. 547). She highlights the emergence of collaborative practice research between academics, practitioners and service-users, but points out that this endeavour will require a 'research-supportive' employing organisation. Orme and Powell (2007) draw attention to the role that Communities of Practice can play in creating a culture for research within and across organisations, and research capacity building between academia and practice. Ian Shaw broadens this out to include exchanges with diverse disciplines and fields such as social and human geography and environmental studies, focusing on the paucity of contemporary urban social work research (Shaw, 2011). At the international level, social work research is essential for the development of theory and generating knowledge for practices in relation to global issues such as child trafficking and refugees (Orme and Karvinen-Niinikoski, 2012).

In the Indigenous context, Linda Tuhiwai Smith (2001) highlights the growing community of Indigenous scholars and researchers who are undertaking Indigenous research and developing Indigenous research protocols and methodologies. She notes that members are positioning themselves as Indigenous researchers informed by critical and frequently feminist approaches to research, and 'are grounded politically in specific Indigenous contexts and histories, struggles and ideas' (p. 4). This is occurring in a context where Indigenous communities and organisations have developed research policies, ethical guidelines and discussion documents, and 'are discussing issues related to control over research activities and the knowledge that research produces' (p. 4).

While we did not ask practitioners in our Irish study directly about their involvement in research, the theme of research emerged in the interviews. Our examples illustrate the diverse forms of research undertaken by practitioners in the course of their practices. Practitioners talked about the key role of research in identifying community needs. This type of research is connected to the process of community profiling that we discussed in Chapter 5. For example, one practitioner who was working on a project to support the families of prisoners and ex-prisoners explained that research was carried out and the families of prisoners came up consistently as a group in the community 'whose needs weren't being met'. Another practitioner in our study expressed:

> Social workers need to be involved in research and identifying needs and gaps and that is very much part of community development because how are you going to respond to needs if you don't identify what the need is and what the gaps are. I put it down to the qualities that are needed... self-awareness, respect and commitment to inclusion and participation... a wider consciousness of the structural inequalities because that, to me, is key, and it is really important for social workers to come up with that consciousness. I am not sure that always happens, my experience I suppose.

She elaborated on the process of setting up a youth café that began with the identification of disadvantaged young people in the area who 'weren't engaging with projects and there were issues, you know, where people saw them as trouble causers etc.' She describes undertaking local research with schools and youth groups and compiling information 'to look at what the needs were'. She elucidates:

> I suppose right from identifying the need, the research – I mean that is community work or community development for me and seeing it right through, identifying the need, the gaps, supporting the people to set up their own service, corporate grants, the admin side of it but not taking over. It is about empowering, about supporting participation and the ultimate aim, if it works is to withdraw from that. I think you have been successful if it can be a sustainable group, the proof will be in the pudding.

She was referring to the idea that the young people themselves would eventually run the project. As discussed in Chapter 5, participation is a distinguishing feature within all stages of the community profiling process.

The use of existing research to inform critical community development practices was highlighted by a practitioner working with a community project in the area of drug addiction:

> Research after research has proved in some way that there is a correlation between poverty and inequality on different levels with drugs and addiction and addiction problems. *We don't want to forget that and we have to keep on saying that.* 'The powers that be' don't want to hear that at the moment. So, in our Drugs Task Force, for us what that means here in our team would be to put value on community development, put value on working around urban regeneration, so it is part of our drug work. Even though it is not giving methadone to some people even though we do that as well. It would mean linking in and working and supporting groups out there who are just doing ordinary community stuff and it is building up their capacity, because in the end, that is the best way to respond to drugs.

Practitioner research: Documenting Practices and Developing Practice Models

In our Irish research, there were stories of practitioners documenting their practices and developing practice models that could be used with other communities. As a social worker in a statutory child protection setting expressed:

A practical example would be the protocol that we came up with – a very short document – but also it is a very friendly structure. A number of agencies buy into this and sign up to operating this protocol that they work together and share information, as appropriate and come up with an action plan for young people identified as at risk. It is very nuts and bolts but a very user friendly way of working together at a lower level than case conferencing but it is to try and name interagency networking sort of work that goes on everyday especially in the informal settings like neighbourhood youth projects or whatever but to try to put a name to that. It is in its infancy but there are other areas around Ireland where it has actually taken off. It is the way forward.

Some of the practitioners were writing about their experiences or identifying the need to 'be feeding back in what it is that we are doing... not just by coming in and talking to students about it (at university) but by writing it down, by recording it, by thinking about it.' One practitioner working with children and families in a rural setting noted: 'Social workers do have stuff to say and a lot of experience... I have noticed that there are better links between universities and practitioners. Sometimes social work practitioners... because they are so overwhelmed, need a bit of light to follow to get them to formulate and structure their experiences in more academic or evaluative terminology'.

The potential for collaborative research between people working in the field and academics was highlighted. For example, one practitioner working in the non-government sector commented,

'I think the research side would be very practical. I think that everyone would benefit from that. The organisation would love it if they are getting any positive research published. It would evidence our work. You guys (academics) would get the publications as well so I think that it would be a win, win, win for everybody, you know.'

In conclusion: Reflection and renewal for sustained critical practices

Processes of conscientisation or critical consciousness-raising are intrinsic to community development, and the means through which people are empowered to enact change. In this chapter, we have drawn on this concept to explore scaffolding practices in a critical community development context. We locate these processes within our critical realist perspective. Our exploration shows that models of critical reflection are important in-built mechanisms for supporting and enabling critical community practices. Practitioners in our own research urged the questioning of underlying assumptions, and the need for constant critical analysis to inform their practices. A range of collective activities, peer support and online professional communities offer opportunities for critical awareness among social workers and foster a collective identity in challenging contexts.

Practitioners can draw on a range of reference points to scaffold their practices within the dynamic, fluid, evolving and recursive processes that characterise community development in late modernity. Self-renewal activities such as self-reflection and maintaining support networks are needed for sustained practices. Nevertheless, we need to recognise that personal pressures and commitments in contemporary contexts may constrain active engagement with a range of collective activities within and across agency contexts.

main points

- Critical consciousness, self-awareness and reflexivity are pivotal ideas to scaffold critical community practices.

- There is a range of approaches and processes at the individual and organisational level that can support practitioners and enable them to stay centred, creative, critical and effective in their work with communities.

- At the individual level, and in collective ways, practitioners develop practice frameworks to organise their thinking and frame actions.

- Communities of practice can foster creativity, critical thinking and collaboration in responses to highly complex social issues within communities that are experiencing disadvantage. It is important that practitioners are aware of the power issues inherent in professional networks.

- Organisational support can facilitate the evolution of multiple communities of practice that can enrich and sustain practitioners in their day-to-day work.

- Models of critical reflection can be important mechanisms for supporting and enabling critical community practices.

- Practitioner researcher has a vital role in the generation of knowledge.

- Which approaches to scaffolding critical practice discussed in this chapter did you find most helpful for your own practice?
- What is the next step you need to take to pursue these ideas for scaffolding your practices?
- Discuss the role of practitioner research and how it might 'empower practitioners by giving them a voice'.

taking it further

- Butcher, H., Banks, S., Henderson, P. and Robertson, J. (2007) *Critical Community Practice*, Bristol: The Policy Press.
- Caniglia, F. and Bourke, P. (2012) *Toolkit for Developing Place-based Responses to Disadvantage*, Queensland: UnitingCare Social Justice.
- Collins, S. (2009) 'Some Critical Perspectives on Social Work and Collectives', *British Journal of Social Work Advance Access*, doi:10.1093/bjsw/bcm097.
- Fook, J. and Gardner, F. (2007) *Practising Critical Reflection. A Resource Handbook*, Maidenhead: McGraw-Hill Education.
- Gilchrist, A. (2009) *The Well Connected Community: A Networking Approach to Community Development,* Second Edition, Bristol: The Policy Press.
- Shdaimah, C., Stahl, R. and Schram, S. (2011) *Change Research: A Case Study on Collaborative Methods for Social Workers and Advocates,* New York: Columbia University Press.
- Stepney, P. and Popple, K. (2008) *Social Work and the Community: A Critical Context for Practice*, Basingstoke: Palgrave Macmillan.
- Westoby, P. and Shevellar, L. (2012) *Learning and Mobilising for Community Development: A Radical Tradition of Community-based Education and Training,* Surrey, UK: Ashgate Publishing Ltd.

Conclusion: New opportunities for social work engagement with critical community development approaches

Introduction

In the conclusion we address the challenges and opportunities for social work practitioners, educators and academics, students and researchers in engaging with community development ideas and approaches.

Prospects for a critical and engaged practice

From its origins in the nineteenth century to its establishment as a profession, social work has always operated at the interface between macro or societal change and those who experience and are affected by social change – their clients or service users. Negotiating this interface has become increasingly challenging as society becomes progressively more complex and subject to a growing range of challenges, risks and threats. Concomitantly, the expectations placed on social workers and the social professions have grown as states have sought ways to address and manage their populations and the multifaceted social and economic issues that affect them.

In the last fifteen years there has been considerable discussion in the social work literature about the potential for a critical and challenging social work practice that can contest and change the dominant neoliberal, professional and managerial discourses that have been pre-eminent for over forty years. The impact of these discourses has been felt throughout the Global North as states wrestle with economic, social and ecological crises that have both local and global causes and consequences. The issue of migration, for instance, is currently receiving considerable attention in the global social work literature, because its causes, consequences and impacts are 'central concerns for social work' (Williams and Graham, 2014, p. 3). Social work academics, practitioners and educators have debated the relative efficacy of radical, structural and critical approaches, argued the comparative merits of ideological and practice-based perspectives, contemplated the significance of structure versus agency, and weighed up the advantages of top-down versus bottom-up responses. All of this discussion and debate has led some social work writers to defend social work by pointing out its distinctive qualities (Broadhurst and Mason, 2012; Jones, 2014), while others have highlighted effective social work practice. In his keynote address to the JSWEC Conference in July 2014, Harry Ferguson argued that the majority of social workers are 'highly ethical', 'really effective' and 'inspirational' practitioners who habitually achieve 'positive outcomes' (Ferguson, 2014) for service users. These varied perspectives underline the existence of a deep-seated and enduring social work tradition of intellectual and applied engagement with the societal changes that surround and affect social work and the profession's response to these changes.

We have argued that critical realism offers a useful and accessible lens through which to view the situation of social work in the twenty-first century. Critical realism seeks a middle way between the polarities of ideology versus practice, structure versus agency and top-down versus bottom-up. In the first place it is sceptical about the influence of ideology, which can be harnessed to justify goals which are detrimental to people's well-being and rights; instead, a critical realist perspective emphasises critical and intellectual engagement combined with practical action. Critical realism acknowledges the existence of social structures or a '"real" social world' (Houston, 2001, p. 858) outside of people's personal experience, but concomitantly emphasises how human agency both influences and shapes these structures. By assuming an intermediate position between extremes, critical realism epitomises an understanding that the social world is both contingent and changing, and reality is a 'dynamic process that draws upon subjective knowledge and understanding' (Stepney and Popple, 2008, p. 162). People function within, shape and respond to, the social world in all sorts of different ways (Houston, 2001). Drawing again on the example of migration, migration has both structural and individual factors, as some people migrate for economic reasons or to escape conflict in their home countries, while others migrate for subjective reasons to reunite families and be with their loved ones (O'Reilly, 2012; Williams and Graham, 2014). Migration is therefore a much more complex phenomenon than it appears at face value, and requires a complex engagement and set of responses from states and from those, including social workers and community development workers, working within the context of the state.

While a critical realist position favours a bottom-up approach, through learning from and working with service users (Stepney and Popple, 2008), it recognises that people in intermediate positions, like social professionals, have an important role to play in effecting change. Social workers and community development workers can use their professionalism to challenge dominant discourses. To illustrate how these key features of critical realism may operate in practice, Pentaraki (2013) argues that social workers have the capacity to operate a dual approach, both as intellectuals who engage themselves and others in critical reflection on 'the contextual political nature of their situation' (p. 706), and as activists who possess a range of social work and community development skills that can be used 'to inaugurate practical solutions' (ibid., p. 707) to social problems.

A social worker is not a 'mere automaton' (Houston, 2001, p. 851), subject to a set of structures, rules or processes. Neither is a social worker 'a "heroic agent" capable of single-handedly effecting individual and social change on a large scale' (Marston and McDonald, 2012, p. 15) and in the face of considerable challenges. The concept of creative activism has enabled us to explore the ways in which social workers and community development workers seek to effect change through engaging critically in the 'nooks and crannies' of their everyday practice, as well as in ways that extend beyond the everyday, and how this critical practice can and does effect change at the individual, community and societal levels. We have seen how 'agency at all levels of policy practice' (Marston and McDonald, 2012, p. 1034) can effect estimable change. The agency of social workers and other social professionals, at individual, organisational, national and global level has contributed to the identification and realisation of social justice goals.

Social work and community development: Emerging possibilities

Community development practice illustrates the dynamic and contingent nature of the social world and the ways in which practitioners respond to it. We have pointed out that community development does not tend to adhere to rigid or hide-bound prescriptions of 'how to do' practice. Ingrid Burkett (2011a, p. 113) refers to the

> variable and contradictory, psychologically and ideologically entangled, rather than singular, ways in which community development workers and organizations react and respond to neoliberalism.

Individuals and organisations do not respond in 'singular, "purist"' (ibid.) or unchanging ways to the challenges posed by neo-liberalism and the working environment that it produces. Instead they react in all sorts of ways; some accept the changing nature of their work, others resist in small but meaningful ways, while others choose overt means including activism and protest in order to seek change. Similar responses are evident in social work; as we have seen, social workers engage with change by either accepting it, accommodating it or by finding ways to struggle against it. A recent study by Evans (2013) highlights that discretion plays a considerable role in social work practice, even in the most rule-bound working environments; while some social workers adhered to the rules, others at all levels and all stages of their careers broke or 'bent' the rules to enable discretion and the exercise of professional judgement. Evans suggests that both forms of response – rule-keeping and rule-bending – represent the exercise of professional and critical judgement rather than unquestioning observance of rules or procedures. These strategies highlight the significance of agency in responding to and tackling the effects of policies, rules and procedures.

We have sought to demonstrate that social work practitioners can and do use community development approaches in a range of contexts, and that the accessibility of these approaches renders them useful in whole or in part, and at all levels of practice, from the individual and local to the global. Possession of a global worldview is increasingly essential for practitioners in the social professions, as they grapple with issues and situations that originate outside of the local context or that have broader implications than a local focus can accommodate. In this context several new or emerging avenues for practice have opened up. These include the growing concern about environmental change and degradation and its current and future effects on the planet, on societies and on communities. Another is the current expansion of conflict in many parts of the world and the repercussions for social work practice, including effects such as forced migration, family break-up and trauma. Practitioners who are involved with these and other issues need a wide-ranging perspective that encompasses their causes, outcomes and effects, as well as the capacity to work in ways that have an effective impact on individuals, groups and communities, and consequently on the wider society. A critical community development approach offers this broad perspective, coupled with a set of values and skills that enable a committed and engaged practice.

Critical directions in social work policy, education and practice

It has been our purpose in this book to explore how a critical community development perspective and approach can be used within the context of social work practice in a range of settings. In the rest of this chapter we will attempt to identify the key ways in which a critical community development perspective and approach may be stimulated and nurtured amongst social work students, practitioners, educators, academics and researchers. Three main areas require attention – these are fostering a critical perspective and engagement in policy, education and practice.

Fostering a critical perspective: Policy

In a study conducted in the early 2000s, Weiss et al. (2006; see also Wood-cock and Dixon, 2005) explored the professional ideologies of graduating social work students in eight countries, the UK, the US, Australia, Brazil, Canada, Israel, Hungary and Zimbabwe. They found substantial differences between students from the eight countries. Students from countries which were formerly colonised (Brazil, Zimbabwe) or which highly prized egali-tarian values (Australia, US, Canada) were more likely to espouse structural or critical perspectives on issues such as the causes of poverty and delin-quency and the goals of social work. While UK students tended to display more consensus and social control perspectives towards these issues, their views were moderate rather than extreme and they favoured state inter-vention over individual or pathological ideas for addressing poverty.

Two main conclusions may be drawn from the results of the Weiss et al. study. Firstly, social work students' attitudes and values tend to be shaped by those of the societies from which they come. The less egalitarian the context, the less likely it is that students will automatically value equality and social justice. Neo-liberalism is the over-riding ideology in most of the countries we have explored in this text, and this set of ideas has had far-reaching consequences for attitudes towards social work, as well as for its policy and practice. Parton (2014b) illustrates how this has happened, in an extreme form, in England.

> While social work in England has been marginalised or excluded
> from a whole range of areas of practice which it has traditionally
> inhabited – such as probation, work with older people and adults,
> and many of the newer family support and community-based
> activities – social work is identified as the profession for taking the
> lead responsibility for child protection. (p. 2053)

Parton argues that policy on child protection is failing to take account of the range of factors that contribute to child maltreatment, including 'social harms … many of which are clearly related to structural inequali-ties' (ibid., p. 13). As we have seen, policy based on neo-liberal ideas tends to individualise social problems and place the responsibility for address-ing them at the feet of individuals, communities and the intermediaries who work between communities and the state; these intermediaries include social workers and community development workers. Policy needs to broaden to take into account what Parton refers to as the *'social'* context to problems such as child abuse and other issues that social workers and community development workers face. Marston and McDonald (2012) point out that many factors influence macro policy but that if social workers are willing to accept uncertainty and to work with 'diverse coalitions and unexpected allies' (p. 15) they can seek policy change.

Fostering a critical perspective: Education

The second conclusion which may be drawn from Weiss et al. is that social work education and training plays a significant role in shaping students' perspectives. Woodcock and Dixon (2005, p. 970) suggest that social work education in the UK may train 'social workers to espouse the statutory role' and encourage 'consensus notions'. This echoes Ferguson and Smith's (2012, p. 991) contention that 'a conservative neo-liberal ideological context' to social work discourages the exploration of critical and structural approaches. Students need to be introduced to broad or structural perspectives in their training and, crucially, to be equipped with the knowledge and skills to realise these perspectives in practice. Weiss, Gal and Katan (2006) point out that policy practice is not taught on many social work training courses internationally and therefore plays a peripheral part in social work practice in several countries. They offer a detailed model of policy practice training in social work education and argue that this model can 'contribute to the production of graduates who are able to integrate their understanding of the impact of social structure and social policy on service users into assessment and intervention' (p. 803). The ability to grasp and integrate the macro and micro contexts is crucial to critical realist practice. We have seen that social workers already engage in policy practice, but a greater emphasis on broader perspectives in social work training would enhance their knowledge of the policy context in which they work, and provide them with the skills to contribute to policy-making.

One of the ways in which students can acquire a global perspective is the opportunity to practice in other contexts from their own. In our own experience as social work and community development educators, students acquire considerable learning from practice placements in other places, particularly but not exclusively countries in the Global South. Vickers and Dominelli (2014) refer to the long-standing contribution that social work students and practitioners have made to development in the Global South, including in the context of disaster response. Students' and practitioners' involvement in these contexts can impart invaluable learning, values and perspectives that are transferable to their own working environments when they return to their own countries. Dominelli (2012b) suggests that social workers need to learn from progressive policy and practice in other places and argues that to 'advocate effectively for structural change, social workers must engage policy-makers and local people in activities that redistribute power and resources to marginalised groups, within a country and outside it' (p. 48).

Fostering a critical perspective: Practice

Social workers need to be given, and to seize, opportunities to practice in a critical way. As we have seen, many social workers take these opportunities in a range of practice settings.

We have attempted to show how social workers use the organisational contexts in which they work to undertake critical and engaged practice. In particular, they are capable of challenging and using dominant discourses to effect change, both within their own organisations and on a wider basis. They can be assisted in these efforts by organisations and managers who are willing to encourage and facilitate environments conducive to critical practice. The learning communities discussed in Chapter 7 are an example of how this can be done in a way which is beneficial to all workers in the organisation, and which can encourage mutual learning and co-operation.

As social workers search for 'fresh understandings, insights, and even explanations' (Jones, 2012, p. 274) of what they do and how they do it, they should consider the potential of social research, which can offer multi-faceted benefits for practitioners. In the first place, research can enable social workers to learn about the individuals, groups and communities with whom they work. In Chapter 5 we identified the significance of community profiling for critical community development practice. This kind of research provides valuable information about the people on whom practice is focused, but it also opens opportunities for engagement with and by service users and communities. By facilitating the voices of service users and community members (Jones, 2012), practitioners are engaging in practice that is both inclusive and empowering.

The results of social research undertaken by social workers and other social professionals can help to inform policy and practice. It is clear from our own research that social workers use the findings of their research in order to influence policy and practice on a range of issues. This type of work is sometimes carried out in addition to their main roles and is often unheralded, yet it can make an appreciable difference in documenting the effects of policy on service users and communities, as well as in making recommendations for improvement or change. It is through this kind of critical practice that social workers can effect significant change in the lives of individuals, communities and societies.

main points

- Critical realism offers a useful and accessible lens through which to view and practice social work in the twenty-first century.

- Through creative activism social workers and community development workers seek to effect change through engaging critically both in and beyond their everyday practice.

- A critical community development approach offers a global perspective and a set of values and skills that enable a committed, critical and engaged practice.

In this chapter we have explored some of the ways in which critical practice can be encouraged in social work policy, education and practice. In terms of your own practice as a social worker, identify:

- An aspect of policy that you would like to change. How would you go about seeking change?
- A context outside of your own practice setting that you would like to learn about or practice in. What would you like to learn? What could this different practice context teach you?
- A piece of research that would enable you to attain a greater understanding of the context in which you are working. How would you approach this research? What could it achieve?

taking it further

- Evans, T. (2013) 'Organisational Rules and Discretion in Adult Social Work', *British Journal of Social Work*, 43, pp. 739–758.
- Ferguson, H. (2014) 'Envisioning Social Work by Putting the Life Back into It: Learning about What Social Workers Do and How They Do It (Well)', Keynote Speech to JSWEC 'Social Work Making Connections' Conference, 23–25 July, 2014, Royal Holloway: University of London.
- Jones, M. (2012) 'Research-minded Practice in Social Work' in P. Stepney and D. Ford (eds) *Social Work Models, Methods and Theories: A Framework for Practice*, Lyme Regis: Russell House Publishing.
- Williams, C. and Graham, M. (2014) 'A World on the Move: Migration, Mobilities and Social Work', *British Journal of Social Work*, 44, Supplement 1, pp. 1–17.
- Weiss, I., Gal, J. and Katan, J. (2006) 'Social Policy for Social Work: A Teaching Agenda', *British Journal of Social Work*, 36(5), pp. 789–806.

Bibliography

Abramovitz, M. (1998) 'Social Work and Social Reform: An Arena of Struggle', *Social Work*, 43(6), pp. 512–526.

Adams, R. (2008) *Empowerment, Participation and Social Work*, Fourth Edition, Basingstoke: Palgrave Macmillan.

Age Action Ireland (2011) *'A Total Indifference to Our Dignity': Older People's Understandings of Elder Abuse*, Dublin: Age Action Ireland.

Agger, B. (1991) 'Critical Theory, Poststructuralism, Postmodernism: Their Sociological Relevance', *Annual Review of Sociology*, 17, pp. 105–131.

Aimers, J. and Walker, P. (2008) 'Is Community Accountability being Overlooked as a Result of Government-Third Sector Partnership in New Zealand?', *Aotearoa New Zealand Social Work*, 3, pp. 14–24.

Aimers, J. and Walker, P. (2011) 'Incorporating Community Development into Social Work Practice within the Neoliberal Environment', *Aotearoa New Zealand Social Work*, 23(3), pp. 38–49.

Allen-Kelly, K. (2010) 'Out of the Wilderness – Australian Social Workers Embrace Their Campaigning Roots', *Australian Social Work*, 63(3), pp. 245–249.

Alston, M. (2013) 'Environmental Social Work: Accounting Gender in Climate Disasters', *Australian Social Work*, 66(2), pp. 218–233.

Alston, M. and Besthorn, F. (2012) 'Environment and Sustainability' in K.H. Lyons, T. Hokenstad, M. Pawar, N. Huegler and N. Hall (eds) *The SAGE Handbook of International Social Work*, London: Sage Publications.

Andrews, J. and Reisch, M. (2002) 'The Radical Voices of Social Workers', *Journal of Progressive Human Services*, 13(1), pp. 5–30.

Arvanitakis, J. (2008) 'Staging Maralinga and Looking for Community (Or Why we Must Desire Community before We Can Find It)', *Research in Drama Education*, 13(3), pp. 295–306.

Atampugre, N. (1998) 'Colonial and Contemporary Approaches to Community Development: A Comparative Overview of Similarities and Differences in West African Experiences', *Community Development Journal*, 33(4), pp. 353–364.

Australian Association of Social Workers (2010) Code of Ethics, Canberra: AASW.

Bailey, R. and Brake, M. (1975) *Radical Social Work*, London: Edward Arnold.

Baines, D. (2007) 'Anti-Oppressive Social Work Practice: Fighting for Space, Fighting for Change' in D. Baines (ed.) *Doing Anti-Oppressive Practice. Building Transformative Politicized Social Work*, Nova Scotia: Fernwood Publishing.

Baker, J., Lynch, K., Cantillon, S. and Walsh, J. (2004) *Equality: From Theory to Action*, Basingstoke: Palgrave Macmillan.

Baldwin, M. (2011) 'Resisting the EasyCare Model: Building a More Radical, Community-based, Anti-authoritarian Social Work for the Future' in M. Lavalette (ed.) *Radical Social Work Today: Social Work at the Crossroads*, Bristol: Policy Press.

Banks, S. (2007) 'Becoming Critical: Developing the Community Practitioner' in H. Butcher, S. Banks, P. Henderson and J. Robertson (eds) *Critical Community Practice*, Bristol: The Policy Press.

Banks, S. (2011) 'Re-Guilding the Ghetto: Community Work and Community Development in the 21st Century' in M. Lavalette (ed.) *Radical Social Work Today: Social Work at the Crossroads*, Bristol: The Policy Press.

Barclay, P. (1982) *Social Workers: Their Role and Task* (*The Barclay Report*), London: Bedford Square Press.

Barnard, H. (2010) *Big Society, Cuts and Consequences: A Thinkpiece*, City University London: Centre for Charity Effectiveness.

Barnardos (2012) *Cutting Them Free: How is the UK Progressing in Protecting Its Children from Sexual Exploitation?* Essex: Barnardos.

Barry, B. (2005) *Why Social Justice Matters*, Cambridge: Polity Press.

Bay, U. (2009) 'Framing Critical Social Work Practices with Rural and Remote Communities' in J. Allan, L. Briskman and B. Pease (eds) *Critical Social Work: Theories and Practices for a Socially Just World*, Sydney, NSW: Allen and Unwin.

Beech, M. (2012) 'The British Welfare State and its Discontents' in J. Connelly and J. Hayward (eds) *The Withering of the Welfare State: Regression*, Basingstoke: Palgrave Macmillan.

Bennett, B. (2013) 'The Importance of Aboriginal and Torres Strait Islander History for Social Work Students and Graduates' in B. Bennett, S. Green, S. Gilbert and D. Bessarab (eds) *Our Voices: Aboriginal and Torres Strait Islander Social Work*, South Yarra: Palgrave MacMillan.

Bennett, B., Zubrzycki, J. and Bacon, V. (2011) 'What Do We Know? The Experiences of Social Workers Working Alongside Aboriginal People', *Australian Social Work*, 64(1), pp. 20–37.

Beresford, P. and Croft, S. (1993) *Citizen Involvement: A Practical Guide for Change*, London: Palgrave Macmillan.

Bertotti, M., Harden, A., Renton, A. and Sheridan, K. (2011) 'The Contribution of a Social Enterprise to the Building of Social Capital in a Disadvantaged Urban Area of London', *Community Development Journal*, 47(2), pp. 168–183.

Besthorn, F. (2014) 'Environmental Social Work: A Future of Curiosity, Contemplation and Connection' in S. Hessle (ed.) *Environmental Change and Sustainable Social Development: Social Work-Social Development Volume II*, Farnham: Ashgate Publishing Ltd.

Besthorn, F. and Meyer, E. (2010) 'Environmentally Displaced Persons: Broadening Social Work's Helping Imperative', *Critical Social Work*, 11(3), pp. 123–138.

Bhaskar, R. (1978) *A Realist Theory of Science*, Brighton: Harvester Press.

Bisman, C. (2004) 'Social Work Values: The Moral Core of the Profession', *British Journal of Social Work*, 34(1), pp. 109–123.

Boal, A. (1979) *Theatre of the Oppressed*, New York: Theatre Communications Group Inc.

Bollens, S. (2000) 'Community Development in Democratic South Africa', *Community Development Journal*, 35(2), pp. 167–180.

Bond, P. (2005) *Elite Transition: From Apartheid to Neoliberalism in South Africa*, Scottsville: University of KwaZulu-Natal Press.

Bradley, K. (2012) 'Big Society and the National Citizen Service: Young People, Volunteering and Engagement with Charities c. 1900–1960' in A. Ishkanian and S. Szreter (eds) *The Big Society Debate: A New Agenda for Social Welfare?* Cheltenham, UK: Edward Elgar.

Brake, M. and Bailey, R. (eds) (1980) *Radical Social Work and Practice*, London: Edward Arnold.

Bratt, R.G. and Rohe, W.M. (2005) 'Challenges and Dilemmas Facing Community Development Corporations in the United States', *Community Development Journal*, 42(1), pp. 63–78.

Breuer, A., Landman, T. and Farquhar, D. (2014) 'Social Media and Protest Mobilisation: Evidence from the Tunisian Revolution', *Democratization*, doi: 10.1080/13510347.2014.885505.

Briskman, L. (2014) *Social Work with Indigenous Communities: A Human Rights Approach*, Second Edition, Annandale, NSW: Federation Press.

Broadhurst, K. and Mason, C. (2012) 'Social Work Beyond the VDU: Foregrounding Co-Presence in Situated Practice, Why Face-to-Face Practice Matters', *The British Journal of Social Work*, doi:10.1093/bjsw/bcs124.

Brookfield, S. (2009) 'The Concept of Critical Reflection: Promises and Contra-dictions', *European Journal of Social Work*, 12(3), pp. 293–304.

Brooks, A. (2013) 'Torture and Terror Post-9/11: The Role of Social Work in Respon-ding to Torture', *International Social Work*, doi: 10.1177/0020872813487932.

Brookes, N., Callaghan, L., Netten, A. and Fox, D. (2015) 'Personalisation and Innovation in a Cold Financial Climate', *British Journal of Social Work*, 45(1), pp. 86–103.

Brueggemann, W.G. (2013) 'History and Context for Community Practice in North America' in M. Weil (ed.) *The Handbook of Community Practice*, Second Edition, Thousand Oaks, CA: Sage Publications.

Buckley, H. (2008) 'Heading for Collision? Managerialism, Social Science, and the Irish Child Protection System' in K. Burns and D. Lynch (eds) *Child Protection and Welfare Social Work: Contemporary Themes and Practice Perspectives*, Dublin: A. & A. Farmar.

Bunyan, P. (2010) 'Broad-based Organizing in the UK: Reasserting the Centrality of Political Activity in Community Development', *Community Development Journal*, 45(1), pp. 111–127.

Bunyan, P. (2012) 'Partnership, the Big Society and Community Organizing: Between Romanticizing, Problematizing and Politicising Community', *Community Development Journal*, 48(1), pp. 119–133.

Burkett, I. (2011a) 'Organizing in the New Marketplace: Contradictions and Opportunities for Community Development Organizations in the Ashes of Neoliberalism', *Community Development Journal*, 46(Supplement 2), pp. 111–127.

Burkett, I. (2011b) 'Appreciating Assets: A New Report from the International Association for Community Development (IACD)', *Community Development Journal*, 46(4), pp. 573–578.

Butcher, H., Banks, S., Henderson, P. and Robertson, J. (2007) *Critical Community Practice*, Bristol: The Policy Press.

Caniglia, F. and Bourke, P. (2012) *Toolkit for Developing Place-based Responses to Disadvantage*, Queensland: UnitingCare Social Justice.

Caniglia, F. and Trotman, A. (2011) *A Silver Lining: Community Development, Crisis and Belonging*, Brisbane: Under 1 Roof.

Carey, M. (2009) '"It's a Bit Like Being a Robot or Working in a Factory": Does Braverman Help Explain the Experiences of State Social Workers in Britain Since 1971?' *Organization*, 16(4), pp. 505–527.

Centre for Social Justice and Community Action and National Coordinating Centre for Public Engagement (2012) *Community-based Participatory Research: A Guide to Ethical Principles and Practice*, Durham University: Authors, available online at www.dur.ac.uk/resources/beacon/CBPREthicsGuidewebNovember2012.pdf [Accessed 26 August 2014].

Chaskin, R. (2008) 'Resilience, Community and Resilient Communities: Conditioning Contexts and Collective Action', *Child Care in Practice*, 14(1), pp. 65–74.

Chaskin, R. (2013) 'Theories of Community' in M. Weil (ed.) *The Handbook of Community Practice*, Second Edition, Thousand Oaks, CA: Sage Publications.

Child Wise Australia (2014) available online at www.childwise.net [Accessed 24 September 2014].

Clarke, J. (2004) 'Dissolving the Public Realm? The Logics and Limits of Neo-liberalism', *Journal of Social Policy*, 33(1), pp. 27–48.

Cleaver, F. (2001) 'Institutions, Agency and the Limitations of Participatory Approaches to Development' in B. Cooke and U. Kothari (eds) *Participation: The New Tyranny?* London: Zed Books.

Collins, S. (2009) 'Some Critical Perspectives on Social Work and Collectives', *British Journal of Social Work Advance Access*, doi: 10.1093/bjsw/bcm097.

Commission for Social Care Inspection (2008) *See Me, Not Just the Dementia: Understanding People's Experiences of Living in a Care Home*, London: CSCI.

Community Development Project (1977) *Gilding the Ghetto: The State and the Poverty Experiments*, London: CDP Interproject Editorial Team.

Community Workers Co-operative (2008) *Towards Standards for Quality Community Work*, Galway: CWC.

Connelly, J. and Hayward, J. (2012) *The Withering of the Welfare State: Regression*, Basingstoke: Palgrave Macmillan.

Cook, B. and Kothari, U. (2001) *Participation: The New Tyranny?* London: Zed Books.

Cooper, J. (2013) 'The Munro Report Two Years On: Social Workers Find Little has Changed', *Community Care*, February 19.

Cornwall, A. (2008) 'Unpacking "Participation": Models, Meanings and Practices', *Community Development Journal*, 43(3), pp. 269–283.

Cornwall, A., Robins, S. and Von Lieres, B. (2011) *States of Citizenship: Contexts and Cultures of Public Engagement and Citizen Action*, University of Sussex, Brighton: Institute of Development Studies.

Corrigan, P. and Leonard, P. (1978) *Social Work Practice under Capitalism: A Marxist Approach*, London: Palgrave Macmillan.

Cortez, C. R. (2005) 'Rights and Citizenship of Indigenous Women in Chiapas: A History of Struggles, Fears and Hopes' in N. Kabeer (ed) *Inclusive Citizenship*, London: Zed Books.

Craig, G. (1989) 'Community Work and the State', *Community Development Journal*, 24(1), pp. 3–18.

Craig, G. (2005) 'Community Capacity-building: Definitions, Scope, Measurements and Critiques', *Paper to the OECD*, Prague, Czech Republic, 8 December, 2005.

Craig, G. (2007) 'Community Capacity-Building: Something Old, Something New...?', *Critical Social Policy*, 27(3), pp. 335–359.

Craig, G. (2010) 'Community Capacity Building: Critiquing the Concept in Different Policy Contexts' in S. Kenny and M. Clarke (eds) *Challenging Capacity Building: Comparative Perspectives*, Basingstoke: Palgrave Macmillan.

Craig, G., Mayo, M., Popple, K., Shaw, M. and Taylor, M. (2011) *The Community Development Reader: History, Themes and Issues*, Bristol: The Policy Press.

Crossley, N. and Ibrahim, J. (2012) 'Critical Mass, Social Networks and Collective Action: Exploring Student Political Worlds', *Sociology,* available online at http://soc.sagepub.com/content/early/2012/03/14/0038038511425560.

Crow, G. and Allan, G. (1994) *Community Life: An Introduction to Local Social Relations*, Hemel Hempstead: Harvester Wheatsheaf.

Cuthbert, D. and Quartly, M. (2012) '"Forced Adoption" in the Australian Story of National Regret and Apology', *Australian Journal of Politics and History*, 58(1), pp. 82–96.

Davies, K., Gray, M. and Webb, S.A. (2014) 'Putting the Parity into Service-user Participation: An Integrated Model of Social Justice', *International Journal of Social Welfare*, 23, pp. 119–127.

De Cruz, H., Gillingham, P. and Melendez, S. (2007) 'Reflexivity, its Meanings and Relevance for Social Work: A Critical Review of the Literature', *British Journal of Social Work*, 37(1), pp. 73–90.

DeFilippis, J., Fisher, R. and Shragge, E. (2006) 'Neither Romance nor Regulation: Re-evaluating Community', *International Journal of Urban and Regional Research*, 30(3), pp. 673–689.

Della Porta, D. and Diani, M. (2006) *Social Movements: An Introduction*, Oxford: Blackwell Publishing.

Denney, D. (2008) 'Risk and the Blair Legacy' in M. Powell (ed.) *Modernising the Welfare State: The Blair Legacy*, Bristol: The Policy Press.

Denzin, N. and Lincoln, Y. (2003) *The Landscape of Qualitative Research: Theories and Issues*, Second Edition, Thousand Oaks, CA: Sage Publications.

Desai, M. and Solas, J. (2012) 'Poverty, Development and Social Justice' in K. Lyons, T. Hokenstad, M. Pawar, N. Huegler and N. Hall (eds) *The SAGE Handbook of International Social Work*, London: Sage Publications.

De Wan, J. (2010) 'The Practice of Politics: Feminism, Activism and Social Change in Ireland' in J. Hogan, Paul F. Donnelly and Brendan K. O'Rourke (eds) *Irish*

Business and Society: Governing, Participating and Transforming in the 21st Century, Dublin: Gill and Macmillan.

Dickens, J. (2011) 'Social Work in England at a Watershed – As Always: From the Seebohm Report to the Social Work Task Force', *British Journal of Social Work*, 41(1), pp. 22–39.

Dominelli, L. (2002) *Anti-Oppressive Social Work Theory and Practice*, Basingstoke: Palgrave MacMillan.

Dominelli, L. (2004a) *Social Work: Theory and Practice for a Changing Profession*, Cambridge: Polity Press.

Dominelli, L. (2004b) 'Practising Social Work in a Globalizing World' in N. Tan and A. Rowlands (eds) *Social Work Around the World III*, Berne, Switzerland: International Federation of Social Workers Press.

Dominelli, L. (2009) 'Anti-Oppressive Practice: The Challenges of the Twenty-First Century' in R. Adams, L. Dominelli and M. Payne (eds) *Social Work: Themes, Issues and Critical Debates*, Third Edition, Basingstoke: Palgrave MacMillan.

Dominelli, L. (2010a) *Social Work in a Globalizing World*, Cambridge: Polity Press.

Dominelli, L. (2010b) 'Globalization, Contemporary Challenges and Social Work Practice', *International Social Work*, 53(5), pp. 599–612.

Dominelli, L. (2012a) *Green Social Work: From Environmental Crises to Environmental Justice*, Cambridge, MA: Polity Press.

Dominelli, L. (2012b) 'Globalisation and Indigenisation: Reconciling the Irreconcilable in Social Work?' in K. Lyons, T. Hokenstad, M. Pawar, N. Huegler and N. Hall (eds) *The SAGE Handbook of International Social Work*, London: Sage Publications.

Dominelli, L. (2013) 'Environmental Justice at the Heart of Social Work Practice: Greening the Profession', *International Journal of Social Welfare*, 22, pp. 431–439.

Dominelli, L. (2014) 'Promoting Environmental Justice through Green Social Work Practice: A Key Challenge for Practitioners and Educators', *International Social Work*, 57(4), pp. 338–345.

Donnelly, L. (2008) 'Thousands of Elderly Abused in Care Homes', *Daily Telegraph*, 4 May.

Ennis, G. and West, D. (2013) 'Community Development and Umbrella Bodies: Networking for Neighbourhood Change', *British Journal of Social Work Advance Access*, doi: 10.1093/bjsw/bct010.

Eriksson, L. (2011) 'Community Development and Social Pedagogy: Traditions for Understanding Mobilization for Collective Self-Development', *Community Development Journal*, 46(4), pp. 403–420.

Eriksson, L. (2013) 'The Understandings of Social Pedagogy from Northern European Perspectives', *Journal of Social Work*, doi: 10.1177/1468017313477325.

Evans, T. (2013) 'Organisational Rules and Discretion in Adult Social Work', *British Journal of Social Work*, 43, pp. 739–758.

Eversole, R. (2013) 'Social Enterprises as Local Development Actors', *Local Economy*, 28(6), pp. 567–579.

Eversole, R., Barraket, J. and Luke, B. (2013) 'Social Enterprises in Rural Community Development', *Community Development Journal*, doi: 10.1093/cdj/bst030.

Fawcett, B. (2009) 'Post-modernism' in M. Gray and S.A. Webb (eds) *Social Work Theories and Methods*, First Edition, London: Sage Publications.

Fell, B. and Fell, P. (2014) 'Welfare Across Borders: A Social Work Process with Adult Asylum Seekers', *British Journal of Social Work*, 44, pp. 1322–1339.

Ferguson, H. (2008) 'Liquid Social Work: Welfare Interventions as Mobile Practices', *British Journal of Social Work*, 38(3), pp. 561–579.

Ferguson, H. (2014) 'Envisioning Social Work by Putting the Life back into it: Learning about What Social Workers do and How They Do it (Well)', *Keynote Speech to JSWEC 'Social Work Making Connections' Conference, 23–25 July, 2014*, Royal Holloway: University of London.

Ferguson, I. (2007) 'Increasing User Choice or Privatizing Risk? The Antinomies of Personalization', *British Journal of Social Work*, 37(3), pp. 387–403.

Ferguson, I. (2008) *Reclaiming Social Work: Challenging Neo-liberalism and Promoting Social Justice*, London: Sage Publications.

Ferguson, I. and Lavalette, M. (2005) '"Another World is Possible": Social Work and the Struggle for Social Justice' in I. Ferguson, M. Lavalette and E. Whitmore (eds) *Globalisation, Global Justice and Social Work*, London: Routledge.

Ferguson, I. and Smith, L. (2012) 'Education for Change: Student Placements in Campaigning Organisations and Social Movements in South Africa', *British Journal of Social Work*, 42, pp. 974–994.

Ferguson, I. and Woodward, R. (2009) *Radical Social Work in Practice: Making a Difference*, Bristol: The Policy Press.

Fitzpatrick, J. (1997) 'In Whose Interests? Community Work, the State and Political Change' in M. Shaw, J. Meagher and S. Moir (eds) *Participation in Community Development: Problems and Possibilities, A Concept Reader in Collaboration with the Community Development Journal*, Edinburgh: Concept.

Fook, J. (2001) 'Identifying Expert Social Work' in I. Shaw and N. Gould (eds) *Qualitative Research in Social Work*, London: Sage Publications.

Fook, J. (2012) *Social Work: A Critical Approach to Practice*, London: Sage Publications.

Fook, J. and Gardner, F. (2007) *Practising Critical Reflection: A Resource Handbook*, Maidenhead: McGraw-Hill Education.

Forde, C. (2009) 'The Politics of Community Development: Relationship with the State' in C. Forde, E. Kiely and R. Meade (eds) *Youth and Community Work in Ireland: Critical Perspectives*, Dublin: Blackhall Publishing.

Forde, C. and Lynch, D. (2014) 'Critical Practice for Challenging Times: Social Workers' Engagement with Community Work', *British Journal of Social Work*, 44(8), pp. 2078–2094.

Foucault, M. (1980) *Power/Knowledge: Selected Interviews and Other Writings, 1972–1977*, New York: Pantheon Books.

Francis, P. (2001) 'Participatory Development at the World Bank: The Primacy of Process' in B. Cooke and U. Kothari (eds) *Participation: The New Tyranny?* London: Zed Books.

Francis, R. (2010) *Independent Inquiry into Care Provided by Mid Staffordshire NHS Foundation Trust January 2005 – March 2009, Volume I*, London: The Stationery Office.

Fraser, H. and Briskman, L. (2005) 'Through the Eye of the Needle: The Challenge of Getting Justice in Australia if You're Indigenous or Seeking Asylum' in I. Ferguson, M. Lavalette and E. Whitmore (eds) *Globalisation, Global Justice and Social Work*, London: Routledge.

Freire, P. (1997) *Pedagogy of the Oppressed*, New York: Continuum.

Freire, P. (2005) *Education for Critical Consciousness*, New York: Continuum.

Fremeaux, I. (2005) 'New Labour's Appropriation of the Concept of Community: A Critique', *Community Development Journal*, 40(3), pp. 265–274.

Fung, A. and Olin Wright, E. (2003) *Deepening Democracy: Institutional Innovations in Empowered Participatory Democracy*, London: Verso.

Gal, J. and Weiss-Gal, I. (2013) 'The "Why" and "How" of Policy Practice: An Eight Country Comparison', *British Journal of Social Work Advance Access*, doi: 10.1093/bjsw/bct179.

Galper, J. (1975) *The Politics of Social Services*, Englewood Cliffs, NJ: Prentice Hall.

Gamble, D.M. and Hoff, M.D. (2013) 'Sustainable Community Development' in M. Weil (ed.) *The Handbook of Community Practice*, Second Edition, Los Angeles: Sage Publications.

Gamble, D. and Weil, M. (2010) *Community Practice Skills: Local to Global Perspectives*, New York: Columbia University Press.

Gane, N. (2001) 'Zigmunt Baumann – Liquid Modernity and Beyond', *Acta Sociologica*, 44(3), pp. 267–275.

Garrett, P.M. (2012) 'Re-Enchanting Social Work? The Emerging "Spirit" of Social Work in an Age of Economic Crisis', *British Journal of Social Work*, doi: 10.1093/bjsw/bcs146.

Garrett, P.M. (2013) 'Active Equality: Jacques Ranciere's Contribution to Social Work's "New Left"', *British Journal of Social Work Advance Access*, doi: 10.1093/bjsw/bct188.

Gee, T. (2011) *Counterpower: Making Change Happen*, Oxford: New Internationalist Publications Ltd.

Geoghegan, M. and Powell, F. (2006) 'Community Development, Partnership Governance and Dilemmas of Professionalisation: Profiling and Assessing the Case of Ireland', *British Journal of Social Work*, 36, pp. 845–861.

Germov, J. (2005) 'Managerialism in the Australian Public Health Sector: Towards the Hyper-Rationalisation of Professional Bureaucracies', *Sociology of Health and Illness*, 27(6), pp. 738–758.

Giddens, A. (1991) *Modernity and Self Identity*, Stanford: Stanford University Press.

Gilchrist, A. (2003) 'Community Development in the UK – Possibilities and Paradoxes', *Community Development Journal*, 38(1), pp. 16–25.

Gilchrist, A. (2009) *The Well Connected Community: A Networking Approach to Community Development*, Second Edition, Bristol: The Policy Press.

Gilchrist, A. and Taylor, M. (2011) *The Short Guide to Community Development*, Bristol: The Policy Press.

Giovannini, M. (2014) 'Indigenous Community Enterprises in Chiapas: A Vehicle for Buen Vivir?', *Community Development Journal*, doi: 10.1093/cdj/bsu019.

Goldenberg, S., Gambino, L., Carrington, D., Randerson, J., Mathieson, K. and Milman, O. (2014) 'Climate Change Marches: Kerry Cites Fight against Ebola and Isis as Thousands Join Protests', 22 September, *The Guardian*, available online at http://www.theguardian.com/environment/2014/sep/21/-sp-climate-change-protest-melbourne-london-new-york-protest [Accessed 23 September 2014].

Goldsworthy, J. (2002) 'Resurrecting a Model of Integrating Individual Work with Community Development and Social Action', *Community Development Journal*, 37(4), pp. 327–337.

Gorski, P. (2013) 'What is Critical Realism? And Why Should You Care?', *Contemporary Sociology: A Journal of Reviews*, 42, pp. 658–669.

Grant-Smith, D. and Matthews, T. (2015) 'Cork as Canvas: Exploring Intersections of Citizenship and Collective Memory in the Shandon *Big Wash Up* Murals', *Community Development Journal*, 50(1), pp. 138–152.

Gray, M. and Lombard, A. (2007) 'The Post-1994 Transformation of Social Work in South Africa', *International Journal of Social Welfare*, 17, pp. 132–145, doi: 10.1111/j.1468-2397.2007.00545.x.

Gray, M., Stepney, P. and Webb, S. (2012) 'Critical Social Work' in P. Stepney and D. Ford (eds) *Social Work Models, Methods and Theories: A Framework for Practice*, Second Edition, Lyme Regis: Russell House Publishing.

Gray, M. and Webb, S. (2008) 'Critical Social Work' in M. Gray and S. Webb (eds) *Social Work Theories and Methods*, First Edition, London: Sage Publications.

Green, D. and McDermott, F. (2010) 'Social Work from Inside and Between Complex Systems: Perspectives on Person-in-Environment for Today's Social Work', *British Journal of Social Work*, 40(8), pp. 2414–2430.

Green, J.J. (2008) 'Community Development as Social Movement: A Contribution to Models of Practice', *Community Development*, 39(1), pp. 50–62.

Griffith, T., Connor, T., Robertson, B. and Phelan, L. (2013) 'Is Mayfield Pool Saved Yet? Community Assets and Their Contingent, Discursive Foundations', *Community Development Journal*, 49(2), pp. 280–294.

Gunn, N. (2006) 'Community Development and Participative Democracy: Constraints and Challenges' in M. Shaw, J. Meagher and S. Moir (eds) *Participation in Community Development: Problems and Possibilities, A Concept Reader in Collaboration with the Community Development Journal*, Edinburgh: Concept.

Gwyther, G. (2000) 'Social Capital and Communitarianism', *Sociological Sites/Sights*, TASA, Adelaide: Flinders University.

Hallstedt, P. and Hogstrom, M. (2009) 'Social Care: A European Perspective' in P. Share and K. Lalor (eds) *Applied Social Care: An Introduction for Students in Ireland*, Dublin: Gill and Macmillan.

Hansen, C. (2013) 'Exploring Dimensions of Critical Reflection in Activist-Facilitator Practice', *Journal of Transformative Education*, 11(1), pp. 70–89.

Hardwick, L. and Worsley, A. (2011) 'The Invisibility of Practitioner Research', *Practice: Social Work in Action*, 23(3), pp. 135–146.

Harlow, E. (2003) 'New Managerialism, Social Service Departments and Social Work Practice Today', *Practice*, 15(2), pp. 29–44.

Harlow, E., Berg, E., Barry, J. and Chandler, J. (2012) 'Neoliberalism, Managerialism and the Reconfiguring of Social Work in Sweden and the United Kingdom', *Organization*, doi: 10.1177/1350508412448222, pp. 1–17.

Harris, J. (2008) 'State Social Work: Constructing the Present from Moments in the Past', *British Journal of Social Work*, 38, pp. 662–679.

Harrison, D. (2009) 'Social Work's Evolution in the United Kingdom: A Study of Community Care and Social Control', *Families in Society*, 90(3), pp. 336–342.

Harrison, G. and Melville, R. (2010) *Rethinking Social Work in a Global World*, Basingstoke: Palgrave Macmillan.

Harvey, D. (2005) *A Brief History of Neoliberalism*, Oxford: Oxford University Press.

Harvey, D., Plummer, D., Pighills, A. and Pain, T. (2013) 'Practitioner Research Capacity: A Survey of Social Workers in Northern Queensland', *Australian Social Work*, 66(4), pp. 540–554.

Hawkins, R. and Maurer, K. (2010) 'Bonding, Bridging and Linking: How Social Capital Operated in New Orleans Following Hurricane Katrina', *British Journal of Social Work*, 40(6), pp. 1777–1793.

Hawkins, R. and Maurer, K. (2012) 'Unravelling Social Capital: Disentangling a Concept of Social Work', *British Journal of Social Work*, 42(2), pp. 353–370.

Hawtin, M. and Percy-Smith, J. (2007) *Community Profiling: A Practical Guide*, Buckingham: Open University Press.

Hay, C. (2004) 'The Normalizing Role of Rationalist Assumptions in the Institutional Embedding of Neoliberalism', *Economy and Society*, 33(4), pp. 500–527.

Hay, C. and Wincott, D. (2012) *The Political Economy of European Welfare Capitalism*, Basingstoke: Palgrave Macmillan.

Hayward, J. (2012) 'From Citizen Solidarity to Self-Serving Inequality: Social Solidarity, Market Economy and Welfare Statecraft' in J. Connelly and J. Hayward (eds) *The Withering of the Welfare State: Regression*, Basingstoke: Palgrave Macmillan.

Health Service Executive (2009) HSE Elder Abuse Service Developments 2008, Dublin: HSE.

Healy, K. (2000) *Social Work Practices: Contemporary Perspectives on Change,* London: Sage Publications.

Healy, K. (2005) *Social Work Theories in Context: Creating Frameworks for Practice*, Basingstoke: Palgrave Macmillan.

Healy, K. (2012) *Social Work Methods and Skills: The Essential Foundations of Practice*, Basingstoke: Palgrave Macmillan.

Healy, K. and Meagher, J. (2004) 'The Reprofessionalization of Social Work: Collaborative Approaches for Achieving Professional Recognition', *British Journal of Social Work*, 34(2), pp. 243–260.

Henderson, P. and Glen, A. (2006) 'From Recognition to Support: Community Development Workers in the United Kingdom', *Community Development Journal*, 41(3), pp. 277–292.

Henkel, H. and Stirrat, R. (2001) 'Participation as Spiritual Duty; Empowerment as Secular Subjection' in B. Cooke and U. Kothari (eds) *Participation: The New Tyranny?* London: Zed Books.

Henriques, P. and Tuckley, G. (2012) 'Ecological Systems Theory and Direct Work with Children and Families' in P. Stepney and D. Ford (eds) *Social Work Models, Methods and Theories: A Framework for Practice*, Second Edition, Lyme Regis: Russell House Publishing.

Hessle, S. (2014) *Environmental Change and Sustainable Social Development: Social Work-Social Development Volume II*, Farnham: Ashgate Publishing Ltd.

Hick, S. and Murray, K. (2008) 'Structural Social Work' in M. Gray and S. Webb (eds) *Social Work Theories and Methods*, First Edition, London: Sage Publications.

Higgins, M. and Goodyer, A. (2014) 'The Contradictions of Contemporary Social Work: An Ironic Response', *British Journal of Social Work*, doi: 10.1093/bjsw/bcu019, pp. 1–14.

Higgins, M., Popple, K. and Crichton, N. (2014) 'The Dilemmas of Contemporary Social Work: A Case Study of the Social Work Degree in England', *British Journal of Social Work*, doi: 1093/bjsw/bcu142, pp. 1–16.

Hodgson, L. (2004) 'Manufactured Civil Society: Counting the Cost', *Critical Social Policy*, 24(2), pp. 139–164.

Hokenstad, T. (2012) 'Social Work Education: The International Dimension' in K. Lyons, T. Hokenstad, M. Pawar, N. Huegler and N. Hall (eds) *The SAGE Handbook of International Social Work*, London: Sage Publications.

Hope, A. and Timmel, S. (1984) *Training for Transformation*, Zimbabwe: Mambo Press.

Houston, S. (2001) 'Beyond Social Constructionism: Critical Realism and Social Work', *British Journal of Social Work*, 31, pp. 845–861.

Houston, S. (2010a) 'Beyond *Homo Economicus*: Recognition, Self-Realisation and Social Work', *British Journal of Social Work*, 40(3), pp. 841–857.

Houston, S. (2010b) 'Prising Open the Black Box: Critical Realism, Action Research and Social Work', *Qualitative Social Work*, 9(1), pp. 73–91.

Houston, S. (2014) 'Beyond Individualism: Social Work and Social Identity', *British Journal of Social Work*, doi: 10.1093/bjsw/bcu097.

Houston, S., Skehill, C., Pinkerton, J. and Campbell, J. (2005) 'Prying Open Spaces for Social Work in the New Millennium: Four Theoretical Perspectives on Transformative Practice', *Social Work and Social Sciences Review*, 12(1), pp. 35–52.

Huegler, N., Lyons, K. and Pawar, M. (2012) 'Setting the Scene' in K. Lyons, T. Hokenstad, M. Pawar, N. Huegler and N. Hall (eds) *The SAGE Handbook of International Social Work*, London: Sage Publications.

Humphries, B. (1997) 'Reading Social Work Competing Discourses in the Rules and Requirements for the Diploma in Social Work, *British Journal of Social Work*, 27, pp. 641–658.

Humphries, B. (2008) *Social Work Research for Social Justice*, Basingstoke: Palgrave Macmillan.

International Association for Community Development (2011) *Strategic Plan 2011–2015: Sustainable Community Development for Global Justice*, Lisboa: IACD.

Ife, J. (1997) *Rethinking Social Work: Towards Critical Practice*, Frenchs Forest, NSW: Pearson Education.

Ife, J. (2002) *Community Development*, Frenchs Forest, NSW: Pearson Education.

Ife, J. (2010) *Human Rights from Below: Achieving Rights through Community Development*, Cambridge: Cambridge University Press.

Ife, J. (2013) *Community Development in an Uncertain World: Vision, Analysis and Practice*, Cambridge: Cambridge University Press.

Ife, J. and Fiske, L. (2006) 'Human Rights and Community Work: Complementary Theories and Practices', *International Social Work*, 49(3), pp. 297–308.

Ingamells, A., Lathouras, A., Wiseman, R., Westoby, P. and Caniglia, F. (2010) *Community Development Practice: Stories, Method and Meaning*, Australia: Common Ground Publishing Pty Ltd.

International Federation of Social Workers (2013) *Statement of Ethical Principles*, available online at www.ifsw.org/policies/statement-of-ethical-principles/ [Accessed 8 December 2013].

International Federation of Social Workers (2014) 'Definition of Social Work', available online at http://ifsw.org/policies/definition-of-social-work/ [Accessed 15 September 2014].

International Federation of Social Workers, International Association of Schools of Social Work and the International Council on Social Welfare (2012) *Global Agenda for Social Work and Social Development: A Commitment for Action*, available online at www.cdnifsw.org/assets/globalagenda2012.pdf [Accessed 11 September 2014].

Ishkanian, A. and Szreter, S. (2012) *The Big Society Debate: A New Agenda for Social Welfare?* Cheltenham, UK: Edward Elgar.

James, I. (2012) *The New French Philosophy*, Cambridge: Polity Press.

Jani, J.S., Ortiz, L., Pierce, D. and Sowbel, L. (2011) 'Access to Intersectionality, Content to Competence: Deconstructing Social Work Education Diversity Standards', *Journal of Social Work Education,* 47(2), pp. 283–301.

Jani, J.S. and Reisch, M. (2011) 'Common Human Needs, Uncommon Solutions: Applying a Critical Framework to Perspectives on Human Behaviour', *Families in Society: The Journal of Contemporary Social Services,* doi: 10.1606/1044-3894.4065.

Jennings, A. (2002) 'Local People Rebuilding Local Economies', *Community Development Journal,* 37(4), pp. 300–315.

Johansson, H. and Hvinden, B. (2007) 'Nordic Activation Reforms in a European Context: A Distinct Universalistic Model?' in B. Hvinden and H. Johansson (eds) *Citizenship in Nordic Welfare States: Dynamics of Choice, Duties and Participation in a Changing Europe*, Abingdon: Routledge.

Johansson, S. (2012) 'Who Runs the Mill? The Distribution of Power in Swedish Social Service Agencies', *European Journal of Social Work,* 15(5), pp. 679–695.

Jones, C., Ferguson, I., Lavalette, M. and Penketh, L. (2006) 'Social Work and Social Justice: A Manifesto for New Engaged Practice, available online at www.liv.ac.uk/sspsw/SocialWorkManifesto.html.

Jones, D., Johannesen, T. and Dodds, I. (2004) 'International Social Work, Globalization and the Environment' in N. Tan and A. Rowlands (eds) *Social Work Around the World III*, Berne: IFSW Press.

Jones, M. (2012) 'Research-minded Practice in Social Work' in P. Stepney and D. Ford (eds) *Social Work Models, Methods and Theories: A Framework for Practice,* Second Edition, Lyme Regis: Russell House Publishing.

Jones, P. (2010) 'Responding to the Ecological Crisis: Transformative Pathways for Social Work Education', *Journal of Social Work Education,* 46(1), pp. 67–84.

Jones, R. (2014) 'The Best of Times, the Worst of Times: Social Work and its Moment', *British Journal of Social Work,* 44(3), pp. 485–502.

Jordan, B. and Drakeford, M. (2012) *Social Work and Social Policy under Austerity,* Basingstoke: Palgrave Macmillan.

Joseph, J. (2010) 'Foucault and Reality' in W. Olsen (ed) *Realist Methodology,* London: Sage Publications.

Kaplan, A. (2002) *Development Practitioners and Social Process: Artists of the Invisible,* London: Pluto Press.

Kenny, S. (1996) 'Contestations of Community Development in Australia', *Community Development Journal,* 31(2), pp. 104–113.

Kenny, S. and Clarke, M. (2010) *Challenging Capacity Building: Comparative Perspectives*, Basingstoke: Palgrave Macmillan.

Kenny, S., Fanany, I. and Rahayu, S. (2013) 'Community Development in Indonesia: Westernization or Doing it Their Way?', *Community Development Journal*, 48(2), pp. 280–297.

Kuecker, G., Mulligan, M. and Nadarajah, Y. (2011) 'Turning to Community in Times of Crisis: Globally Derived Insights on Local Community Formation', *Community Development Journal*, 46(2), pp. 245–264.

Kullberg, K. (2013) 'From Glass Escalator to Glass Travelator: On the Proportion of Men in Managerial Positions in Social Work in Sweden', *British Journal of Social Work*, 43(8), pp. 1492–1509.

Laenui, P (2007) 'Welcome Remarks', Paper presented at the 'Indigenous Voices in Social Work: Not Lost in Translation', First Indigenous Social Work Conference, Makaha Resort, Oahu, Hawaii, 4–7 June 2007.

Landvogt, K. (2012) 'Poverty Finds a Voice: Dialogic Learning and Research through Theatre in Melbourne' in L. Shevallar and P. Westoby (eds) *Learning and Mobilising for Community Development: A Radical Tradition of Community-based Education and Training*, Aldershot: Ashgate Publishing Ltd.

Lathouras, A. (2010) 'Developmental Community Work – A Method' in A. Ingamells, A. Lathouras, R. Wiseman, P. Westoby and F. Caniglia (eds) *Community Development Practice: Stories, Method and Meaning*, Australia: Common Ground Publishing Pty Ltd.

Lathouras, T. (2013) 'The Power of Structural Community Development to Unlock Citizen-Led Change', The Les Halliwell Address, *Queensland Community Development Conference*, Deception Bay, Queensland, 31 October 2013.

Lavalette, M. (2011) *Radical Social Work Today: Social Work at the Crossroads*, Bristol: The Policy Press.

Lavalette, M. (2013) 'Popular Social Work, Official Social Work and Social Movements', *Socialno Delo*, 52(2–3), pp. 113–127.

Lavalette, M. and Ioakimidis, V. (2011) 'International Social Work or Social Work Internationalism? Radical Social Work in Global Perspective' in M. Lavalette (ed.) *Radical Social Work Today: Social Work at the Crossroads*, Bristol: The Policy Press.

Lawler, J. and Harlow, E. (2005) 'Postmodernization: A Phase We're going through? Management in Social Care', *British Journal of Social Work*, 35, pp. 1163–1174.

Ledwith, M. (2001) 'Community Work as Critical Pedagogy: Re-envisioning Freire and Gramsci', *Community Development Journal*, 36(3), pp. 171–182.

Ledwith, M. (2005) *Community Development: A Critical Approach*, Bristol: The Policy Press.

Ledwith, M. (2007) 'Reclaiming the Radical Agenda: A Critical Approach to Community Development', *Concept*, 17(2), pp. 8–13.

Ledwith, M. (2011) *Community Development: A Critical Approach*, Second Edition, Bristol: The Policy Press.

Ledwith, M. and Springett, J. (2010) *Participatory Practice: Community-based Action for Transformative Change*, Bristol: The Policy Press.

Lee, J. (1994) *The Empowerment Approach to Social Work Practice*, New York: Columbia University Press.

Lee, S. and Woodward, R. (2012) 'From Financing Social Insurance to Insuring Financial Markets: The Socialisation of Risk and the Privatisation of Profit in an

Age of Irresponsibility' in J. Connelly and J. Hayward (eds) *The Withering of the Welfare State: Regression*, Basingstoke: Palgrave Macmillan.

Lenette, C., Cox, L. and Brough, M. (2013) 'Digital Storytelling as a Social Work Tool: Learning from Ethnographic Research with Women from Refugee Backgrounds', *British Journal of Social Work Advance Access*, doi: 10.1093/bjsw/bct184, pp. 1–18.

Lenette, C. and Ingamells, A. (2014) 'Mind the Gap! The Growing Chasm between Funding-driven Agencies, and Social and Community Knowledge and Practice', *Community Development Journal*, doi: 10.1093/cdj/bsu024.

Leonard, L. (2007) 'Towards an Understanding of a Territorial Resource Dispute: The "Shell to Sea" Campaign in North Mayo', *Irish Journal of Sociology*, 16(1), pp. 80–96.

Leung, T.T.F., Yip, N.M., Huang, R. and Wu, Y. (2012) 'Governmentality and the Politicisation of Social Work in China', *British Journal of Social Work*, 42(6), pp. 1039–1059.

Leung, Z., Lam, C., Yau, T. and Chu, W. (2010) "Re-empowering Social Workers through the Online Community: The Experience of SWForum in Hong Kong', *Critical Social Policy*, 30, pp. 48–73.

Levin, I. (2010) 'Discourses within and about Social Work', in L. Dominelli (ed.) *Revitalising Communities in a Globalising World*, Aldershot: Ashgate Publishing Ltd.

Levin, L., Goor, Y. and Tayri, M. (2013) 'Agency Advocacy and Organisational Development: A Feasible Policy Practice Alliance', *British Journal of Social Work*, 43, pp. 522–541.

Lingam, L. (2013) 'Development Theories and Community Development Practice: Trajectory of Change' in M. Weil (ed.) *The Handbook of Community Practice*, Second edition, Thousand Oaks, CA: Sage Publications.

Lloyd, A. (2010) 'The Will of the State and the Resilience of the Community Sector in a Time of Crisis: Obliteration, Compliance or an Opportunity for Renewal?' *Working for Change: The Irish Journal of Community Work*, 2, pp. 44–63.

Lonne, B., Harries, M. and Lantz, S. (2012) 'Workforce Development: A Pathway to Reforming Child Protection Systems in Australia', *British Journal of Social Work*, doi: 10.1093/bjsw/bcs064, pp. 1–19.

Lopez, M. (2000) *The Origins of Multiculturalism in Australian Politics 1945–1975*, Melbourne: Melbourne University Press.

Lorenz, W. (2001) 'Social Work Responses to "New Labour" in Continental European Countries', *British Journal of Social Work*, 31(4), pp. 595–609.

Lorenz, W. (2006) *Perspectives on European Social Work: From the Birth of the Nation State to the Impact of Globalisation*, Opladen: Barbara Budrich Publishers.

Lorenz, W. (2008) 'Towards a European Model of Social Work', *Australian Social Work*, 61(1), pp. 7–24.

Loughran, H. and McCann, M. (2013) 'Employing Community Participative Research Methods to Advance Service User Collaboration in Social Work Research', *British Journal of Social Work Advance Access*, doi: 10.1093/bjsw/bct113.

Louis, W.R., Duck, J.M., Terry, D.J. and Lalonde, R.N. (2010) 'Speaking Out on Immigration Policy in Australia: Identity Threat and the Interplay of Own Opinion and Public Opinion', *Journal of Social Issues,* 66(4), pp. 653–672.

Lovett, T. (1995) *Community Development, Education and Community Relations,* Jordanstown: Community Research and Development Centre, University of Ulster at Jordanstown.

Lundy, C. and Van Wormer, K. (2007) 'Social and Economic Justice, Human Rights and Peace: The Challenge for Social Work in Canada and the USA', *International Social Work,* 50, pp. 727–739.

Lymbery, M. (2010) 'A New Vision for Adult Social Care? Continuities and Change in the Care of Older People', *Critical Social Policy,* 30(1), pp. 5–26.

Lymbery, M. (2012a) 'Social Work and Personalisation', *British Journal of Social Work,* 42(4), pp. 783–792.

Lymbery, M. (2012b) 'Social Work and Personalisation: Fracturing the Bureau-Professional Compact?' *British Journal of Social Work,* 44(4), pp. 795–811.

Lymbery, M. (2014) 'Austerity, Personalisation and Older People: The Prospects for Creative Social Work Practice in England', *European Journal of Social Work,* 17(3), pp. 367–382.

Lynch, D. and Burns, K. (2008) 'Introduction: Contexts, Themes and Future Directions in Irish Child Protection and Welfare Social Work' in K. Burns and D. Lynch (eds) *Child Protection and Welfare Social Work: Contemporary Themes and Practice Perspectives,* Dublin: A. & A. Farmar.

Lynch, D. and Forde, C. (2006) 'Social Work within a Community Discourse: Challenges for Teaching', *Social Work Education,* 25(8), pp. 851–862.

MacLeod, J. and Byrne, C. (2012) 'It's Only a Garden! A Journey from Community Building to Community Organising and Back Again', *New Community Quarterly,* 10(38), pp. 36–44.

McDonald, C. and Chenoweth, L. (2009) '(Re)Shaping Social Work: An Australian Case Study', *British Journal of Social Work,* 39, pp. 144–160.

McGhee, J. and Waterhouse, L. (2011) 'Locked Out of Prevention? The Identity of Child and Family-Oriented Social Work in Scottish Post-Devolution Policy', *British Journal of Social Work,* 41(6), pp. 1088–1104.

McMaster, K. (2004) 'Facilitating Change through Group Work' in J. Maidment and R. Egan (eds) *Practice Skills in Social Work and Welfare,* Crows Nest: Allen and Unwin.

McMenamin, B. (2003) 'Global Actions to Prevent Child Exploitation: The ECPAT Experience' in W. Weeks, W.L. Hoatson and J. Dixon (eds) *Community Practices in Australia,* Frenchs Forest: Pearson Education Australia.

Mandell, J. (2010) 'Picnics, Participation and Power: Linking Community Building to Social Change', *Community Development,* 41(2), pp. 269–282.

Manthorpe, J., Stevens, M., Hussein, S., Neath, H. and Lievesley, N. (2011) *The Abuse, Neglect and Mistreatment of Older People in Care Homes and Hospitals in England: Observations on the Potential for Secondary Data Analysis,* London: Department of Health.

Mantle, G. and Backwith, D. (2010) 'Poverty and Social Work', *British Journal of Social Work,* 40, pp. 2380–2397.

Marston, G. and McDonald, C. (2012) 'Getting Beyond "Heroic Agency" in Conceptualising Social Workers as Policy Actors in the Twenty-first Century', *British Journal of Social Work,* 42(6), pp. 1022–1038.

Martin, D.G., Hanson, S. and Fontaine, D. (2007) 'What Counts as Activism? The Role of Individuals in Creating Change', *Women's Studies Quarterly,* 35(3/4), pp. 78–94.

Martin, G. (2001) 'Social Movements, Welfare and Social Policy: A Critical Analysis', *Critical Social Policy,* 21(3), pp. 361–383.

Marx, G. and McAdam, D. (1994) *Collective Behaviour and Social Movements,* Englewood Cliffs: Prentice-Hall.

Mayo, M. (1974) 'Community Development: A Radical Alternative?' in G. Craig, K. Popple, M. Mayo, M. Shaw and M. Taylor (eds) *The Community Development Reader: History, Themes and Issues,* Bristol: Policy Press.

Mayo, M. (1994) *Communities and Caring: The Mixed Economy of Welfare,* Basingstoke: Palgrave Macmillan.

Mayo, M. (2002) 'Community Work' in R. Adams, L. Dominelli and M. Payne (eds.) *Social Work: Themes, Issues and Critical Debates,* Second Edition, Basingstoke: Macmillan.

Mayo, M. (2005) *Global Citizens: Social Movements and the Challenge of Globalisation,* London: Zed Books.

Mayo, M. (2009) 'Community Work' in R. Adams, L. Dominelli and M. Payne (eds) *Social Work: Themes, Issues and Critical Debates,* Second Edition, Basingstoke: Palgrave Macmillan.

Meade, R. (2009) 'Community Development: A Critical Analysis' in C. Forde, E. Kiely and R. Meade (eds) *Youth and Community Work in Ireland: Critical Perspectives,* Dublin: Blackhall Publishing.

Meagher, J. (2006) 'Participation: Problems, Paradoxes and Possibilities' in M. Shaw, J. Meagher and S. Moir (eds) *Participation in Community Development: Problems and Possibilities. A Concept Reader in Collaboration with the Community Development Journal,* Edinburgh: Concept.

Mendes, P. (2005) 'The History of Social Work in Australia: A Critical Literature Review', *Australian Social Work,* 58(2), pp. 121–127.

Mendes, P. (2007) 'Social Workers and Social Activism in Victoria, Australia', *Journal of Progressive Human Services,* 18(1), pp. 25–44.

Mendes, P. (2008a) 'Teaching Community Development to Social Work Students: A Critical Reflection', *Community Development Journal,* 44(2), pp. 248–262.

Mendes, P. (2008b) 'Integrating Social Work and Community Development Practice in Victoria, Australia', *Asia Pacific Journal of Social Work and Development,* 18(1), pp. 14–25.

Mendes, P. (2009) 'Retrenching or Renovating the Australian Welfare State: The Paradox of the Howard Government's Neo-liberalism', *International Journal of Social Welfare,* 18(1), pp. 102–110.

Mendes, P. and Binns, F. (2012) 'The Integration of Community Development Values, Skills and Strategies within Rural Social Work Practice in Victoria, Australia', *Community Development Journal,* 48(4), pp. 605–622.

Menzies, K. and Gilbert, S. (2013) 'Engaging Communities' in B. Bennett, S. Green, S. Gilbert and D. Bessarab (eds) *Our Voices: Aboriginal and Torres Strait Islander Social Work*, South Yarra: Palgrave MacMillan.

Mertens, D. (2009) *Transformative Research and Evaluation*, New York: The Guilford Press.

Midgley, J. (2001) 'Issues in International Social Work: Resolving Critical Debates in the Profession', *Journal of Social Work*, 1(1), pp. 21–35.

Midgley, J. (2004) 'The Complexities of Globalization: Challenges to Social Work' in N. Tan and A. Rowlands (eds) *Social Work Around the World III*, Berne, Switzerland: International Federation of Social Workers Press.

Midgley, J. and Livermore, M. (2005) 'Development Theory and Community Practice' in M. Weil (ed.) *The Handbook of Community Practice*, First Edition, Thousand Oaks, CA: Sage Publications.

Miller, C. and Ahmad, Y. (1997) 'Community Development at the Crossroads: A Way Forward', *Policy and Politics*, 25(3), pp. 269–284.

Mlcek, S. (2013) 'Are We Doing Enough to Develop Cross-cultural Competencies for Social Work?' *British Journal of Social Work*, doi: 10.1093/bjsw/bct044.

Mooney, G. (2006) '"United We Swim": Community Action and the Fight to Save Govanhill Pool', in M. Shaw, J. Meagher and S. Moir (eds) *Participation in Community Development: Problems and Possibilities, A Concept Reader in Collaboration with the Community Development Journal*, Edinburgh: Concept.

Morley, C. and MacFarlane, S. (2010) 'Repositioning Social Work in Mental Health: Challenges and Opportunities for Critical Practice', *Critical Social Work*, 11(2), pp. 46–59.

Mowbray, M. (2005) 'Community Capacity Building or State Opportunism?' *Community Development Journal*, 40(3), pp. 255–264.

Mullaly, R. (1997) *Structural Social Work: Ideology, Theory and Practice*, Toronto: Oxford University Press.

Muller, L. (2014) *A Theory for Indigenous Australian Health and Human Services Work: Connecting Indigenous Knowledge and Practice*, Crows Nest, NSW: Allen and Unwin.

Munro, E. (2011) *The Munro Review of Child Protection: A Child-centred System*, London: The Stationery Office.

Murphy, J. (2011) 'Obama Anti-Poverty Programs begin to take Shape', *City Limits*, available online at http://www.citylimits.org/news/articles/4353/obama-anti-poverty-programs-begin-to-take-shape/1 [Accessed 27 April 2013].

Mynott, E. (2005) '*Compromise, Collaboration and Collective Resistance: Different Strategies in the Face of the War on Asylum Seekers*' in I. Ferguson, M. Lavalette and E. Whitmore (eds) *Globalisation, Global Justice and Social Work*, London: Routledge.

NASC (2013) *In from the Margins: Roma in Ireland: Addressing the Structural Discrimination of the Roma Community in Ireland*, Cork: NASC.

Newman, J. and Tonkens, E. (2011) *Participation, Responsibility and Choice: Summoning the Active Citizen in European Welfare States*, Amsterdam: Amsterdam University Press.

Nyamu-Musembi, C. (2005) 'Towards an Actor-orientated Perspective on Human Rights' in N. Kabeer (ed) *Inclusive Citizenship*, London: Zed Books.

O'Brien, C. (2012) 'Social Work and the Media in Ireland: A Journalist's Perspective' in D. Lynch and K. Burns (eds) *Children's Rights and Child Protection: Critical Times, Critical Issues in Ireland*, Manchester: Manchester University Press.

Ohmer, M.L. and Brooks, F. (2013) 'The Practice of Community Organizing: Comparing and Contrasting Conflict and Consensus Approaches' in M. Weil (ed.) *The Handbook of Community Practice*, Second Edition, Thousand Oaks, CA: Sage Publications.

Ohmer, M.L., Sobek, J., Texeira, S.M., Wallace, J.M. and Shapiro, V.B. (2013) 'Community-based Research: Rationale, Methods, Roles, and Considerations for Community Practice' in M. Weil (ed.) *The Handbook of Community Practice*, Thousand Oaks, CA: Sage Publications.

O'Keeffe, M., Hills, A., Scholes, S., Constantine, R., Tinker, A., Manthorpe, J., Biggs, S., Erens, B. (2007) *UK Study of Abuse and Neglect of Older People: Prevalence Survey Report*, UK National Centre for Social Research.

Oliver, C. (2012) 'Critical Realist Grounded Theory: A New Approach for Social Work Research', *British Journal of Social Work*, 42, pp. 371–387.

O'Reilly, K. (2012) *International Migration and Social Theory*, Basingstoke: Palgrave Macmillan.

Orme, J. (2008) 'Feminist Social Work' in M. Gray and S. Webb (eds) *Social Work Theories and Methods*, First Edition, London: Sage Publications.

Orme, J. and Karvinen-Niinikoski, S. (2012) 'Social Work Research' in K. Lyons, T. Hokenstad, M. Pawar, N. Huegler and N. Hall (eds) *The Sage Handbook of International Social Work*, Thousand Oaks, CA: Sage Publications.

Orme, J. and Powell, J. (2007) 'Building Research Capacity in Social Work: Process and Issues', *British Journal of Social Work*, 38, pp. 988–1008.

O'Sullivan, N. (2012) 'The Rationale for the Retreat from the Welfare State', in J. Connelly and J. Hayward (eds) *The Withering of the Welfare State: Regression*, Basingstoke: Palgrave Macmillan.

Pain, H. (2011) 'Practice Research: What it is and its Place in the Social Work Profession', *European Journal of Social Work*, 14(4), pp. 545–562.

Pain, R., Whitman, G., Milledge, D. and Lune Rivers Trust (no date) *Participatory Action Research Toolkit: An Introduction to Using PAR as an Approach to Learning, Research and Action*, available online at www.dur.ac.uk/resources/beacon/PARtoolkit.pdf [Accessed 26 August 2014].

Parton, N. (1994) 'Problematics of Government, (Post) Modernity and Social Work', *British Journal of Social Work*, 24, pp. 9–32.

Parton, N. (2009) 'From Seebohm to Think Family: Reflections on 40 Years of Policy Change of Statutory Children's Social Work in England', *Child and Family Social Work*, 14(1), pp. 66–78.

Parton, N. (2014a) 'Privatising Child Protection: How the State is becoming more Authoritarian', *The Guardian*, available online at http://www.theguardian.com/social-care-network/2014/may/29/privatising-child-protection-state-authoritarian [Accessed 8 August 2014].

Parton, N. (2014b) 'Social Work, Child Protection and Politics: Some Critical and Constructive Reflections', *British Journal of Social Work*, 44(7), pp. 2042–2056.

Paterson, K. (2010) 'Community Engagement: For Whom?' in A. Emejulu and M. Shaw (eds) *Community Empowerment: Critical Perspectives from Scotland*, The Glasgow Papers, Edinburgh: Community Development Journal.

Payne, M. (1997) *Modern Social Work Theory*, Second Edition, Basingstoke: Palgrave.

Payne, M. (2005) *The Origins of Social Work: Change and Continuity*, Basingstoke: Palgrave MacMillan.

Pearce, J. (2010) *Participation and Democracy in the Twenty-First Century City*, Basingstoke: Palgrave Macmillan.

Pearce, J., Howard, J. and Bronstein, A. (2010) 'Editorial: Learning from Latin America', *Community Development Journal*, 45(3), pp. 265–275.

Pentaraki, M. (2013) '"If We Do not cut Spending, We will end up like Greece": Challenging Consent to Austerity through Social Work Action', *Critical Social Policy*, 33, pp. 700–711.

Perold, H., Graham, L.A., Mavungu, E.M., Cronin, K., Muchemwa, L. and Lough, B.J. (2013) 'The Colonial Legacy of International of International Voluntary Service', *Community Development Journal*, 48(2), pp. 179–196.

Popple, K. (1995) *Analysing Community Work, Its Theory and Practice*, Berkshire: Open University Press.

Popple, K. (2000) 'Community Development and the Voluntary Sector in the New Millennium: The Implications of the Third Way in the UK', *Community Development Journal*, 35(4), pp. 391–400.

Popple, K. (2006) 'Community Development in the 21st Century: A Case of Conditional Development', *British Journal of Social Work*, 36, pp. 333–340.

Popple, K. (2007) 'Community Development Strategies in the UK' in L. Dominelli (ed) *Revitalising Communities in a Globalising World*, Aldershot: Ashgate Publishing Ltd.

Powell, F. (2001) *The Politics of Social Work*, London: Sage Publications.

Powell, F. and Geoghegan, M. (2005) 'Reclaiming Civil Society: The Future of Global Social Work?' *European Journal of Social Work*, 8(2), pp. 129–144.

Pozzuto, R. and Arnd-Caddigan, M. (2008) 'Social Work in the US: Sociohistorical Context and Contemporary Issues', *Australian Social Work*, 61(1), pp. 57–71.

Preece, D.V. (2009) *Dismantling Social Europe: The Political Economy of Social Policy in the European Union*, Boulder, CA: First Forum Press.

Price, V. and Simpson, G. (2007) *Transforming Society? Social Work and Sociology*, Bristol: Policy Press.

Putnam, R. (2000) *Bowling Alone: The Collapse and Revival of American Community*, New York: Simon and Schuster.

Pyles, L. (2009) *Progressive Community Organizing: Reflective Practice in a Globalizing World*, New York: Taylor and Francis Group.

Pyles, L. and Harding, S. (2012) 'Discourses of Post-Katrina Reconstruction: A Frame Analysis', *Community Development Journal*, 47(3), pp. 335–352.

Ramon, S. and Maglajlic, R. (2012) 'Social Work, Political Conflict and Displacement' in K.H. Lyons, T. Hokenstad, M. Pawar, N. Huegler and N. Hall (eds) *The SAGE Handbook of International Social Work*, London: Sage Publications.

Ratcliffe, P. (2012) '"Community Cohesion": Reflections on a Flawed Paradigm', *Critical Social Policy*, 32(2), pp. 262–281.

Reed, B. (2005) 'Theorising in Community Practice: Essential Tools for Building Community, Promoting Social Justice and Implementing Social Change' in M. Weil (ed.) *The Handbook of Community Practice*, First Edition, California: Sage Publications.

Reisch, M. (2013) 'What is the Future of Social Work?' *Critical and Radical Social Work*, 1(1), pp. 67–85.

Reisch, M. and Andrews, J. (2002) *The Road Not Taken: A History of Radical Social Work in the United States*, New York: Brunner-Routledge.

Reisch, M. and Jani, J.S. (2012) 'The New Politics of Social Work Practice: Understanding Context to Promote Change', *British Journal of Social Work*, 42, pp. 1132–1150.

Reisch, M., Ife, J. and Weil, M. (2013) 'Social Justice, Human Rights, Values, and Community Practice' in M. Weil (ed.) *The Handbook of Community Practice*, Second Edition, Thousand Oaks, CA: Sage Publications.

Rigby, P. and Whyte, B. (2013) 'Children's Narrative within a Multi-centred, Dynamic Ecological Framework of Assessment and Planning for Child Trafficking', *British Journal of Social Work*, doi: 10.1093/bjsw/bct105.

Ritchie, A. and Woodward, R. (2009) 'Changing Lives: Critical Reflections on the Social Work Change Programme for Scotland', *Critical Social Policy*, 29(3), pp. 510–532.

Rogowski, S. (2011) 'Managers, Managerialism and Social Work with Children and Families: The Deformation of a Profession?' *Practice: Social Work in Action*, 23(3), pp. 157–167.

Rogowski, S. (2012) 'Social Work with Children and Families: Challenges and Possibilities in the Neo-Liberal World', *British Journal of Social Work*, 42, pp. 921–940.

Room, G.J. (1995) 'Poverty in Europe: Competing Paradigms of Analysis', *Policy and Politics*, 23(2), pp. 103–113.

Ruch, G., Turney, D. and Ward, A. (2010) *Relationship-based Social Work: Getting to the Heart of Practice*, London: Jessica Kingsley.

Rush, M. and Keenan, M. (2013) The Social Politics of Social Work: Anti-Oppressive Social Work Dilemmas in Twenty-First-Century Welfare Regimes, *British Journal of Social Work Advance Access*, doi: 10.1093/bjsw/bct014.

Ryder, A. (2013) 'Snakes and Ladders: Inclusive Community Development and Gypsies and Travellers', *Community Development Journal*, 49(1), pp. 21–36.

Saad-Filho, A. and Johnston, D. (2005) *Neoliberalism: A Critical Reader*, London: Pluto Press.

Sage, D. (2012) 'A Challenge to Liberalism? The Communitarianism of the Big Society and Blue Labour', *Critical Social Policy*, 32(3), pp. 365–382.

Sawicki, J. (1991) *Disciplining Foucault: Feminist, Power and the Body*, New York: Routledge.

Sayer, A. (2012) 'Power, Causality and Normativity: A Critical Realist Critique of Foucault', *Journal of Political Power*, 5(2), pp. 179–194.

Schaffner Goldberg, G. (2012) 'Economic Inequality and Economic Crisis: A Challenge for Social Workers', *Social Work*, 57(3), pp. 211–224.

Seebohm, P., Gilchrist, A. and Morris, D. (2012) 'Bold but Balanced: How Community Development Contributes to Mental Health and Inclusion', *Community Development Journal*, 47(4), pp. 473–490.

Segal, U. and Heck, G. (2012) 'Migration, Minorities and Citizenship' in K. Lyons, T. Hokenstad, M. Pawar, N. Huegler and N. Hall (eds) *The SAGE Handbook of International Social Work*, London: Sage Publications.

Sewpaul, V. (2006) 'The Global-Local Dialectic: Challenges for African Scholarship and Social Work in a Post-Colonial World', *British Journal of Social Work*, 36, pp. 419–434.

Share, M. (2010) 'Capacity Building and Urban Regeneration in Dublin, Ireland' in S. Kenny and M. Clarke (eds) *Challenging Capacity Building: Comparative Perspectives*, Basingstoke: Palgrave Macmillan.

Shaw, I. (2011) 'Social Work Research – An Urban Desert?' *European Journal of Social Work*, 14(1), pp. 11–26.

Shaw, M. (2003) '*Gilding the Ghetto* (1977) CDP Inter-Project Editorial Team, London. *In and Against the State* (1979) London Edinburgh Weekend Return Group, Pluto Press, London', Classic Texts, *Community Development Journal*, 38(4), pp. 361–366.

Shaw, M. (2011) 'Stuck in the Middle? Community Development, Community Engagement and the Dangerous Business of Learning for Democracy', *Community Development Journal*, 46(S2), pp. 128–146.

Shaw, M. and Martin, I. (2000) 'Community Work, Citizenship and Democracy: Re-making the Connections', *Community Development Journal*, 35(4), pp. 401–413.

Shdaimah, C., Stahl, R. and Schram, S. (2011) *Change Research: A Case Study on Collaborative Methods for Social Workers and Advocates*, New York: Columbia University Press.

Shevellar, L. (2011) '"We Have to Go Back to Stories": Causal Layered Analysis and the Community Development Gateaux', *Community Development*, 42(1), 3–15, doi: 10.1080/15575331003611599.

Shevellar, L., Sherwin, J. and Mackay, G. (2012) 'A Re-imagined Identity: Building a Movement in Brisbane for the Practice of Social Role Valorisation' in P. Westoby and L. Shevellar (eds) *Learning and Mobilising for Community Development. A Radical Tradition of Community-based Education and Training*. Surrey, UK: Ashgate Publishing Ltd.

Shipman, J. and Powell, J.L. (2005) '"Modernist" Sociology in a "Postmodern" World?' *International Journal of Sociology and Social Policy*, 25(10/11), pp. 1–13.

Shragge, E. (2013) *Activism and Social Change: Lessons for Community Organising*, Toronto: University of Toronto Press.

Sites, W. (1998) 'Communitarian Theory and Community Development in the United States', *Community Development Journal*, 33(1), pp. 57–65.

Sites, W., Chaskin, R. and Parks, V. (2007) 'Reframing Community Practice for the 21st Century: Multiple Traditions, Multiple Challenges', *Journal of Urban Affairs*, 29(5), pp. 519–541.

Slater, T. (2012) 'The Myth of "Broken Britain": Welfare Reform and the Production of Ignorance', *Antipode*, doi: 10.1111/anti.12002, pp. 1–22.

Slevin, A. (2010) 'Rossport: From Community Action to Movement for Social Change', *Working for Change: The Irish Journal of Community Development*, 2, pp. 126–147.

Solas, J. (2008a) 'What Kind of Justice does Social Work Seek?' *International Journal of Social Work,* 51(6), pp. 813–822.

Solas, J. (2008b) 'Social Work and Social Justice: What Are We Fighting for?' *Australian Social Work,* 61(2), pp. 124–136.

Solomon, B.B. (1976) *Black Empowerment: Social Work in Oppressed Communities,* New York: Columbia University Press.

Somerville, P. (2011) *Understanding Community: Politics, Policy and Practice,* Bristol: The Policy Press.

Spicker, P. (2012) 'Personalisation Falls Short', *British Journal of Social Work,* doi: 10.1093/bjsw/bcs063, pp. 1–17.

Stacey, L. (2009) *Whose Child Now? Fifteen Years of Working to Prevent the Exploitation of Children in the UK,* Ilford, Essex: Barnardos.

Steger, M.B., and Roy, R.K. (2010) *Neoliberalism: A Very Short Introduction,* Oxford: Oxford University Press.

Stepney, P. (2006) 'The Paradox of Reshaping Social Work as "Tough Love" in the Nordic Welfare States', *Nordisk Sosialt Arbeid,* 26(4), pp. 293–305.

Stepney, P. (2012) 'An Introduction to Social Work Theory, Practice and Research' in P. Stepney and D. Ford (eds) *Social Work Models, Methods and Theories: A Framework for Practice,* Second Edition, Lyme Regis: Russell House Publishing.

Stepney, P. and Ford, D. (2012) *Social Work Models, Methods and Theories: A Framework for Practice,* Second Edition, Lyme Regis: Russell House Publishing.

Stepney, P. and Popple, K. (2008) *Social Work and the Community: A Critical Context for Practice,* Basingstoke: Palgrave Macmillan.

Stepney, P. and Popple, K. (2012) 'Community Social Work' in P. Stepney and D. Ford (eds) *Social Work Models, Methods and Theories: A Framework for Practice,* Second Edition, Lyme Regis: Russell House Publishing.

Stones, R. (2008) 'Introduction' in R. Stones (ed.) *Key Sociological Thinkers,* Second Edition, Basingstoke: Palgrave Macmillan.

Strier, R. and Binyamin, S. (2013) 'Introducing Anti-Oppressive Social Work Practices in Public Services: Rhetoric to Practices', *British Journal of Social Work,* 1–18, doi: 10.1093/bjsw/bct049.

SWAN – Social Work Action Network (2014) available online at www.socialworkfuture.org [Accessed 24 September 2014].

Taylor, V. (1997) 'The Trajectory of National Liberation and Social Movements: The South African Experience', *Community Development Journal,* 32(3), pp. 252–265.

Taylor, V. and Van Willigen, M. (1996) 'Women's Self-Help and the Reconstruction of Gender: The Postpartum Support and Breast Cancer Movements', *Mobilization,* 1(2), pp. 123–142.

Teater, B. and Baldwin, M. (2012) *Social Work in the Community: Making a Difference,* Bristol: The Policy Press.

Tew, J. (2006) 'Understanding Power and Powerlessness: Towards a Framework for Emancipatory Practice in Social Work', *Journal of Social Work,* 6(1), pp. 33–50.

Thompson, N. (2002) 'Social Movements, Social Justice and Social Work', *British Journal of Social Work,* 32, pp. 711–722.

Thompson, N. (2010) *Theorizing Social Work Practice,* Basingstoke: Palgrave Macmillan.

Thornham, H. and Parry, K. (2015) 'Constructing Communities: The Community Centre as Contested Site', *Community Development Journal*, 50(1), pp. 24–39.

Throssell, H. (1975) *Social Work: Radical Essays*, Brisbane: University of Queensland Press.

Tonkens, E. (2011) 'The Embrace of Responsibility: Citizenship and Governance of Social Care in the Netherlands' in J. Newman and E. Tonkens (eds) *Participation, Responsibility and Choice: Summoning the Active Citizen in Western European Welfare States*, Amsterdam: Amsterdam University Press.

Toseland, R. and Rivas, R. (2011) *An Introduction to Group Work Practice*, Seventh Edition, Boston: Pearson.

Tovey, H. (2009) 'Theorising "Community"' in C. Forde, E. Kiely and R. Meade (eds) *Youth and Community Work in Ireland: Critical Perspectives*, Dublin: Blackhall Publishing.

Travis, A. and Watt, N. (2013) 'Offenders Face Supervision by Private Firms', *The Guardian*, 9 May, p. 1.

Treatment Action Campaign (2014) available online at www.tac.org.za [Accessed 24 September 2014].

Tudor, R. (2013) 'Social Work in the Quake Zone: Supporting the Sustainable Development of Christchurch's Eastern Communities', *Aotearoa New Zealand Social Work*, 25(2), pp. 18–26.

Tuhiwai Smith, L. (2001) *Decolonizing Methodologies: Research and Indigenous Peoples*, Dunedin: University of Otago Press.

Turbett, C. (2014) *Doing Radical Social Work*, Basingstoke: Palgrave Macmillan.

Turner, R.S. (2008) *Neo-Liberal Ideology: History, Concepts and Policies*, Edinburgh: Edinburgh University Press.

UK Federation for Community Development Learning (2009) *National Occupational Standards for Community Development*, available online at www.fcdl.org.uk [Accessed 28 March 2013].

Uluorta, H.M. (2008) 'Welcome to the "All-American" Fun House: Hailing the Disciplinary Neo-liberal Non-subject', *Millennium – Journal of International Studies*, 36(2), pp. 241–265.

Van Berkel, R. and Hornemann Moller, I. (2002) *Active Social Policies in the EU: Inclusion through Participation?* Bristol: Policy Press.

Van Heugten, K. and Daniels, K. (2001) 'Social Workers who Move into Private Practice: The Impact of the Socio-economic Context', *British Journal of Social Work*, 31, pp. 739–755.

Varley, T. and Curtin, C. (2002) 'Communitarianism Populism and the Politics of Rearguard Resistance in Rural Ireland', *Community Development Journal*, 37(1), pp. 20–32.

Vickers, T. and Dominelli, L. (2014) 'Students' Involvement in International Humanitarian Aid: Learning from Student Responses to the 2004 Tsunami in Sri Lanka', *British Journal of Social Work*, doi: 10.1093/bjsw/bcu052.

Voss, K. and Williams, M. (2012) 'The Local in the Global: Rethinking Social Movements in the New Millennium', *Democratization*, 19(2), pp. 352–377.

Walker, S. (2001) 'Tracing the Contours of Postmodern Social Work', *British Journal of Social Work*, 31, pp. 29–39.

Wallace, J. and Pease, B. (2011) 'Neoliberalism and Australian Social Work: Accommodation or Resistance?' *Journal of Social Work,* 11(2), pp. 132–142.

Webb, S.A. (2006) *Social Work in a Risk Society: Social and Political Perspectives,* Basingstoke: Palgrave Macmillan.

Webb, S.A. (2010) '(Re) Assembling the Left: The Politics of Redistribution and Recognition in Social Work', *British Journal of Social Work,* 40, pp. 2364–2379.

Webber, R. and Jones, K. (2012) 'Implementing "Community Development" in a Post-disaster Situation', *Community Development Journal,* 48(2), pp. 248–263.

Weil, M. and Ohmer, M. (2013) 'Applying Practice Theories in Community Work' in M. Weil (ed) *The Handbook of Community Practice,* Second Edition, Thousand Oaks, CA: Sage Publications.

Weiss, I., Gal, J. and Katan, J. (2006) 'Social Policy for Social Work: A Teaching Agenda', *British Journal of Social Work,* 36(5), pp. 789–806.

Welbourne, P. (2011) 'Twenty-first Century Social Work: The Influence of Political Context on Public Service Provision in Social Work Education and Service Delivery', *European Journal of Social Work,* 14(3), pp. 403–420.

Wenger, E. (1998) *Communities of Practice: Learning, Meaning and Identity,* Cambridge: Cambridge University Press.

Wenger, E. (2006) Communities of Practice: A Brief Introduction, available online at www.ewenger.com/theory/communities_of_practice_intro.htm.

Wenger, E., McDermott, R. and Snyder, W. (2002) *Cultivating Communities of Practice: A Guide to Managing Knowledge,* Boston: Harvard Business School.

Westheimer, J. and Kahne, J. (2004) 'What Kind of Citizen? The Politics of Educating for Democracy', *American Educational Research Journal,* 41(2), pp. 237–269.

Westoby, P. (2010) 'Story of Working with Southern Sudanese Refugees within Brisbane and Logan' in A. Ingamells, A. Lathouras, R. Wiseman, P. Westoby and F. Caniglia (eds) *Community Development Practice: Stories, Method and Meaning,* Australia: Common Ground Publishing Pty Ltd.

Westoby, P. and Botes, L. (2013) '"I work with the Community, Not the Parties!" The Political and Practical Dilemmas of South Africa's State-Employed Community Development Workers', *British Journal of Social Work,* 43, pp. 1294–1311.

Westoby, P. and Ingamells, A. (2011) 'Teaching Community Development Personal Frameworks', *Social Work Education,* doi: 10.1080/02615479.2010.550913.

Westoby, P. and Kaplan, A. (2014) 'Foregrounding Practice – Reaching for a Responsive and Ecological Approach to Community Development – A Conversational Inquiry into the Dialogical and Developmental Frameworks of Community Development', *Community Development Journal,* 49(2), pp. 214–227.

Westoby, P. and Shevellar, L. (2012) *Learning and Mobilising for Community Development: A Radical Tradition of Community-based Education and Training,* Surrey, England: Ashgate Publishing Limited.

Weyers, M. (2011) 'The Habits of Highly Effective Community Development Practitioners', *Development Southern Africa,* 28(1), pp. 87–98.

Whelan, M. (1989) 'Training and Professionalisation in Community Work' in Combat Poverty Agency *Community Work in Ireland: Trends in the 80s, Options for the 90s,* Dublin: Combat Poverty Agency.

Williams, C. and Graham, M. (2014) '"A World on the Move": Migration, Mobilities and Social Work', *British Journal of Social Work,* 44(Supplement 1), pp. 1–17.

Wilson, A. and Beresford, P. (2000) '"Anti-Oppressive Practice": Emancipation or Appropriation?' *British Journal of Social Work,* 30, pp. 553–573.

Wint, E. and Sewpaul, V. (2008) 'Product and Process Dialectic: Developing an Indigenous Approach to Community Development Training', *Journal of Community Practice,* 7(1), pp. 57–70.

Wood, M. (1994) 'Should Tenants Take Over? Radical Community Work, Tenants Organisations, and the Future of Public Housing' in S. Jacobs and K. Popple (eds) *Community Work in the 1990s,* Nottingham: Spokesman.

Woodcock, J. and Dixon, J. (2005) 'Professional Ideologies and Preferences in Social Work: A British Study in Global Perspective, *British Journal of Social Work,* 35(6), pp. 953–973.

Yerbury, H. (2012) 'Vocabularies of Community', *Community Development Journal,* 47(2), pp. 184–198.

Zubrzycki, J. and Crawford, F. (2013) 'Collaboration and Relationship Building in Aboriginal and Torres Strait Islander Social Work' in B. Bennett, S. Green, S. Gilbert and D. Bessarab (eds) *Our Voices: Aboriginal and Torres Strait Islander Social Work,* South Yarra: Palgrave MacMillan.

Index

Bessarab, D., 74–75
Besthorn, F. H., 55
Bhaskar, R., 69
Big Society, 6, 23, 37–38
Bonds or ties, community as, 5
Botes, L., 38
Bottom-up participatory process
  in community capacity-building, 37
  in critical and engaged practice, 145
  critical realist practice aligned with,
    69, 72
  empowerment as, 15
  in Friere's model of problem-posing,
    124
  in grassroots movement, 9, 16, 81–82
  in green social work, 55
  in Ife's Framework of Human Service
    Delivery, 45 46
  in post-modern feminism, 68
  post-modernism linked to, 18, 68–69
  power coming from, 73
  in social work activism, 116, 119
  versus top-down intervention, 94
Bourke, P., 131, 133
Brake, M., 62
Britain. *See also* United Kingdom (UK)
  anti-racist and anti-discriminatory
    practice approaches in, 64
  radical social work in, 62–63
  Urban Programmes in, 84
  working-class self-help in, tradition
    of, 82
Brooks, A., 113, 117
Buen vivir (good living), 89
Butcher, H., 124

C
Cameron, D., 25
Caniglia, F., 5, 131, 133
Case studies
  ECPAT/Childwise, 119–120
  social work responses to militarism
    and violence, 117–119
  SWAN, 120–121
Celtic Tiger, 76

Centrelink, 31, 32–33, 38, 39
Chandler, J., 26
Change agents, 19
Chaskin, R., 10, 34, 35
Chenoweth, L., 12, 31, 32
Citizen, in participation, 115–116
Citizenship
  community development and, in
    activism, 111–116
  shifting forms of, 113–116
  top-down intervention and, 112
Climate change, 54, 56
Coalition government, 6, 25, 29
Codes of ethics, 13–14
Collective action, 11
Collins, S., 64, 115, 132, 133
Communitarianism, 34–38
  issues and opportunities, 36–38
  Third Way policies and, 34–35
Communities of practice, 127,
    130–133, 139, 142
Community
  challenging neo-liberalism, London
    Citizens and, 86–87
  critical practice in, emerging
    opportunities for, 51–56
  as enduring site of change and
    resistance, 85–87
  as intervention (*See*
    Communitarianism)
  meanings of, 5–6
  as place, 5–7
  as political unit, 6
  social work and, 5–7
  understandings of, 5
Community action approach, 8–9, 112
Community as enduring site of change
    and resistance, 85–87
Community as place, 5–7
Community as political unit, 6
Community development, 7–20
  approaches to, in UK, 8–9
  characteristics of, 10–11
  as collective action, 11
  community work and, 7–8

Glasgow City Council, 9
Global Agenda for Social Work and Social Development: A Commitment for Action (IFSW, IASSW and ICSW), 4–5, 55–56
Globalisation
  advocacy and, 74
  in changing landscape of social work practice, 4
  changing social work practice, 30–33
  community-based solutions to challenges of, 9, 33
  conceptions of community and, 5
  green social work and, 54
  indigenisation and, 74, 98
  social work activism and, 117
  social work responses to the adverse impacts of, 50, 54, 56
Global North, 24, 84, 98, 144
Govanhill swimming pool, 9, 112
Grassroots, community development as, 9, 81–83
Gray, M., 25, 59, 94
Green, S., 74–75
Green social work, 54–56, 91

H
Hanson, S., 111, 112
Harlow, E., 26
Healy, K., 42–43, 44, 47, 50, 53, 59–60, 64, 66–67, 68, 73, 102, 103, 126, 134, 135
Henderson, P., 124
Henkel, H., 15
HIV/AIDS, 111, 112, 113
Houston, S., 29, 69–70
Human rights, 74–78
  in Australia, 51
  citizenship linked to, 113–114
  critical practice strategies and, 76–77
  external reference points and, 134
  framework, 78, 116–117
  green social work and, 54
  Ife's post-modernist practice linked to, 68

militarisation and armed conflict and, 117
political activism and, 117–119
as principle in social work based on, 12, 75–76
research activism and, 135
social work theory and, 59, 63
in UK, 29
values and, 14
Human rights groups, 103
Humphries, Beth, 135

I
Ife, Jim, 14, 15, 50, 53, 59, 71, 72
  on community centers, 82
  empowerment defined by, 78
  Framework of Human Service Delivery, 44–46
  on perspectives to view social problems or issues, 102
  on political role for social workers, 103
  on postcolonial perspectives, 75
  on post-modernist practice, 68
  on social movements, 115
  on social workers as human rights workers, 118
Immigration, 26–27, 74, 97, 103
Indigenisation, 74, 98
Induced self-help, 36
Ingamells, A., 97–98, 127
Inquiry, The, 62
Institutional discourses. *See* Dominant discourses
International Association for Community Development (IACD), 13, 14
International Association of Schools of Social Work (IASSW), 4–5
International Council on Social Welfare (ICSW), 4–5
International Federation of Social Workers (IFSW), 4–5, 12
Intervention, community development as, 9–10, 20, 83–85
Ireland, 49

motivation in, 107–108
opportunity in, 106
Political activism, 117–119
Popple, K., 8, 17–18, 52, 53, 59, 69, 126, 138
Post-modernism, 18, 68–69
Post-modern period, 47
Post-modern theory
  discourse and, 42, 47
  in social work theory, 68–69
  theoretical perspective on, 18
Pozzuto, R., 31
Practice. *See* Critical practice in social work
Practice discourses, 43
Practice frameworks, 59, 66, 67, 76, 126–127
Practice research, 135, 138–139
  service users and, 138–139, 150
Practitioner-led research (PLR), 138
Practitioner perspectives
  on human rights and critical practice strategies, 76–78
  on values, theories and practices, 70–73
Practitioner research, 124, 125
  developing theory and knowledge for practices with communities, 138–140
  documenting practices and developing practice models, 140–141
Principles and values, 12–13
Professional Association of Social Workers (PASW), 116
Professional Capabilities Framework (PCF), 3
Professional discourses, 43, 44–45, 49–50, 107, 144

R
Radical social change, 30, 64
Radical social work, 12
  activism in research and practice and, 110
  in Britain, 62–63
  community development practice and, 63

oppression and, 64, 66
social work activists and, 101
in social work theory, 68
Radical Social Work, 63
Rahayu, S., 14
Rancieres, J., 109–110
Reflection, 91–93. *See also* Critical reflection
Reflexivity, 64, 125, 135
Reisch, M., 43, 110, 114
Research. *See* Practice research
Research activism, 124, 135, 137
  conceptualising activism in, 109–111
  critical reflection and, 136, 138
  human rights and, 135
  social justice and, 135, 138
  in USA, 110
Robertson, J., 124
Roma community in Dublin, 95–96
Rush, M., 66

S
Scaffolding practices. *See also* Community development in critical practice, scaffolding
  consciousness-raising in, 123–124
  social workers' as researchers for social change, 135–137
  social workers' engagement with collective activities, 133–135
Scandinavian welfare state, 24
Schram, S., 135
Self-help
  Britain's tradition of working-class self-help, 82
  communal, 34
  community involvement in, 9
  CSW and, 53
  discourse, 37
  induced, 36
  in Kulin initiatives, 87
  model of community development, 8
  programmes, 85
  women's self-help movements, 114
Self-reliance, 87

landscape, 3–4
policy and managerialism, impact of, 28–33
regional differences, 3
Social Work Action Network (SWAN), 120–121
Social work activism. *See also* Case studies
globalisation and, 117
new and emerging forms of, 116–121
social workers as activists, 101–111
Social work engagement with critical community development approaches, 144–150
critical and engaged practice, prospects for, 144–146
critical directions, 147–150
education and, critical directions in, 149
introduction, 144
policy and, critical directions in, 148
practice and, critical directions in, 149–150
social work and community development, emerging possibilities in, 146–147
Social workers
as activists, 101–111 (*See also* Social work activism)
policy practice engagement, 106–109
as social policy activists, 105–109
Social work policy, fostering critical perspectives, 147–150
on education, 149
on policy, 148
on practice, 149–150
Social work practice
around the world, 30–31
in Centrelink, 32–33
in the UK, 28–30
Social Work Reform Board, 3
Social Work Research for Social Justice (Humphries), 135
Social Work Theories in Context (Healy), 60

Social work theory, 59–79
advocacy, empowerment and human rights in, 74–78
anti-oppressive practice, 64
complexities of power in, 73–74
critical realist practices in, 69–74
ideas in social work, ebb and flow of, 61–67
introduction, 59
making connections between values, theories and practices, 59–61
mechanisms of oppression, 65–67
post-modern orientations in, 68–69
practitioner's account of, 76–78
structural social work for transforming social order, 67–68
values, theories and practices, practitioner perspectives on, 70–73
as a way forward, 78
Solas, J., 15, 118
Solomon, B. B., 74
South Africa, 50, 110–111, 114
Sowbel, L., 44
Springett, J., 16, 91–92, 93, 95
Stahl, R., 135
Stepney, P., 17–18, 25, 52, 53, 59, 69, 126, 138
Stirrat, R., 15
Stolen Generation, 74
Story-telling, 95
Structural social work, 20, 59, 66, 67–68
Sweden, social work in, 2, 26, 107
Systems theories, 20, 63, 93

T
Taken-for-granted assumptions, 6, 68
Technical assistance model of community development, 8
Theatre of the oppressed, 95
THEMBA ('There Must Be an Alternative'), 111
Third Way, 23, 34–35
Top-down intervention
versus bottom-up participatory process, 94

Lightning Source UK Ltd.
Milton Keynes UK
UKHW021132020721
386521UK00005B/896